AN INTRODUCTION TO PROGRAMMING USING ALICE

by Charles W. Herbert

COURSE TECHNOLOGY
CENGAGE Learning

Australia • Brazil • Japan • Korea • Mexico • Singapore • Spain • United Kingdom • United States

COURSE TECHNOLOGY
CENGAGE Learning™

**An Introduction to Programming
Using Alice**

Charles W. Herbert

Publisher: Bob Woodbury

Senior Product Manager: Tricia Coia

Development Editor: Jill Batistick

Product Marketing Manager: Brian Berkeley

Editorial Assistant: Allison Murphy

Production Editor: Danielle Chouhan

Cover Designer: Abigail Scholz

Manufacturing Coordinator: Justin Palmeiro

Copy Editor: Judi Silver

Proofreader: Christine Clark

Indexer: Elizabeth Cunningham

Compositor: GEX Publishing Services

For product information and technology assistance, contact us at
Cengage Learning Customer & Sales Support, 1-800-354-9706

For permission to use material from this text or product, submit all requests online at **cengage.com/permissions**
Further permissions questions can be emailed to
permissionrequest@cengage.com

ISBN-13: 978-1-4188-3625-2

ISBN-10: 1-4188-3625-7

Course Technology
25 Thomson Place
Boston, Massachusetts 02210
USA

Cengage Learning is a leading provider of customized learning solutions with office locations around the globe, including Singapore, the United Kingdom, Australia, Mexico, Brazil, and Japan. Locate your local office at: **international.cengage.com/region**

Cengage Learning products are represented in Canada by Nelson Education, Ltd.

For your lifelong learning solutions, visit **course.cengage.com**

Purchase any of our products at your local college store or at our preferred online store **www.ichapters.com**

Printed in China
4 5 6 7 8 9 10 09 08

▪▪▪▪ BRIEF CONTENTS

▪▪▪▪▪ TABLE OF CONTENTS

CHAPTER EIGHT

■ ■ ■ ■ ■ PREFACE

An Introduction to Programming Using Alice is not about Alice, it's about computer programming. The book is intended to provide a first exposure to the concepts of object-oriented programming and algorithm development for students with little or no experience programming computers. It is based on National Science Foundation funded research exploring the use of virtual reality programming in introductory computer courses throughout the United States.

Why Alice?

In today's world, what teenager in his or her right mind is going to read through the instruction manual that comes with a DVD player, which may be bigger than the player itself, before attempting to use the device? Today, young people learn by exploring, by playing with a device to make it do what they want it to do. Unfortunately, such a learning style can separate them from the "nuts and bolts" of the technology they are using. They learn enough to perform a few tasks that are necessary to make the device function as desired, but they are less likely to understand how or why the device works the way it does. This can easily lead to frustration with technology when it is necessary to go beyond the basic functions of a device. Today's students can do things with a computer, but they are less likely to understand the underlying technology as much as young people did a few years ago. Is this learning style related to a decline in Computer Science enrollments?

This phenomenon about technology is nothing new. It happens in part because most technology, like computing, becomes more complex as time goes by. What percentage of teenage boys who owned a car in the late 1950's knew how to change the car's oil? What is that percentage today? I'll bet it's significantly less. One recent television commercial laments the fact that we change our car's oil today with a credit card rather than with a wrench. This happens with almost every technology. As a technology becomes more sophisticated, people become further removed from the underlying foundations of that technology[1].

Yet, can we afford to let this happen with computing and related technology? According to almost all informed sources, such as the United States Department of Labor and the National Science Foundation, the demand for a technically competent workforce, and particularly for people who have degrees in what the National Science Foundation calls the STEM disciplines—Science, Technology, Engineering and Mathematics—will not decrease in the coming years, while at the same time the United States Department of Education tells us that the number of people majoring in these disciplines, and in computing in particular, is decreasing. Today a smaller percentage of students entering college are choosing to study computers and computer-related technology than at any time since 1996.[2] Is this a good thing or a bad thing for our society? Why is this happening? What can we, as educators, do about it? Enter Alice.

[1] For a wonderful discussion about how this effects teachers and educational technology, see Larry Cuban's book on educational technology—*Teachers and Machines: The Classroom Use of Technology Since 1920*. Teachers College Press (1986) ISBN: 080772792X

[2] See the Computer Research Association 2005 Taulbee Study at *http://www.cra.org/CRN/articles/may05/taulbee.html*

I've heard some teachers say that it is extremely difficult to teach object-oriented programming because the concepts of object-oriented programming are so complex. Do you believe that? I think that any student of average intelligence who reads the first 500 or so words of Chapter 1 of this text will have a fundamental understanding of what objects are and what object-oriented programming is all about. It won't be a deep understanding, but it's a start. That's what I believe: the best way to teach complicated ideas is to expose our students to them gently, and then to gradually add more and more detail until one day they realize they've learned quite a bit. To be sure, the process can be long and sometimes tedious, but we need to motivate students along the way, to keep them moving, to keep them interested. Some folks call this the curriculum spiral, in which we expose our students to ideas at a simple level, and then revisit them again and again, each time going a little deeper, each time motivating them to want to go even deeper. The educational psychologist Jerome Bruner wrote:

> "...I was struck by the fact that successful efforts to teach highly structured bodies of knowledge like mathematics, physical sciences, and even the field of history often took the form of a metaphoric spiral in which at some simple level a set of ideas or operations were introduced in a rather intuitive way and, once mastered in that spirit, were then revisited and reconstrued in a more formal or operational way, the mastery at this stage then being carried one step higher to a new level of formal or operational rigour and to a broader level of abstraction and comprehensiveness. The end stage of this process was eventual mastery of the connexity and structure of a large body of knowledge." [3]

The Russian educational philosopher Vygotsky compared learning to the growth of a tree. Where does the new growth on an oak tree occur each year? It starts from the places where the last growth occurred in the previous season—buds spring forth from the spot where the tree was last growing. The growth is slow, yet steady. If a large and heavy branch were to suddenly appear, the structure of the tree might not be able to support it, and it would fall off and die. If not enough growth occurs then the tree might not be healthy for other reasons. Vygostsky called the place where new growth occurs the "zone of proximal development." [4] He said that, if nothing else, it is the job of teachers to help our students advance in the zone of proximal development—to carefully, steadily and continuously maintain intellectual growth from where they are to where we want them to be. Early in the semester I tell my students about Vygotsky's ideas and later often warn them to "stay in the zone."

For persistent learning to take place, it needs to be interesting (maybe even fun), relevant to other things that students have already learned, and well paced. I believe that Alice is an excellent tool to help us achieve these ends in teaching computer programming. But I also

[3] Bruner, J (1960) The Process of Education, Cambridge, Mass.: Harvard University Press, ISBN: 0674710010 (1977 reprint)
[4] See Vygotsky, L. S. (1978). *Mind in society: The development of higher psychological processes.* Vera John-Steiner (Editor). Cambridge, MA: Harvard University Press. ISBN: 0674576292 Vygotsky actually defines the zone of proximal development for a child as the difference between the actual development level as determined by individual problem solving and the potential development level as determined through problem solving under the guidance of adults or more knowledgeable peers.

believe that's not the most important thing about Alice. You see, as students manipulate objects in Alice, they are considering placement and motion in three-dimensional space and time. They begin to think about acceleration, one object's orientation relative to another, and things like how to make the path of a moving object, such as a baseball, look like it does in the real world. They begin to persistently explore ideas that are pretty fundamental to most of science, technology, engineering and mathematics. What made Archimedes, or Da Vinci, or Wilbur Wright think about these things? What are we doing to make our students think about them? How much more can our students do empowered by the *desire* to explore such ideas coupled with the *ability* to explore them with the tools of modern computing? Enter Alice.

Anthropologist Fred Erikson, among others, has pointed out that learning occurs in a social environment.[5] He says we should consider the social environment in the classroom, and whether or not it fosters learning. Are our students learning from one another as well as from the teacher? Are they talking to each other in class about what they're learning? Are they talking to each other outside of class about what they're learning? Does the social environment of our classrooms welcome women and minority students to learn about computing? Does it encourage borderline students to make the effort to "get over the hump," or does it send the message that computer programming is only for the most brilliant among us? Enter Alice.

There is some research to show that the use of Alice changes the social environment of the classroom in fundamentally positive ways. In fact, there are many ways to teach and learn computer programming. Java is a good tool for modern object-oriented, event-driven, concurrent, network-based, multi-tiered, enterprise-wide, client-server computing—but it is a difficult language to start to learn. Visual Basic.NET, C++, C#.NET, and any number of other modern languages aren't much easier to learn. Enter Alice.

Alice by itself isn't all that useful if our goal is to train people so that they can become professional computer programmers. Companies don't use Alice to write payroll programs or operating systems. Students who wish to become professional programmers still need to learn languages like Java, Visual Basic and so on. Alice isn't intended to replace them; it is intended to position students so that they can learn them better. There is some research to show that using Alice for a few weeks and then switching to Java for the remainder of the semester results in better Java programmers than if Java is used for the entire semester. The important things about using Alice are that it allows students to get started quickly learning the concepts of modern programming and that it motivates them early in the process to want to learn those things and more.

Good teachers are good teacher for many reasons. Many of them are intelligent people who have spent a lifetime thinking about teaching and learning and have worked with other intelligent people who have done the same. Of course, as young people, they were probably influenced by their own good teachers, including their parents. But most of all, they are probably good teachers because they enjoy teaching—they get something out of it. They also want

---

[5] See Erickson, Fred "Transformation and School Success: The Politics and Culture of Educational Achievement." Anthopology and Education Quarterly (American Anthropological Association) 18, (1987): 335–356

their students to get something out of it. They want them to enjoy learning. They want their students to be good students. Alice is one of the best tools I have ever worked with to help make this happen.

Alice is an object-oriented system of programming. The objects in Alice exist in a three-dimensional virtual world, much like a modern video game. In fact, the virtual word itself is an object in Alice—it has properties, and methods that can be used to manipulate those properties. In some ways, Alice is just like other modern object-oriented programming systems that use languages such as Java, C++, or Visual Basic, and in some ways, it is different. The Alice language has a grammar and syntax like other programming languages, but, as you will see, it is constructed in such a way that we don't need to memorize the grammar and syntax of the language in order to write computer programs. As students are learning Alice, they can concentrate on learning about the ideas of computer programming, such as the logic of computer programming, instead of having to worry about the spelling and grammar of a new language at the same time.

The virtual world of Alice is one that students can see. Like the real world, it has three-dimensional space and time, and the objects have properties just like physical objects, such as color, size, position, what direction an object is facing, and so on. We have a "camera" in Alice that allows us to see the virtual world on a computer screen, just like we might view a movie or a video game. This ability to see what happens to objects in our virtual world also makes it easier to learn computer programming with Alice than with many other programming systems. If we try to program a white rabbit to run around in a circle in our virtual world, and instead it simply stays in one spot and spins around in a circle, we can see that happening on the screen. We can get instant feedback from viewing the way Alice runs the programs we have created. Not every programming system is so easy to use. Often it is necessary to go through a process known as "compiling" before we can run a program.

In summary, there are three things about Alice that make it easier to learn programming by using Alice than most other systems of programming. First, Alice is constructed in such a way that we do not need to learn the grammar and syntax of a strange new language and can instead focus our attention on the concepts of programming; second, Alice provides visual feedback that allows students to see the effects of their programming; and third, Alice, provides rapid feedback shortening the creative cycle of conceptualization, implementation, and results. Alice is also fun and interesting to use, which never hurts when one is trying to learn something new. The use of Alice fosters persistent learning about computer programming, and perhaps more importantly, about many concepts fundamental to all of science, technology, engineering and mathematics.

Organization of the Text

Each chapter in this text is composed of two parts: lecture and tutorial (lab). The lecture part includes reading material for the student. For the most part, the reading material is relatively brief and is intended to establish a foundation for the lab component. Each of the readings is approximately 750 to 1,500 words long.

The lab component includes hands on tutorials in Alice, and sometimes related work intended to help them explore the concepts of the lesson. The lab component consists of one or more hands-on step-by-step tutorials, followed by review questions and open-ended exercises the students should be able to complete on their own, either individually, or in groups, once they understand the step-by-step exercise. The step-by-step exercises contain notes directing the students' attention to what they should be learning as they carry out the exercise. It is not enough to complete the steps in the exercise; each student should understand what was done, why it was done, and be able to repeat the exercise without the directions.

The book is organized in eight chapters, with goals as follows:

- Chapter 1—*An Introduction to Alice and Object Oriented Programming*

   Goal: The student will develop an understanding of the basic concepts of object-oriented programming and become familiar with the Alice interface.

- Chapter 2—*Developing Methods in Alice*

   Goal: The student will learn to create methods in Alice that demonstrate the application of good modular design.

- Chapter 3—*Events in Three-Dimensional Space*

   Goal: The student will learn to create events in Alice that manipulate objects in three-dimensional space and the Alice camera showing viewers those objects.

- Chapter 4—*The Logical Structure of Algorithms*

   Goal: The student will develop an understanding of the logical structure of algorithms.

- Chapter 5—*Boolean Logic in Programming*

   Goal: The student will develop an understanding of Boolean logic and its application in computer programming and algorithm development.

- Chapter 6—*Text and Sound in Alice Worlds*

   Goal: The student will learn to use text, graphic images, and sound as objects in Alice programs.

- Chapter 7—*Recursive Algorithms*

   Goal: The student will develop a basic understanding of recursion in computer programming, and learn to create and manipulate recursive algorithms in Alice.

■ Chapter 8—*Lists and Arrays in Alice*

Goal: The student will develop an understanding of the concept of a data structure and learn to implement the simple data structure known as a list in Alice.

Chapter 3 on event-driven programming precedes the chapters introducing algorithmic structures and Boolean logic for three reasons: first, because of the increasing importance of events in modern computer software; second, because students seem to enjoy working with events more than branching and looping; and third, because Alice handles events in such a simple, easy-to-use way. In practice, Chapters four and five could easily be covered before Chapter three.

Chapters 7 and 8 present topics that are not covered by everyone in an introductory programming course. They are intended to provide students with a first exposure to recursion and to data structures. Some preliminary work with developmental math and English students has shown that the chapters work in making this material accessible to them.

The text can be used for :

■ An introduction to the concepts of object-oriented programming during the first several weeks of a semester in which Java or a similar "real" programming language is used for the remainder of the semester. This is the way Java is being used in many places, with most teachers reporting that at the end of the semester they had actually covered more Java material than if they had not used Alice.

■ A semester-long course in programming and problem solving for the general student population. Such a course has been shown to be remarkably successful in helping "borderline" students succeed academically. It is especially helpful for students in developmental mathematics and English.

■ A programming component for a general computer literacy or applications course. The National Research Council and other groups have suggested that all college graduates should have been exposed to computer programming, yet currently less than ten percent of college students are required to take a course in programming. Not much can be done with Java or C++ in three weeks, but Alice and the material in the first few chapters of this book can be used to provide a basic understanding of objects and algorithms.

Acknowledgements

No book is really written by a single person, particularly a technically-oriented textbook like this one. I'd like to thank those who contributed directly to the development of the book, and those who contributed indirectly by shaping the ideas embodied in the text. I hope the final product does them justice.

Jill Batistick was the person with whom I worked most closely. She edited each part of the book as it was written and served as a mediator between me and everyone else who worked on the text. Tricia Coia was the Senior Product Manager who kept things moving along in a professional manner. If it wasn't for her this book probably would have published about three years later than it was. Tricia, Jill and I formed a three-person team linked via the Internet to develop and produce this book.

Cliff Brozo, Monroe College; Michael Galea, Washtenaw Community College; Larry Langellier, Moraine Valley Community College; Tom McCullough, Hillsborough Community College; Jo Ann Smith, formerly of Harper College; and Judith Zaplatynsky, Harper College reviewed the chapters as they were written. The final product was influenced greatly by their guidance, with entire chapters reshaped, a new one added, and one deleted, based on their comments. They took the time to serve as the guinea pigs trying each exercise as it was first written and identifying what worked and what didn't work. I'm very grateful for their efforts and insights.

Judi Silver was the book's Copy Editor—one of the unsung heroes of the publishing industry who serves as guardian of the English language and makes sure that sentences present coherent ideas. Peter Boivin, Susan Whalen, and Marianne Snow were the official testers for the technical material in the text. They made sure that the exercises really worked, and that words or phrase describing Alice matched the actual software. I'm grateful for their thoroughness, their competence, and their concern for the material. They actually had to take the time to learn Alice along the way, and in several cases their input shaped critical ideas in the text. I should also point out that Course Technology's commitment to excellence includes testing and editing that goes beyond that found in most publishing companies.

Abby Scholz deserves recognition for the time and effort she put into the outstanding cover for this book. I think it is one of the best I've seen, incorporating John Tenniel's 19th-century artwork into an exciting modern design. John Tenniel was the original illustrator for both of Lewis Carol's *Alice* books: *Alice's Adventures in Wonderland* and *Through the Looking Glass*. The image of the White Rabbit near the beginning of Tutorial 2B and elements of the cover design are from an original copy of his work secured by Drew Strawbridge.

I'd like to thank Randy Pausch, Dennis Cosgrove, and Caitlin Kelleher for their contribution in the form of the foreword for this book and for their efforts on behalf of Computer Science educators and students in developing Alice. Although he did not contribute directly to this text, Matt Conway's efforts in developing Alice and the ideas behind it, especially as presented in his doctoral dissertation, also deserve recognition. In addition, there are a host of people from the University of Virginia and Carnegie Mellon University who have shaped the development of Alice, and consequently this book and others. The Alice startup screen says that Alice is a "free gift to you from Carnegie Mellon University". I and many others who are teaching and learning about computers are truly grateful to all of those who helped to provide that gift.

Steve Cooper and Wanda Dann, co-authors with Randy Pausch of the only other Alice book currently on the market, deserve recognition for their seminal work in making Alice a tool for teaching computer programming and for their leadership in the National Science Foundation research into the effectiveness of Alice. They, perhaps as much or more than any else, are changing the way introductory computer programming is taught. Bill Taylor, from Camden County College, one of our co-PI's with the NSF, has also done a lot of pioneering work, creating the first Alice course aimed at serving developmental students in a community college setting.

This book was influenced by my colleagues at Community College of Philadelphia, especially by two groups of faculty—the Curriculum Facilitation Team (CFT) and the Alice Team. For more than eight years I served as a member of Community College of Philadelphia's CFT, which helps faculty from various disciplines develop courses and curricula. We would meet weekly to discuss our work and education in general, under the direction of Elaine Atkins, a leader in putting sound educational theory into practice. The University of Pennsylvania recently recognized her as the outstanding faculty member of the year for her work in their Graduate School of Education. Long conversations with her, Wendy Blume, Miles Grossbard, Carol La Belle, and Larry MacKenzie have contributed to the educational outlook behind this book. All of them, as well as Addie Butler, Doug Fenwick and Jim Oswald, have helped me to become a better writer and a better teacher.

Ed Baker, Joewanna Freeman, Charles McGinley, Dan Melamed, and Jim Watson are my colleagues on the Alice team who have been meeting to discuss Alice almost weekly for more than two years. Charles, Jim and I, along with Mike Hearn, Steve Horwitz, Fred Goldberg, Frank Gutekunst and Ray Sweeney, have been discussing how to teach introductory programming for more than 20 years. Charles was especially interested in Alice and has contributed many ideas to this text. Mardi Holliday is currently our Department Chair, and I'm grateful for her support of our work. Before coming to the College, she served for years as a disaster recovery specialist at IBM—excellent preparation for being a department chair. I'm also grateful to the more than 40 members of the faculty at CCP who are currently teaching with Alice. Their feedback has been invaluable.

Alice is a hot topic these days, and several companies wanted to publish this book. I chose Course Technology, because of the influence of the people from Course that I've met and worked with over the years—Kye Morrow, Bill Lisowski, Dave West, Drew Strawbridge and Bob Woodbury among them. All of them are very nice people, but what struck me about them most is their professionalism, their competence, and their enthusiasm for education and computing. Kye is our college's Course Technology Sales Rep, our first contact with the company. We are lucky in Philadelphia to have had excellent reps from almost all of the textbook companies with whom we do business, but Kye is one of the best and her encouragement made this book happen. Bill Lisowski is her boss, and he has always been there for us as well. Dave West was the company president at the time this project got started, and he is the kind of guy to make things happen. His positive, forward-looking vision and his dedication to providing a quality product for our students are infectious. Drew was the first editor at Course Technology with whom I worked. He recognized from the beginning that this wasn't just another programming book, but a new approach to teaching programming, and created an environment to develop things that way. Bob is a true professional in the publishing industry and a real gentleman, and Course Technology is fortunate to have him.

I'd like to thank my teachers at LaSalle Institute in Troy, New York. When I was 13 years old someone donated a DEC PDP-8 computer to the school. For an hour every day, between the time classes ended and the time track practice began, I was allowed to play with the machine, which had 4 Kilobytes of memory. I remember the wonderful day when the school spent thousands of dollars to upgrade to an 8 K memory. I am a computer professional today because of the influence of the Christian Brothers at LaSalle during those years.

Finally, I'd like to thank several people in my family. My wife, Daphne, who happens to be a Professor of English, not only provided all of the moral support one comes to expect from such a wonderful spouse, but proved to be an excellent proof reader as well. She also kept our household together while I spent many hours keeping up (catching up, really) with deadlines along the way. Of course this work was greatly influenced by my parents, George and Marlene Herbert. My father was a teacher and the Athletic Director for more than 30 years in the Maplewood School District, near Albany New York, so I grew up in a home centered on education. His mother, my grandmother Irene Fitzpatrick Herbert, taught me about the importance of education by her example. She was a teacher for more than 50 years, starting in a one-room school house in Grafton, New York in 1926. The building is still there. Early in her career she moved to the Blue Creek School in Latham, New York, which at the time was also a rural one-room school house. By the time she retired it had become part of one of the largest school districts in New York. That year a new invention appeared in her 4th grade classroom—an Apple computer. I often think about the amazing changes she saw in her career as a teacher and wonder about what our students will see in the nest 50 years.

Read This Before You Begin

This text is a stand-alone product with a CD that includes Alice version 2.0 (04/05/2005). The Alice software can also be found at *www.Alice.org*, the official Alice Web site.

Each chapter of this book has clearly stated objectives, one or more readings related to those objectives, and several hands-on tutorials. A chapter summary, review questions, and further exercises are included at the end of each chapter. Note that Appendix A of this text contains technical information about the Alice software, which is easy to install and use.

Note that the text was quality assurance tested using Alice v. 2.0 (04/05/2005) on Windows 2000 and Windows XP.

Student Data Files These are provided on the Course Technology Web site at *course.com* and on the CD that accompanies this book. The student data files contain all of the Alice worlds, image files, and so on that are needed within the tutorials.

Solution Files Solutions to the review questions and exercises found in the book are provided on the Course Technology Web site at *course.com*. The solutions are password protected. The solution files contain the completed Alice worlds that are the final product of each tutorial.

■ ■ ■ ■ ■FOREWORD

Note from the author: I asked Randy Pausch, Dennis Cosgrove, and Caitlin Kelleher to tell us about the development of Alice, the current state of affairs regarding Alice, and where things seem to be headed in the future. The sections that follow are what they wrote in reply. We've also included their individual bios at the end of this foreword.

All About Alice

So far there have been three distinct phases in the development of Alice, the *Goggles and Gloves* phase, the *"rapid prototyping 3D graphics* phase," and the *Teaching Introductory Programming* phase.

The *Goggles and Gloves* phase started in the early 1990's at the University of Virginia, where Randy was on the faculty, heading a 20-person User Interface Group investigating the boundary where people and technology interact. We were trying to make virtual reality more accessible by developing improved interfaces and lower-cost human computer interaction hardware and software. The paper *Virtual Reality on Five Dollars a Day,* which was published in the April 1991 edition of the ACM SIGCHI's journal *Human Factors in Computing Systems,* describes some of our work. It's available online through *www.alice.org*, where we provide links to publications related to our work on Alice.

We call that first phase the *Goggles and Gloves* phase because we really were focusing on the development of virtual reality systems in which the participant (the term *user* really doesn't seem to capture the sense of it; Disney Imagineering uses the term "guest") enters a virtual world by putting on a VR helmet and gloves. One mantra was "If it doesn't have a glove, it's not VR." At the time, virtual reality was in its infancy. So, in addition to developing VR interfaces, we were working on software systems to test the interfaces. One of our early reseach projects was SUIT, the *Simple User Interface Toolkit*, to which Matt Conway and Rob DeLine contributed heavily. Matt was instrumental in recognizing that vocabulary matters—that the choice of names for behaviors is critically important in a system for novices. His work was very influential in shaping the direction of the development work that led to the Alice system we have today. His doctoral dissertation, *Alice: Easy-to-Learn 3D Scripting for Novices* should be required reading for people interested in how to design systems for novices. It's available on the Web at *www.alice.org*.

The language for programming VR systems required one to think in terms of X,Y,Z coordinates, and to use terms like *translate*, *scale*, and *rotate* to describe things happening in a virtual world. On the early Silicon Graphics machines, angles were measured in integers representing tenths of a degree, so commands like *rotate -3600* were common. A person needed fairly advanced mathematics skills to program graphical objects in a 3D system. Engineers and physicists had the keys to get in, but many other intelligent, talented and creative people, such as artists, and filmmakers, did not. Matt saw that the language of VR was a part of the problem and that if we could change the language, then VR systems would be easier to use, and thus more accessible for novices and more powerful for experts at the same time. In his dissertation he wrote that "the tradeoff between power and simplicity is often a false one." He led us in discovering that using more everyday terms terms like *move*, *turn*, and *resize* instead of technically-oriented terms like *translate*, *rotate*, and *scale* could go a long way toward achieving the powerful simplicity that would become one of the hallmarks of Alice. *Turn left 1 revolution* makes sense to a lot more people than *rotate X -3600.*

The first version of Alice emerged as an easy-to-use scripting system for building virtual worlds. The system itself was a combination of C and Python code, with which one could rapidly create virtual worlds by iterating Python scripts. Over the years, the programming features of Python have been replaced with dragging and dropping code elements.

It's important to note that even early versions of Alice could not have been created without the efforts of a dedicated team of people. In particular, PhD student Rich Gossweiler, was responsible for the implementation of the very early versions of Alice, and its co-system DIVER. Tommy Burnette was also responsible for a great deal of the early Alice software implementation. A complete listing of people who have contributed to the Alice project over the years is available at *www.alice.org* .

At about this time (the mid 1990's) our work was funded by a variety of sources, including the National Science Foundation (NSF) and the Defense Advanced Research Projects Agency (DARPA). These are two of the most amazing agencies in the federal government, when it comes to return on investment of public money. A while back, NSF and DARPA asked for funding to explore using computers as tools for communication among educators, scientists, and engineers, and the result is the Internet. We believe that any time they ask for money, Congress should jump at the chance to spend public funds so wisely. One day one of the people from the Department of Defense who was overseeing our project said that we should forget about the virtual reality hardware and concentrate on the software we were building. He argued that our most important contribution was the way in which our software could be used as a rapid development system for 3D graphics prototyping.

During the summer and fall of 1995, Randy spent a sabbatical at Walt Disney Imagineering's Virtual Reality Studio working on the "Aladdin" project which was featured at EPCOT Center and, later, at DisneyQuest. The experience working with the Imagineering team helped to make it clear that we were moving into a realm of work that would require both artists and engineers. In the spirit of bringing artists and engineers together, Randy created a course called "Building Virtual Worlds" in which teams of artists and engineers work together to create interactive virtual worlds. In the Spring of 1997, the research group moved to Carnegie Mellon University, in order to take advantage of the fairly unique cross-disciplinary focus at CMU. However, no story of the Alice system would be complete without acknowledging how gracious the University of Virginia was in allowing us to continue work on Alice seamlessly, by allowing us to transfer our funding and research to another university, and we are very grateful for their support. We have fond memories of the University of Virginia and highly recommend it to students looking for a great place to go to school.

Over the next few years we gradually moved into the third phase of our work as we developed better ways to build virtual worlds. Alice became a workhorse for the "Building Virtual Worlds" course, which was then being taught at Carnegie Mellon, for several years, finally realizing our dream of allowing "a 1,000 creative flowers to bloom." However, with respect to making 3D graphics programming easier, we slowly began to realize that we had the problem inside-out. Instead of thinking about how to improve programming to make 3D graphics more accesible, it started to become clear that 3D graphics could make programming more accesible. A seminal event occured one day when Randy was on a family trip to DisneyWorld. His ten year old nephew Christopher spent the day working with Alice on a laptop as they drove. Chris programmed 3D graphics for eight hours straight, never really having trouble with the 3D part, but constantly asking for help about "where the commas and semicolons had to go." In Randy's words: "I immediately realized that this was a problem we could solve." Some work had already been done on the drop and drag interface, but now the creation of a drag and drop interface for creating Alice programs became a priority.

Wanda Dann and Steve Cooper both became important contributors to the future of Alice at about this time. Wanda, who teaches Computer Science at Ithaca College, and Steve, who teaches at St. Joseph's University, have long been interested in how visualization can be used to teach object-oriented programming concepts. They began to work with us to shape Alice as a better tool to teach introductory programming. We were all beginning to recognize that Alice works well for teaching introductory programming for three primary reasons: minimization of the problems of syntax, the ability to see the results of object-oriented programming in a live virtual world, and the motivation provided by working in such an exciting environment. Since 1999 Steve and Wanda's efforts developing educational materials based on Alice, testing Alice in the classroom, and providing feedback to Dennis and company as the software was refined have been instrumental in shaping the current look and feel of Alice.

In addition to helping students with the technical hurdles, Alice is allowing us to begin changing the ways in which we introduce students to computer programming. The way we teach computer programming hasn't changed much in the past 50 years, despite the fact that the way we use computers has. The first computers that appeared in the middle of the 20th century were literally used to help bombs hit their targets. The early high-level programming language, FORTRAN, was designed to help scientists and engineers with their number crunching. Today, how many high school students are excited about writing code to generate the first 10 Fibonacci numbers? Using Alice, students learn the basics of programming while creating animated stories and games. Wanda Dann has been a strong proponent for using Alice to introduce programming through storytelling at the college-level, and Caitlin has been studying using the activity of storytelling in Alice to interest middle-school girls in learning to program. In addition to being more motivating than assignments like sorting a list of numbers, creating animated stories helps to make computer programming seem less foreign. Not many people are familiar with the concept of mathematical algorithms, but everyone is familiar with storytelling. By using Alice to tell story in a virtual world, young people become engaged in linear sequencing, modular development, and planning before implementation—three of the most important skills for early success in computer programming.

One highly desirable side effect of using Alice to introduce programming through storytelling is that more young women are attracted to the discipline. It's no secret that Computer Science, unlike Law and Medicine, has failed to attract women in significant numbers. Currently, women constitute less than one-third of all Computer Science majors in the US, and less than one-fourth of those earning Ph.Ds in Computer Science. According to Caitlin's research (her dissertation, when completed, will be available at *www.alice.org*), Alice has the power to begin to change that; thereby changing the culture of the Computer Science classroom and workplace.

So where do things stand now? Well, Chuck Herbert's programming textbook is only the second book to use Alice as a tool to teach programming. The Dann, Cooper and Pausch book was the first. Course Technology's Alice CourseCard is the first widely available reference material for Alice 2.0. More material is sure to follow as the number and type of schools using Alice increases. Last year we knew of approximately 30 colleges and universities using Alice. This year we are aware of about 60 colleges and universities and at least that many high schools, as well—and there are probably more folks using Alice that we don't know about.

Currently most people who use Alice seem to be doing so to teach introductory programming, although it is starting to be used in other disciplines. The most widespread educational model for the use of Alice is to use Alice for the first half of an introductory programming course, followed by the use of Java or a similar commercial programming language in the second half of the semester. That model seems to be working remarkably well in places like Duke University, the University of Mississippi, Haverford College, and here at Carnegie Mellon.

Within the past three years other models for the use of Alice have emerged, particularly in the community colleges, and in courses other than computer programming. Here are just a few of the efforts we know about:

> ■ Bill Taylor is leading a group of faculty members at Camden County College in New Jersey who are studying the use of Alice in problem solving and programming courses for students in developmental Mathematics and English courses. Their preliminary work has shown that Alice is an effective tool for improving the overall academic performance of developmental students.

- Chuck Herbert is leading a team of 40 faculty members at Community College of Philadelphia exploring the use of Alice for a programming module in computer literacy and applications courses. Their preliminary work shows that the use of Alice in such courses is attracting new students to computer-related disciplines.

- Sharon Wavle at Tompkins Cortland County College in New York is offering an online programming course using Alice.

- For each of the past two Fall semesters, 1,300 freshman engineering students at Virginia Tech have used Alice as a tool to explore programming and problem solving in their introductory engineering course.

- ITESM, a 33-campus, 80,000 student high-end University in Mexico has been using Alice,and reports very similar results to the American experience, giving us hope that the storytelling approach works in a fairly culture-independent way.

The most common question people ask us these days is about the future of Alice. Right now, the 04/05/2005 Version of Alice 2.0 is reasonably stable and reliable, and runs on Windows and the Macintosh. There are no plans develop it further. Instead, work is beginning on Alice 3.0. How will Alice 3.0 be different? Well, to start with, one thing about it will be the same— it will continue to be provided free of charge to the public from Carnegie Mellon University. The University has been very gracious in supporting us, and we are committed to maintaining Alice as an open source, non-commercial, piece of software. This "purity" is important; many students have worked hard over the years to contribute to the Alice effort, and we believe it must continue to be "for the people." All of Randy Pausch's royalties from the Dann, Cooper and Pausch book are donated by him to Carnegie Mellon, to help support the software development. We are glad to hear that Chuck Herbert has also pledged a portion of his royalties from this book to the Alice effort. We had various corporate sponsors over the years, most notably Intel and Microsoft, and we are pleased to say that Electronic Arts (EA) is a major sponsor of Alice version 3.0.

We expect that Alice 3.0 will be a pure Java implementation, and that you will be able to dump the Java code for an Alice 3.0 world and then work with it in Java. That's a big change from Alice 2.0, which does not create Java code, but works more like an interpreter that directly executes Alice methods. This should serve several purposes, including helping to make the transition form Alice to Java smoother in introductory programming courses.

You can expect the new version of Alice to be more truly object-oriented than the current version. Alice 2.0 is a good tool to introduce the concept of an object as a collection of properties and methods, but it does not provide the ability to create true class-level methods, true inheritance, or the overriding necessary for polymorphism. Alice 3.0 should have some, if not all, of these features.

Caitlin's work has shown that users, especially young people, can do more and learn more with objects that have higher order primitive methods, such as walk, sit, and touch instead of just move, turn, and so on. There will probably be more methods that manipulate objects and their sub-parts together, and the gallery of available objects will probably be richer that the current Alice gallery.

The overall look and feel of Alice will also probably be less toy-like. Anyone who has used Alice for more than a few minutes knows it's not a toy, but it *looks* like a toy. The new version should still be easy to use, but people probably won't think "Fisher Price" when they first see it.

The team that started working on virtual reality interfaces years ago at the University of Virginia had no idea that our work would lead to Alice and that it would become such an important tool in Computer Science education. As is the case with many NSF funded projects, the taxpayers have gotten more than their money's worth, but just not in the way one would have thought reading the original proposals. Such is the path of science and exploration. Now that we know where we are headed, our goal is to make Alice the vehicle of choice for someone's first exposure to computer programming, for everyone—worldwide—from 5th grade through college.

> Randy Pausch
> Dennis Cosgrove
> Caitlin Kelleher
> Carnegie Melon University,
> December 2005

Randy Pausch is a Professor of Computer Science, Human-Computer Interaction, and Design at Carnegie Mellon University, where he co-founded the university's Entertainment Technology Center (etc.cmu.edu). He leads the research group at CMU that is responsible for the development of Alice. This groups' mission is "to explore and develop the mechanisms by which humans can more effectively and enjoyably interact with technology, and to have fun while doing so."

Dennis Cosgrove is a Senior Research Programmer at Carnegie Mellon University, where he has spent the last several years as the primary software architect and implementer for Alice 2.0. He was one of the principal developers of the earlier PC/Windows 95 Alice implementation at the University of Virginia. In addition to his work on Alice, he has contributed to the development of an eye-tracking system that allows quadriplegics to interact with a computer.

Caitlin Kelleher has been working as Graduate Research Assistant at Carnegie Mellon University since 1999. By the time you read this she will have finished her Ph.D. in Computer Science. Her thesis work has been based on creating a programming system that is attractive to middle school girls by focusing on storytelling. She developed the online, stencil-based tutorials that are part of the current Alice software.

1

AN INTRODUCTION TO ALICE AND OBJECT-ORIENTED PROGRAMMING

After finishing this chapter, you should be able to:

☐ Provide a brief definition of the following terms: algorithm, class, computer program, event, function, Integrated Development Environment (IDE), instance, instantiation, method, method parameter, object, object-oriented programming (OOP), programming language, property, and state of an object

☐ Run the Alice software and locate and describe the following components of the Alice interface: World window, Object tree, Details area, Editor area, Events area, menu bar, trash can, clipboard, Play button, Undo button, Redo button

☐ Load and play an existing Alice world

☐ Create a new Alice world by adding objects to a blank world, positioning them, and using simple methods to animate those objects

☐ Print the code for Alice methods and events

1

OBJECT-ORIENTED PROGRAMMING AND ALICE

An **algorithm** is a step-by-step process. A computer program is a set of instructions telling a computer how to perform a specific task. As such, every **computer program** is an algorithm. Early computers were far less complex than computers are today—their memories were smaller and their programs were much simpler. To help manage the growing complexity of computers, computer scientists have introduced the notion of **objects** and object-oriented programming An object is anything that is manipulated by a computer program. It is possible for modern computers to manipulate many objects at the same time.

An object can be something in the physical world or even just an abstract idea. An airplane, for example, is a physical object that can be manipulated by a computer. Almost all commercial aircraft today, Boeing 777s, Airbus 330s, and so on, have autopilots—computers with programs that can fly the plane. The autopilot is a computer that manipulates an object in the physical world. To the computer, the airplane is an object.

Most objects that computers manipulate are not physical objects. A bank transaction is an example of an object that is not physical. There is a set of activities that can be called a transaction, there may be physical money that changes hands, and there is usually a paper record of the transaction; however, the transaction itself is simply a concept, or an idea. It is an object, but not a physical object.

Whether an object exists in the physical world doesn't matter much in terms of what happens inside a computer. To a computer, an object is simply something that can be represented by data in the computer's memory and manipulated by computer programs. The data that represents the object is organized into a set of **properties**. Each property describes the object in some way. For example, the weight of an airplane, its location, the direction in which it's facing, and so on are all properties of the airplane. A computer manipulates an object by changing some of its properties or some of the properties of its sub-parts. For instance, the autopilot might change the angle of a wing flap (a sub-part), which in turn affects the entire airplane.

Sometimes the hardware in a computer can translate these changes in properties into actions that affect the physical world—as an airplane's autopilot does—and sometimes the changes in an object only affect information in the computer's memory and have no direct effect on the physical world. For example, when a bank deposit is recorded on a computer, the amount of money in the bank balance property of the bank account object is changed, but there is no other immediate effect on the physical world.

The programs that manipulate the properties of an object are called the object's **methods**. We can think of an object as a collection of properties and the methods that are used to manipulate those properties. The values stored in the properties of an object at any one time are collectively called the **state of an object.** This modern approach to computer programming is known as **object-oriented programming**, or **OOP** for short.

A **computer programming language** is a particular set of instructions for programming a computer, along with the grammar and syntax for using those instructions. Most modern computer programming languages are object-oriented languages, in which programs are organized into a set of methods that manipulate the properties of objects stored in a computer. To understand any object-oriented system of programming, you need to know something about how that system handles objects and about the language that is used in methods to manipulate objects in that system.

Learning to program a computer is often a difficult task because of the need to learn about programming concepts and the language of programming at the same time. It's also difficult because people find it hard to visualize all of the changes that are occurring as a computer program runs. Alice can make it easier to learn to program a computer by helping with both of these problems.

Alice is an object-oriented system of programming. The objects in Alice exist in a three-dimensional virtual world, much like a modern video game. In fact, the virtual world itself is an object in Alice—it has properties and methods that can be used to manipulate those properties. Alice is somewhat like other modern object-oriented programming systems that use languages, such as Java, C++, or Visual Basic, but, as you will see, it is constructed so that you don't need to memorize the grammar and syntax of the language in order to write computer programs. As you are learning Alice, you can concentrate on learning about the ideas of computer programming, such as the logic of your algorithms, instead of having to worry about the spelling and grammar of a new language at the same time.

The virtual world of Alice is one that you can see. Like the real world, it has three-dimensional space (and time), and each object has properties just like physical objects have properties; these include color, size, position, the direction in which the object is facing, and so on. Alice has a **camera** that allows you to see its virtual world on a computer screen, just as you might view a movie or a video game. This ability to see what happens to objects in your virtual world makes it easier to learn computer programming with Alice than with almost any other system of programming. For instance, if you try to program a white rabbit to run around in a circle, and instead he simply stays in one spot and spins, you can see that happening on the screen. You can get instant feedback from viewing the way Alice runs the programs you have created. Not every programming system is so easy to use. Often it is necessary to go through a process known as compiling before you can run a computer program.

NOTE □ □ □ | For more information on compilers, interpreters, and computer languages, see Appendix C of this book.

In summary, there are three things about Alice that make it easier to learn programming by using Alice than almost any other system of programming:

- Minimal memorization of syntax—Alice is constructed in such a way that you do not need to learn the grammar and syntax of a strange new language and can instead focus your attention on the concepts of computer programming.
- Visualization—Alice allows you to see the effects of your programs and any changes you make to them.
- Rapid feedback—Alice provides rapid feedback, which you may get at any time by simply starting your virtual world and watching what happens.

You will also find that Alice is fun and interesting to use, which never hurts when one is trying to learn something new.

TUTORIAL 1A—EXPLORING THE ALICE INTERFACE

In this tutorial, you will explore the Alice interface, and then load and play an Alice world. Before starting, you should have a computer system with the Alice software properly installed. Fortunately, installing Alice is easy. The software is available freely from The Stage Three Development Team at Carnegie Mellon University via their Web site at *www.alice.org* and is also on the CD that accompanies this book. See Appendix A for further instructions on acquiring, installing, and starting the Alice software.

Anyone attempting this exercise should have experience using a computer. You certainly don't need to be an expert, but you should have some experience with things like word processing and accessing the Internet so that you are familiar with Windows, a mouse, a keyboard, and a printer.

NOTE □ □ □ | A six-page laminated CourseCard for Alice version 2.0, which summarizes Alice features and commands, is available from Thomson Course Technology—ISBN 1-4188-4675-9. It will prove useful as you learn to use Alice, and later as a command reference.

1. Start the Alice software. You will see the Welcome to Alice! dialog box overthe front of the Alice Integrated Development Environment (IDE), as shown in Figure 1-1. If Alice opens without showing you the Welcome to Alice! dialog box, click **File**, and then click **New World** to open this window. An **IDE** is a computer program that is used to write other computer programs. Most modern programming languages have IDEs with everything you need to create and run computer programs. Alice is no exception, but its IDE is simpler than most. The Alice IDE is often called the **Alice interface**.

NOTE□ □ □ | There is a *Show this dialog at start* check box in the lower-left corner of the Welcome to Alice! dialog box. It should be checked so that the Welcome to Alice! dialog box will appear when Alice starts.

FIGURE 1-1: The Alice Interface with the Welcome to Alice! dialog box

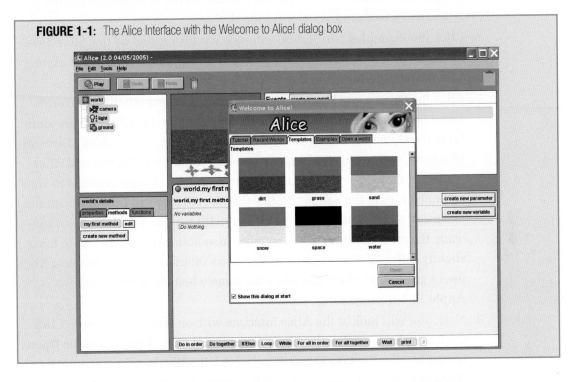

2. Notice that the Welcome to Alice! dialog box has five tabs: Tutorial, Recent Worlds, Templates, Examples, and Open a world. You may get back to this dialog box at any time while using Alice by clicking **File** on the menu bar, and then clicking **New World** or **Open World**. Let's look at each of these tabs before continuing.

3. Click the **Tutorial** tab and you will see four Alice tutorials. You won't use the tutorials now, but you may want to come back to them later as an exercise on your own. When you are ready to use the tutorials, either click the tutorial you would like to run, or click the large **Start the Tutorial** button to follow them in order. They were created by the developers of Alice to help people learn the system. They are quite easy to follow.

4. Click the **Recent Worlds** tab. You will see thumbnail sketches of the most recently saved Alice worlds. If no worlds have been saved since the Alice software was installed on your system, this tab will say *no recent worlds*.

5. Click the **Templates** tab. Alice comes with six blank templates for starting a new virtual world—dirt, grass, sand, snow, space, and water. Each of the templates includes a texture for the surface, which is called the ground in Alice, and a background color for the sky.

6. Click the **Examples** tab. Several example worlds created by the Alice developers are provided with the Alice software. We'll come back to the examples tab later in this tutorial.

7. Click the **Open a world** tab. This tab is used to access other Alice worlds saved on your computer. In Figure 1-2, you can see this tab. It is very similar to the Open File dialog boxes seen in other programs, such as Microsoft Windows, with navigation icons across the top, a list of folders and Alice worlds from the current directory in the middle, and some controls to view and open files at the bottom. Notice that the Alice world files end with the extension .a2w. These files were created with version 2.0 of the Alice software, the most recent version. You may also notice that the interface looks slightly different than most other Windows interfaces. This is because Alice uses a generic interface that looks the same when using the Windows, Apple, or Unix operating systems.

8. Next, you will look at the Alice interface with an Alice world open. Click the **Examples** tab, click the lakeSkater thumbnail, and then click the **Open** button to open the **lakeSkater** Alice world. It will take a few seconds for Alice to load all of the elements of the world. You will see the names of the elements flash past in a small window in the center of the screen while this happens. When Alice is finished loading the world, your screen should resemble Figure 1-3.

FIGURE 1-2: The Open a world tab in the Welcome to Alice! dialog box showing eight folders and three Alice world files

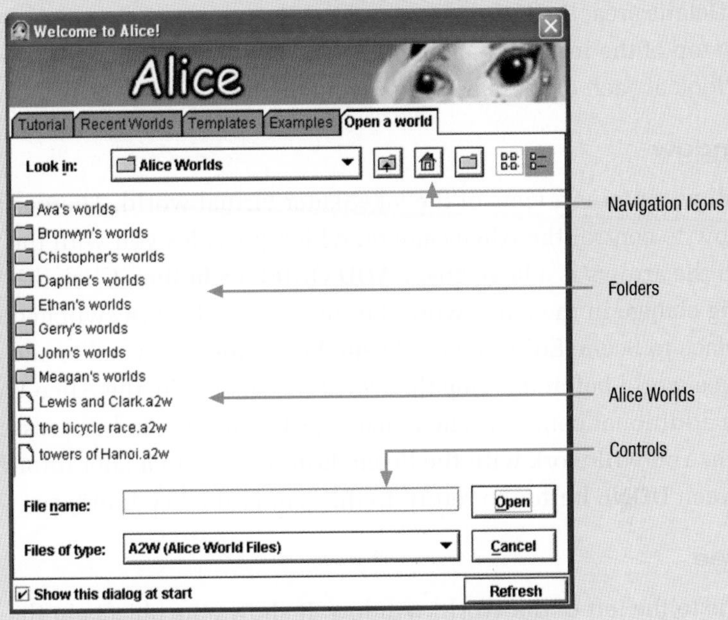

Navigation Icons

Folders

Alice Worlds

Controls

FIGURE 1-3: The Alice Interface after loading the lakeSkater example world

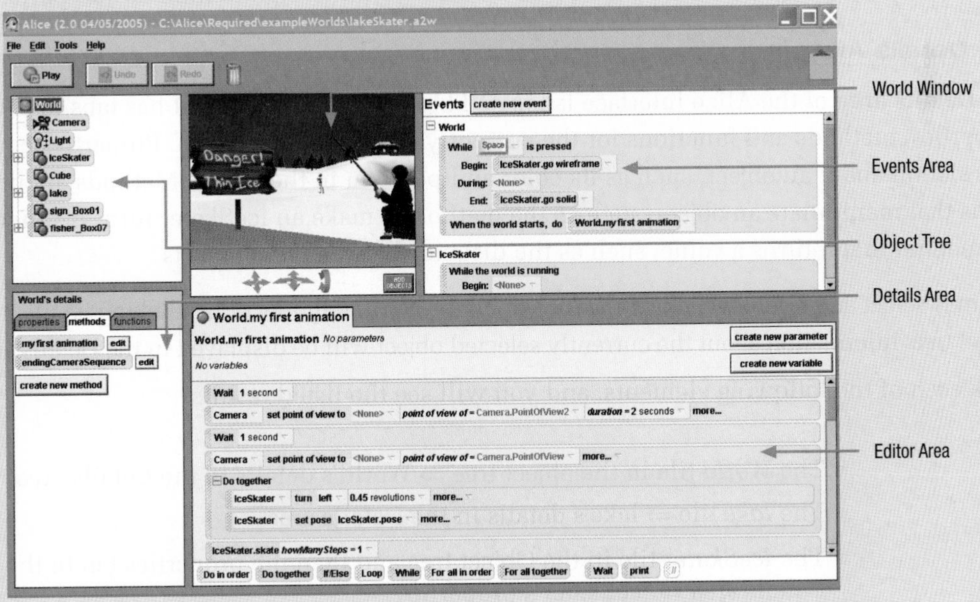

World Window

Events Area

Object Tree

Details Area

Editor Area

THE MAIN WORK AREAS OF THE ALICE INTERFACE

The Alice interface has five main work areas, as shown in Figure 1-3: the World window, the Object tree, the Details area, the Editor area, and the Events area. There are also several elements across the top of the interface—a menu bar, three control buttons, a trash can, and a clipboard. Let's look at each of these before playing the lakeSkater world.

The World Window

The **World window** contains a view of the lakeSkater virtual world. There is a set of arrows below the window to control the Alice camera, which provides you with the view in the window. Next to the arrows is a large green **ADD OBJECTS button**. Click this button, and you will see a big change in the Alice world because you will have switched from the standard Alice interface to Scene Editor mode. **Scene Editor mode** is used to add and position objects in an Alice world before playing the world. In this mode, the Alice World window is larger and has additional controls. The Alice object galleries can be accessed at the bottom of the screen. You will work with the Scene Editor mode in a later tutorial. For now, click the large green **DONE button** to return to the standard Alice interface.

The Object Tree

The **Object tree** is to the left of the World window. It shows the objects in the current Alice world organized as a tree of tiles, with a tile for each object. The plus sign next to an object shows that it has sub-parts, which may be seen by clicking the plus sign. Click the *plus sign* to see the sub-parts of the IceSkater, and then click the *minus sign* to hide its sub-parts.

The Details Area

The **Details area** of the Alice interface is located below the Object tree. It has tabs to show properties, methods and functions for the currently selected Alice object. Properties contain information about an object, such as its color and position in the world. Methods are programs that manipulate an object, such as the method to make an IceSkater turn. A **function** is a method that returns a value, such as the distance between two objects.

You may select an object by clicking that object in the World window or by clicking its tile in the Object tree. Information about the currently selected object will be displayed in the Details area.

Click each of the following elements, and you will see the listed results:

- The *World* tile in the object tree ⇒ World's details in the Details area
- The *lake* tile ⇒ lake's details in the Details area
- The *IceSkater* tile in the Object tree and then the properties tab in the Details area ⇒ IceSkater's properties
- The *methods* tab ⇒ IceSkater's methods
- The *functions* tab ⇒ IceSkater's functions

The Editor Area

The largest area of the Alice interface is the **Editor area**, which is to the right of the Details area. Here, methods are assembled and edited by clicking and dragging tiles from other parts of the interface. The bottom of the Editor area has a row of logic and control tiles that can be used to put branching, looping, and other logical structures into the algorithms that will make up an object's methods. Most of the time that you spend working with Alice will be spent using the Editor area.

The Events Area

The **Events area** in Alice is above the Editor area. This part of the interface shows existing events and is used to create new events. An **event** consists of a condition, called an **event trigger**, and the name of a method, called an **event handler**. Whenever the event trigger occurs, the event handler is called into action. For example, you might want the sound of a splash to occur if an ice skater falls through the ice. Falling through the ice would be the event trigger, and the method that makes the splash sound would be the event handler.

Some events, such as causing a method to run when a key is pressed, provide user interaction for an Alice world. The flight simulator world that can be accessed through the examples tab is an interactive world that you might want to take a look at after finishing this chapter. Events are covered in detail in Chapter 3.

OTHER ELEMENTS OF THE ALICE INTERFACE

In addition to the main work areas that you have just explored, the Alice interface also has two icons, three buttons, and a menu bar near the top of the screen. These are identified in Figure 1-3 and are discussed in the following sections.

Alice Tools for Deleting and Copying

The Trash can icon and the Clipboard icon near the top of the screen are used for editing Alice worlds.

You can delete an item in an Alice world, such as an object or instruction tile, by dragging and dropping it in the Alice trash can. You can also right-click an object or tile, and select *delete* from the menu that appears.

You can copy an item by dragging and dropping it onto the Clipboard icon in the top-right corner of the interface, and then dragging it from the Clipboard icon and dropping it in its new location. You can also duplicate a method tile by right-clicking it and selecting *make copy* from the menu that appears, but this does not work with Alice objects.

The Undo and Redo buttons near the top-left corner of the interface are also useful for editing an Alice world. You can undo the last change you made by clicking the *Undo* button. The effects of the Undo button can be reversed by using the Redo button. Alice can remember the last several dozen changes that you made. The Ctrl+Z and Ctrl+Y shortcut keys can also be used for Undo and Redo, although there are no shortcut keys for cut, copy, and paste.

Alice Menus

The Alice interface has a menu bar at the top of the screen with four menus: File, Edit, Tools, and Help. The menus are used far less in Alice than in many other computer programs. For now, you will look at only a few of the items on these menus. All of the features on the Alice menus are listed in Appendix B.

File Menu   The Alice File menu has commands for opening, closing, and saving Alice worlds, as well as options to export an Alice world as a movie file or as an HTML Web page. You will use these options in later tutorials throughout this book.

Edit Menu   Currently the only option on the Alice Edit menu is Preferences, which is used to change settings for the Alice software. Appendix B of this book lists and describes these settings. The most important thing to know for now is that the Alice Edit menu is not used to edit Alice methods in the same way that the Edit menu can be used to edit elements, such as documents, in Microsoft Word. Instead, Alice emphasizes the use of a drag-and-drop interface, which uses the editing icons and buttons described in the previous sections of this chapter.

Tools Menu   The Alice Tools menu contains three options: World Statistics, Text Output, and Error Console. The Text Output option allows you to see system messages generated as you play Alice worlds, and the Error Console can be used to look at detailed Alice error messages. Both of these are rather sophisticated, and are not very useful for novice programmers. The World Statistics option allows you to see statistics, such as the number of objects in a world, the time the world has been open, and many other useful items. Only some of the information here will be meaningful to you until you learn more about Alice and computer graphics.

Help Menu   The Help menu does not contain an option to look up the features of Alice as you might expect. By not providing a way to look up features, the developers of Alice were hoping to encourage people to learn about Alice by experimenting with it.

The Help menu does have three options: Tutorials, Example Worlds, and About Alice. Example Worlds and Tutorials will both take you back to the Welcome to Alice! dialog box . The About Alice option will give you general information about the development of Alice and has a link to the Alice Web site *www.alice.org*, where you can find out more about Alice.

NOTE □ □ □   From time to time you may encounter errors while using the Alice software. The Alice error message box contains a button to submit a bug report to the Stage 3 Development Team at Carnegie Mellon University. Reporting errors will help to improve future versions of Alice, and in some cases a member of the team may contact you directly. You may also submit bugs and suggestions about Alice through the Alice Web site. They want to hear from the users of Alice.

TUTORIAL 1B—PLAYING AN ALICE WORLD

In this tutorial, you will experiment with playing an Alice world. Alice worlds fit into two different categories—some Alice worlds are interactive the way a video game is, while others are simply run and viewed like a video tape. In either case, experienced Alice users refer to "playing" an Alice world the way most software developers talk about "running" a computer program.

The Alice world that you will play in this tutorial is the lakeSkater world used in Tutorial 1A. It is not an interactive world, but is more like watching a video of an ice-skater's performance. If you have just finished Tutorial 1A and still have the lakeSkater world open, then continue with the steps that follow. If you do not have the lakeSkater world open, then before starting this tutorial you need to run the Alice software and open the lakeSkater example world. The lakeSkater example world can be found on the Examples tab of the Welcome to Alice! dialog box that appears when you start the Alice software.

1. There are three buttons near the top of the Alice interface, labeled *Play*, *Undo*, and *Redo*, *Undo* and *Redo* are used for editing, as described in Tutorial 1A. The Play button is used to play the current Alice world. When this button is clicked, the world will play in a larger version of the World window, with player controls at the top of the window, as shown in Figure 1-4. Click the **Play** button now and watch the show unfold. Let the world play through to the end at least once before proceeding.

FIGURE 1-4: The World window with the lakeSkater world running

2. Notice that the new window has a speed slider control and five buttons across the top of the window in which the Alice world plays. The buttons are labeled *Pause, Resume, Restart, Stop,* and *Take Picture.*

3. The *Restart* button is used to begin playing the current world again from the beginning. The *Pause* and *Resume* buttons work like the pause and play buttons on a VCR or DVD player. Click the **Restart** button now to restart the lakeSkater world, and then experiment with the *Pause* and *Resume* buttons.

4. The speed slider is used to change the speed of the world while it is playing. Restart the world, and experiment with the speed slider control.,

5. The *Take Picture* button captures an image of the currently playing world and saves it in a data file. Restart the world and click the *Take Picture* button to take a picture of the world. An Image captured and stored dialog box will appear, showing you the full path name of the file that was saved. The stored image file can be viewed and used as any other computer image file can be. Appendix C has more information on changing the settings for Alice's screen capture function. Click **OK** to close the dialog box.

6. The *Stop* button stops the world that is currently playing and returns you to the standard Alice interface. Once the *Stop* button is pressed, you will need to click the standard interface's *Play* button to replay the world. Try this now. After you have finished experimenting, click the **Stop** button one last time to return to the standard Alice interface.

Alice is a graphics intensive program that can use a lot of a computer's memory, so you should exit the Alice program when it is not in use. Now that you are finished with this tutorial, you should exit the Alice program.

1. Click **File** on the menu bar, and then click **Exit**.

2. If you have made any changes to the current world since it was last changed, a Save World? dialog box will appear, asking you if you want to save the world first. If this happens when you attempt to exit Alice after viewing the lakeSkater world, click **No** so that you do not change the saved example world.

NOTE □ □ □ | While you are viewing or editing an Alice world, a dialog box will appear every 15 minutes, warning you that you have not saved your Alice world. If this happens while you are playing an Alice world, such as in Tutorial 1B, then it's probably safe to ignore the warning. If it happens while you are creating or editing your own Alice world, then it's probably a good idea to save your world.

TUTORIAL 1C—CREATING YOUR FIRST ALICE WORLD

In this tutorial, you will create, play, and save a new Alice world. You should have finished Tutorials 1A and 1B before starting. You will create an Alice world in which a bunny will move from the right side of the screen to the center, turn to face the camera, and then say "Hello, World!" This is an Alice equivalent of the "Hello, World!" program that students traditionally write as their first program in a new programming language.

NOTE ▫ ▫ ▫ | The tutorial begins with the Alice software closed. If you have an Alice world open, then exit Alice before continuing.

1. Start the Alice software.
2. In the Welcome to Alice! dialog box, click the **Tutorials** tab. If the Welcome to Alice! dialog box does not open automatically, click **File** on the menu bar, and then click **New World**. You should now see the *Templates* tab of the Welcome to Alice! dialog box, as shown in Figure 1-5.

FIGURE 1-5: The templates tab with six templates for new Alice worlds

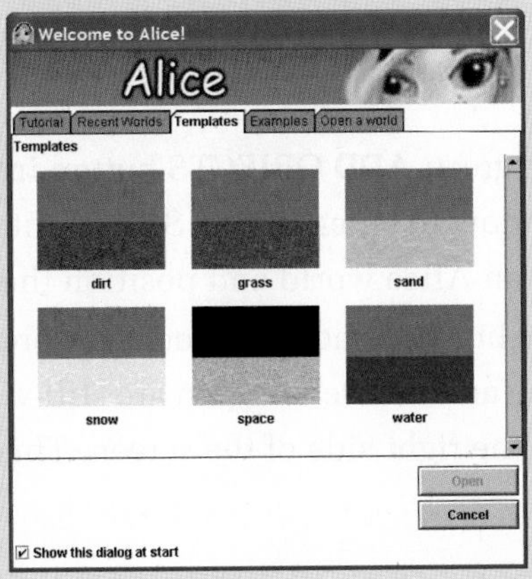

3. Thumbnail sketches for six new world templates are now available—dirt, grass, sand, snow, space, and water. The templates appear to be very simple with a texture for the ground and a background color for the sky, but looks can be deceiving. There is actually a great deal of computer programming behind a new Alice world, with a camera, ambient light, and other elements already in place. Click the **grass** thumbnail, and then click the **Open** button.

A new Alice world based on the grass template is now open, and you can see the standard Alice interface that you used earlier in the chapter. Notice that the Object tree in the upper-left part of the interface contains the four tiles that appear in every Alice world: world, camera, light, and ground, as shown in Figure 1-6. You can see from the way the tree is organized that the other objects are sub-objects of the world.

FIGURE 1-6: The Object tree after starting a new world

The new world also has the default event—When the world starts, do world.my first method—in the Events area, and a blank default method—world.my first method—in the Editor area.

ADDING OBJECTS TO AN ALICE WORLD

The next several steps will introduce you to the Alice object galleries and the process of adding objects to an Alice world. Many people get carried away with creating big Alice worlds with many objects when they first start to use Alice. In this tutorial, you will start with a very small Alice world with a minimum number of objects. Objects are added to an Alice world in Scene Editor mode.

1. Click the large green **ADD OBJECTS** button in the bottom-right corner of the World window to enter Alice's Scene Editor mode, which is used to add objects to an Alice world and position them.
2. Note that the Alice interface now looks different, as shown in Figure 1-7. The Object tree and the Details area are still visible on the left, but there is a new area on the right side of the screen. This new area is called the Scene Editor.

The Scene Editor has new controls, a larger world window, and object galleries on the bottom. The Scene Editor replaces the Events area and the Editor area when you are in Scene Editor mode.

Let's look at the Alice object galleries. There are two object galleries: a **Local Gallery** provided with the Alice software, and a **Web Gallery** maintained by the Stage Three Development Team at Carnegie Mellon University. (You need an active Internet connection to use the Web Gallery.) The Local Gallery is visible at the bottom of the screen in Scene Editor mode, as shown in Figure 1-7. The galleries are organized as a tree of folders containing related objects. You can navigate the tree of galleries by clicking a gallery folder to enter that gallery, or by using the gallery navigation bar, which is just above the galleries.

FIGURE 1-7: The Alice Interface in Scene Editor mode

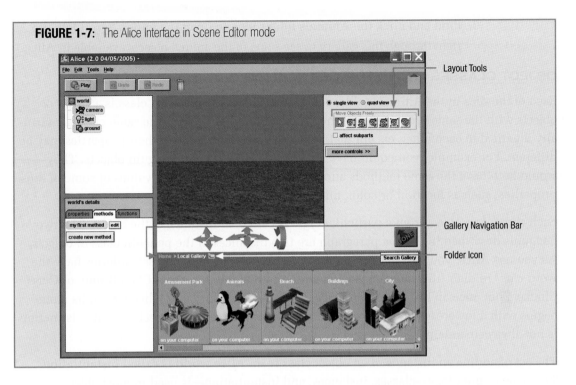

1. You should already be able to see the Local Gallery. You are going to explore the galleries a bit before preparing to add objects to your new world. Click the **folder** icon in the gallery navigation bar to move up one level in the tree of galleries, so that you can see the top level in the tree, as seen in Figure 1-8. Two icons are visible: one for the Local Gallery and one for the Web Gallery.

FIGURE 1-8: The top level in the tree of object galleries

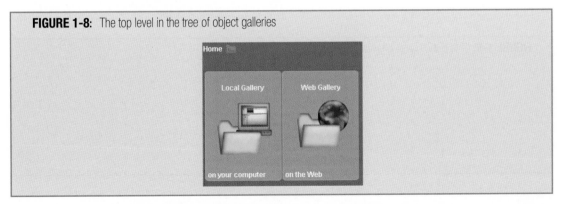

2. Click the **Local Gallery** icon to go back to the Local Gallery. Scroll left and right through the Local Gallery using the scroll bar below the gallery folders, and you will see some of the many categories of objects available in Alice.

3. Find and click the **Animals folder** icon to open the folder. Scroll left and right through this gallery to see some of the animal objects available in Alice.

OBJECT CLASSES AND INSTANCES IN ALICE

Each of the tiles in the Animals folder represents a **class** of objects. A class is a group of objects with the same properties and the same methods. Objects in the same class are virtually identical to each other, except that the values stored in some of their properties may be different. For example, you could have an Alice world with two Penguin objects. They would both have the same methods and the same properties, but the values of some of those properties, such as location or color, might be different.

Each copy of an object from a particular class is called an **instance** of the object. The two penguins described in the last paragraph are two instances of the penguin class of objects. As you use Alice, you will notice that the object class tiles in the object galleries have the word *class* in their title and each begins with a capital letter, such as Class Bunny or Class Chicken, but once an instance of an object is placed in a particular Alice world, its name begins with a lowercase letter. Of course, it is possible to rename objects, so this distinction is not always maintained.

The act of adding an instance of an object class to an Alice world is called **instantiation**. The same terminology—classes, instances, and instantiation—is used in most object–oriented programming languages.

You are going to add an instance of the first object in the first object folder in the Local Gallery to your new Alice world. You are going to instantiate a Bunny class object.

1. Click the **Class Bunny** icon. A window with information about Bunny class objects, like the one in Figure 1-9, should appear.

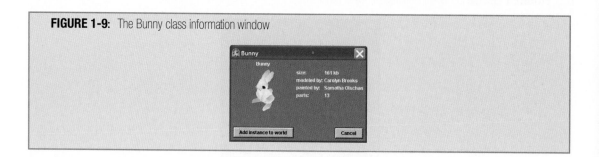

FIGURE 1-9: The Bunny class information window

2. Click the **Add instance to world** button to put a bunny into the world. This is sometimes called dropping an object into the world. You should see a bunny appear in the center of the World window.

3. There is a second way to add an object to an Alice world. You can click an object class tile and drag it into place in the World window. Try this now: drag and drop a **chicken** tile into your Alice world. This approach lets you place the new object wherever you would like on the ground in the world window, but does not show you the object's information window first.

4. You should now have an Alice world with two objects—a bunny and a chicken. Notice that tiles for the new objects have also been added to the object tree. You really don't need the chicken for the rest of this exercise. To delete the chicken, right-click the object or the object's tile in the Object tree and select **delete** from the menu that appears.

POSITIONING OBJECTS

The **layout tools** to the right of the World window in Scene Editor mode can be used to manipulate objects. This area contains the seven standard tools listed in Table 1-1.

TABLE 1-1: The seven Scene Editor layout tools

Button	Name	Function
	Pointer tool	Selects an object and moves the object parallel to the ground
	Vertical tool	Moves an object up or down
	Turn tool	Turns an object along its X-Y plane parallel to the ground
	Rotate tool	Rotates an object forward or backward (Z-axis rotate)
	Tumble tool	Freely turns and rotates an object in any direction
	Resize tool	Changes the size of an object
	Duplicate tool	Creates a new instance of the same object

1. The Pointer tool is already selected, so experiment a bit by using the pointer to click the bunny and move it around the screen. Notice that you can move the bunny on the ground with the pointer, but you cannot use the pointer to turn the bunny, rotate it, or move it up and down.

2. Click the **Rotate** tool and try turning the bunny a few times. You may be tempted to use the other tools, but please wait—for now they'll only confuse things. You can come back and experiment with them after you've finished this chapter.

3. Before closing Scene Editor mode, you need to properly position the bunny in its starting position for the new Alice world you are creating. Remember, in this world, the bunny will move from the right side of the screen to the center, turn to face the camera, and then say "Hello, World!" Position the bunny using the pointer and then the rotate tool, so that it is near the right side of the window, facing toward the viewer's left, as shown in Figure 1-10.

FIGURE 1-10: The bunny in position

4. After the bunny is in position, click the large green **DONE** button to close the Scene Editor and go back to the standard Alice interface.

ADDING SOME ACTION

The next step is to add some motion to your world. You can start with something simple—making the bunny move across the screen—and then add a little more action. To make things happen in your world, you need to use methods for the objects. In the Editor area, you already have the default method, which is `world.my first method`. The full name of every method has two parts: the name of the object associated with the method (which comes before the period) and the name of the method itself (which comes after the period).

1. Click the **World** tile in the Object tree in the upper-left corner of the interface.

2. Click the **methods** tab in the Details area. You will see that the name of the method in the Details area is simply `my first method`, but in the Editor, you see the full name of `world.my first method`.

The default event can be seen in the Event area on the top-right side of the interface. In Figure 1-11, you can see the tile for the default event, which shows that the event trigger is *When the world starts*, and the event handler is world. *my first method*. Any instructions you add to *world.my first method* will be executed when the world starts to play.

FIGURE 1-11: The default event

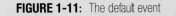

When the world starts, do   world.my first method

3. Click the **bunny** tile in the Object tree. Now you can see information about the bunny in the Details area. You should be able to see the bunny's methods. You create new code for Alice objects by dragging tiles for objects, other methods, and control structures into the method you are currently editing. You get object tiles from the Object tree, method tiles from the methods tab in the Details area, and logic and control tiles from the bottom of the Editor area.

4. Make sure that the methods tab is selected in the Details area, and then find and drag the **bunny move** tile into the middle of *world.my first method* in the Editor area.

5. A short menu will appear asking you to choose the direction and amount you want the bunny to move. Select **forward** for the direction, and then **1 meter** for the amount.

NOTE □ □ □   Information that you must give to a method whenever you use the method is called a **method parameter**. Direction and amount are two parameters for the move method.

6. To test your world, click the **Play** button near the upper-left corner of the Alice interface. You will see the bunny move. It's not much, but it's a start. Click the **Restart** button to play the world again, and then click the **Stop** button to return to the standard Alice interface.

NOTE □ □ □   In this short tutorial, you are going to play the new world several times before saving it. However, when you are working on your own worlds, it is best to save the world *before* playing it.

7. To change the amount the bunny moves, click the **1 meter** parameter in the move tile in your new method, and then choose one of the values in the drop-down menu that appears. You can also click **other** and then enter a number on the calculator-style keypad that appears. Try changing the

amount a few times and then playing the world after each change until you can make the bunny move approximately to the middle of the screen.

8. Let's add a few more instructions. First, find the bunny turn to face method tile. It's in the Details area about 11 or 12 tiles below the bunny move tile that you just used. You will probably need to scroll down to see it. The parameter for this tile will be the object you want the bunny to face. Click and drag the **bunny turn to face** tile into the Editor area below the *bunny move* tile, and choose **camera** as the object you want the bunny to face.

9. Next, you are going to add two tiles to make the bunny speak, and then save the method. First, find and drag the **bunny say** tile into the Editor area below your other two instructions. The parameter for this method is the phrase you want the bunny to say. This parameter is a string parameter, which contains a string of characters from the keyboard. When the parameter menu appears, click **other**, and then type **Hello, World!** in the *Enter a string* input box that appears, and then click **OK**.

Why "Hello, World!"? One of the most useful and popular programming languages ever created was the C programming language developed at AT&T labs in the 1970s. The "Hello, World!" program first appeared in a C language book written by two AT&T software developers, Brian Kernighan and Dennis Ritchie. Dr. Kerninghan, who is now a professor at Princeton University, actually wrote the first "Hello World!" program for a tutorial on an earlier programming language. Ever since then, it has been the custom for someone programming in a new language to write a version of the "Hello, World!" program as his or her first program. Congratulations, you've just done that in a new language! Let's add one more instruction before saving the program.

To add additional methods and save your world:

1. After the say *Hello, World!* tile in your program, add another bunny say tile to make the bunny say "Hello, Dr. Kerninghan!"

2. Now play your world again (several times if you'd like), and when you are finished, click the **Stop** button to return to the Alice interface.

3. To save the world you created, click the **File** menu and then click **Save World**. Notice that Alice has File menu options to Save World and to Save World As. The first time you try to save a new world, you will see the Save World As dialog box, as shown in Figure 1-12. This dialog box looks like similar Save As dialog boxes in other Windows programs, such a Microsoft Word, with a navigation bar and other controls.

FIGURE 1-12: The Save World As dialog box

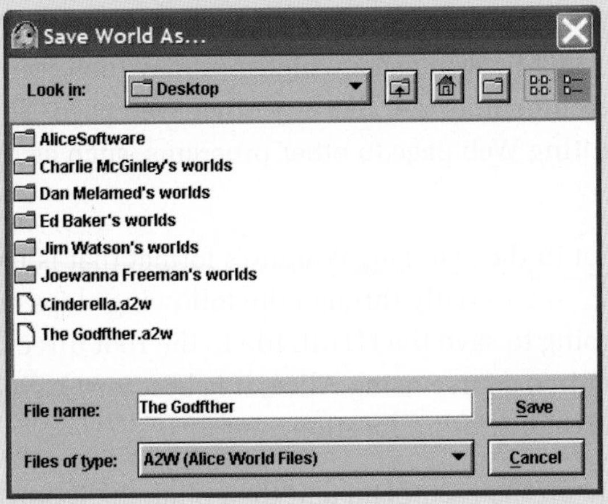

4. You should decide where you want to save the world, and then navigate the computer's tree of directories to find the right directory.

NOTE □ □ □ | The default location for saving Alice files is the Windows desktop, but you may save files wherever you wish. If you are in a course using Alice, please find out where your instructor would like you to save your files, because this may depend on how your classroom computers are configured. If you are working on your own, it is suggested that you save them someplace where they will be easy to find, and that you remember (or write down) where you saved each file. Appendix C contains more information about changing the default settings for the save command.

5. Type the name **hello world**, with no punctuation, in the *File name* input box. Notice that the file type shown below the *File name* input box is A2W (Alice World Files). This indicates that the file you save will end in the extension .a2w, for Alice version 2 World. You should not change this. Click the **Save** button to save your world.

CLOSING AND RELOADING A SAVED WORLD

Next, let's close the Alice program and then try to open your saved world.

1. Click **File** on the menu bar, and then click **Exit**. The Alice program will close.
2. Reopen the Alice software. Click the **Recent Worlds** tab in the Welcome to Alice! dialog box, and then open the **hello world** program. If the name of a world you want to open does not appear on the *Recent Worlds* tab, you can click the **Open a world** tab and look for your world in the tree of directories.

TUTORIAL 1D—PRINTING CODE FROM AN ALICE WORLD

Before you finish this chapter, let's try printing the code from your "Hello World!" program. Alice code is saved as an HTML Web page, which you may then print on a printer, send to someone as an e-mail attachment, or use like any other Web page. You can also cut and paste items from the resulting Web page to other programs, such as Microsoft Word or PowerPoint.

This feature of Alice is not in the standard Windows format that is familiar to most people. Thus, it can be confusing, so go slowly through the following steps and pay careful attention as you do. You are going to save the HTML file to the root directory on the C: disk drive. If you are a student in a course using Alice, it is best to ask your teacher whether you should use the C: disk drive or another location.

1. Click **File** on the menu bar, and then click the **Export Code For Printing** option. The Export to HTML dialog box, as shown in Figure 1-13, should appear.

FIGURE 1-13: The Export to HTML dialog box

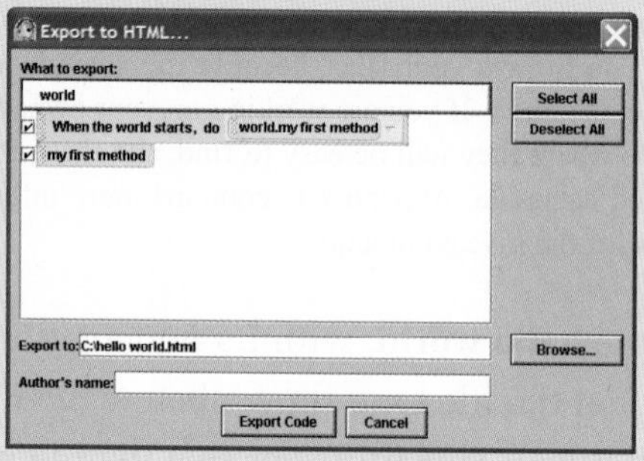

2. Notice that you need to tell the computer what to print. In Figure 1-13 you can see that you have only two items in your world that you can print. The first is the default event, when the world starts, do world.my first method, and the second is the default method, my first method. The code for an Alice world consists of the code for all of its events, and for all of its methods, but Alice lets you decide what parts of that code you want to print. In this exercise, you will print everything because you only have a small amount of code, but with large Alice worlds you may choose to print just a few items at a time. Make sure that the boxes in front of both items are checked.

3. You now need to tell Alice where you want to save the HTML file. This is the tricky part. There is a browse button, but it does not work as you might expect, so avoid it for now. You are going to save the file in the root directory of the C: disk drive (or in another location if so directed by your instructor). Enter the full path name of the new HTML page in the *Export to*: input box, as shown in Figure 1-13. Use the full path name, such as "C:\hello world.html" (or another name if directed to do so by your instructor).

4. You also need to add your name as the author of the code. Type your name in the *Author's name* input box.

5. Once you have entered the full path name for your new file and your name as the author of the file, click **Export Code** to create the new HTML document. Now you can find the document where you saved it and open it in a Web browser to look at your code. You can also copy the code to another location, such as on a USB memory chip or other device. You simply open and print the HTML page to print your code, just as you would for other HTML documents.

CHAPTER SUMMARY

This chapter consisted of an introduction followed by four hands-on tutorials. The introduction discussed the following:

- ☐ An algorithm is a step-by-step process; computer programs are algorithms.

- ☐ Most modern computer programming languages are object-oriented languages in which programs are organized as a set of methods that manipulate the properties of objects stored in a computer.

- ☐ An object can be anything that is manipulated by a computer, and consists of properties that contain information about the object and methods that can be used to manipulate an object's properties.

- ☐ The values stored in the properties of the object at any one time are called the state of the object.

- ☐ A class of objects is a collection of all objects that have the same properties and methods.

- ☐ Each individual object in a class is called an instance of that class.

- ☐ Alice is an object-oriented system of programming in which objects exist in a three-dimensional virtual world, which can be seen on a computer screen.

- ☐ Alice makes it easier to learn programming because of minimal memorization of syntax, visualization, and rapid feedback.

In Tutorial 1A, you explored the Alice interface, which has five main work areas—the World window, the Object tree, the Details area, the Editor area, and the Events area, as well as a menu bar, a Play button, an Undo button, a Redo button, a trash can, and a clipboard.

In Tutorial 1B, you learned to load and play an Alice world, and to use the speed slider control and the Pause, Resume, Restart, Stop and Take Picture buttons that appear when a world is playing.

In Tutorial 1C, you learned to create your own simple Alice world. You learned how to add objects from the object gallery, position them in the virtual world with the Scene Editor layout tools, and add instructions to the default method that is initiated by the default event.

In Tutorial 1D, you learned that Alice code may be exported to an HTML Web page and then viewed or printed from the Web page.

REVIEW QUESTIONS

1. **Define the following terms:**

☐ algorithm	☐ function	☐ method parameter
☐ class	☐ IDE	☐ object
☐ computer program	☐ instance	☐ OOP
☐ computer programming language	☐ instantiation	☐ property
	☐ method	☐ state of an object
☐ event		

2. List and describe the five tabs in the Welcome to Alice! dialog box that appear when the Alice software is first started.

3. Describe the role of each of the five main areas of the Alice interface: the World window, the Object tree, the Details area, the Editor area, and the Events area.

4. What is the difference between a method and a function?

5. Briefly describe how to do each of the following:
   a. Add an object to an Alice world.
   b. Delete an object from an Alice world.
   c. Change the value of a method parameter.
   d. Capture and store an image of an Alice world while it is playing.
   e. Save an Alice world.
   f. Print the code from an Alice world.

6. What is the difference between the Pause and Stop buttons in the window for a playing Alice world?

7. What is the function of the speed slider control in Alice?

8. What is the difference between the standard Alice interface and Scene Editor mode?

9. List and describe the function of the following Scene Editor layout tools: the Pointer tool, the Vertical tool, the Turn tool, the Rotate tool, and the Tumble tool.

10. Alice methods have full method names, such as `robot.dance`. Describe the meaning of the two different parts of the full method name.

EXERCISES

1. It can be very difficult for people to write clear and complete algorithms, such as a set of directions. We often take things for granted when writing directions and use our intelligence to interpret poorly written directions. For example, directions often contain clauses like "turn left at the third red light." But what if one of the lights is green? Does it count? Would a person even ask this question, or just make an assumption about what the writer meant? How would a computerized robot handle such a problem? Try writing a detailed set of directions for a simple everyday process, such as making a pot of coffee, then exchange your directions with another student. Critique each other's directions to see if they are clear and complete. Did the writer make assumptions that caused steps to be left out of the algorithm?

2. E-mail the HTML Web page that you saved with the code for your world to someone, such as your teacher or another person who will be impressed that you are beginning to learn three-dimensional, interactive, virtual reality programming with modern high-speed digital electronic computers. It might be best to send it as an attachment to a message.

3. Open the "hello world" Alice world that you saved as part of Tutorial 1C, and add some additional animation to the world. You may want to experiment with the methods to make the bunny move, turn, and roll. See if you can do the following:

    a. Make the bunny jump up and down.
    b. Make the bunny jump up, turn one revolution, and then land.
    c. Make the bunny jump up, roll one revolution, and then land.
    d. Make the bunny move and turn several times to go around in a full circle (or polygon).

    What is the difference between turn and roll? What difference does it make if you change the order of instructions in a particular world? When you are finished, click Tools on the menu bar, and then click World Statistics to see how long your Alice world has been open.

4. The methods available for the Bunny class of objects are called "primitive methods" and are available for all Alice objects. Certain classes of objects, such as the Penguin class, have additional methods available. Try starting a new world with a penguin and experiment with some of its user-created methods. These methods include `wing_flap`, `glide`, `jump`, `jumping`, `walk`, and `walking`.

5. Try creating, playing, and saving another Alice world on your own. While doing so, follow these two pieces of advice:

    a. Follow McGinley's Rule for New Programmers: K.I.S.S.—Keep it Small and Simple. You should be encouraged to experiment, but be careful about getting in over your head. Try a few simple things with only a few objects to get started.
    b. Try to plan what you will do in the world before you start working on it. Keep in mind the Rule of the Six P's: Proper Prior Planning Prevents Poor Performance. Many developers of Alice worlds like to outline or storyboard their work first. They draw a series of a few simple sketches of what they would like to try to make the objects in the world do. Professional programmers also use pseudo-code and flowcharts, which you will learn about in later chapters, to design the algorithms that methods will follow.

6. Try planning and creating a simple Alice world as part of a team of students. How does this experience differ from working on your own?

7. Alice has tool tips that appear if you place the mouse pointer on one of the tools, buttons, or tabs on the Alice interface and leave it still for more than two seconds. Table 1-1 in Tutorial 1C shows how the Scene Editor tools can be used to manipulate objects, but the table doesn't tell you everything. The tool tip for the pointer tool in the Scene Editor mode tells you several additional ways to use the Alice pointer. See if you can find out what they are.

8. There are many Web sites that contain useful information about computer technology. Here are two for you to try: *www.webopedia.com* and *www.wikipedia.com*. Both are free online encyclopedias. Webopedia focuses on computer technology and provides a brief definition of terms and links to other sites. Wikipedia is more general. A Wikipedia is a free Web-based encyclopedia written collaboratively by volunteers. Pick a few of the terms from this lesson, such as algorithm, object-oriented programming, or IDE, and see what you can find out. You can also look up people, such as Brian Kerninghan. The Wikipedia page at *http://en.wikipedia.org/wiki/Hello_world_program* has the

"Hello, World!" program in dozens of different computer languages. The ACM "Hello World" project page on Louisiana Tech's Web site at *http://www2.latech.edu/~acm/HelloWorld.shtml* has 204 different examples of the "Hello, World!" programs.

9. *Building Virtual Worlds* is a course taught in the Entertainment Technology Department at Carnegie Mellon University. A Web site for the course can be accessed at *http://www.etc.cmu.edu/bvw/*. The site includes sample worlds created with different software, including Alice. Visit the site if you would like to learn more about creating virtual worlds or to see some of the worlds created by more experienced students majoring in Computing and Entertainment Technology.

10. In Lewis Carroll's original story about Alice in Wonderland, why did Alice follow the rabbit down the hole? What does her motivation have to do with creating successful virtual worlds? How is this related to one's education? The name Alice comes from the Lewis Carroll novels *Alice's Adventures in Wonderland* and *Through the Looking Glass and What Alice Found There*. Electronic editions of both, with the original text and the original illustrations by John Tenniel can be found in the Electronic Text Center of the University of Virginia Library at *http://etext.lib.virginia.edu/toc/ modeng/public/CarAlic.html and http://etext.lib.virginia.edu/toc/modeng/public/CarGlas.html.* The Electronic Text Center also contains thousands of other works of literature that are available online, including the complete works of Shakespeare, the King James version of the Bible, the Koran, and the Book of Mormon. Their main page is on the Web at *http://etext.lib.virginia.edu*.

2 DEVELOPING METHODS IN ALICE

After finishing this chapter, you should be able to:

☐ Provide brief definitions of the following terms: CamelCase, coding, encapsulated methods, integration test, method header, modular development, off-camera, parameter, primitive methods, program development cycle, reusable code, test for correctness, testing shell, top-down design, unit test, user-defined methods, and variable

☐ Describe the processes known as top-down design and modular development, including why they are often used together, how organizational charts are involved, and some of the advantages of modular development of new software

☐ List and describe the steps in a simple program development cycle

☐ Describe the difference between primitive methods and user-created methods in Alice, and show how to run primitive methods to directly position objects and manipulate the camera in an Alice world

☐ Create new methods in Alice in a manner that demonstrates good top-down design and modular development

☐ Create and demonstrate the use of generic methods in Alice that contain method parameters

TOP-DOWN DESIGN AND MODULAR DEVELOPMENT

The process of developing methods for objects is mostly a process of developing algorithms because each method is an algorithm. Algorithm development has a long history in the world of mathematics, in which algorithms are step-by-step solutions to well-defined mathematical problems, such as finding the least common denominator of two fractions. Traditional approaches to mathematical problem solving have been applied to many different disciplines that rely on mathematics, such as engineering, the physical and social sciences, and computer programming. Generally, a problem must be clearly specified, so that once a solution has been developed, it can be compared to the specifications to determine its correctness.

It's easier to solve smaller problems than it is to solve big ones, so good mathematicians often start solving a problem by trying to break a large algorithm into parts that are more manageable. This process of decomposition is sometimes called a **divide and conquer** approach to problem solving. In this approach, a problem is broken into parts, those parts are solved individually, and then the smaller solutions are assembled into a big solution. Computer programmers do the same thing when developing new software.

This process is also known as **top-down design** or **top-down development**, which starts at the top with one concept or big idea and then breaks that down into several parts. If those parts can be further broken down, then the process continues. The end result is a collection of small solutions, called modules, which collectively contain the overall solution to the original problem.

Let's look at an example of top-down development. Imagine that you want to write a computer program to process the payroll for a large company. Your big idea is named "Payroll." What would you need to do if you were going to process a payroll? Generally, you would need to get some data, perform some calculations, and output some results. Figure 2-1 shows Payroll broken down into these three modules.

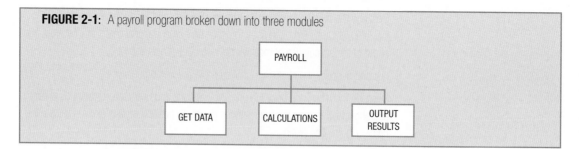

FIGURE 2-1: A payroll program broken down into three modules

You can go further in decomposing the problem. There are two different sets of data—old data, such as a list of employees, and new data, such as the number of hours each person worked during a specific week. The old data will probably be read in from a database on the hard disk drive, while the new data will be entered into the system for the first time, so the Get Data module can be broken down further into Get Old Data and Get New Data. If the Calculations and Output Results modules are broken down in a similar manner, and then the sub-modules of those modules are broken down, and so on, then the final design might look something like the one in Figure 2-2. Such a diagram is called an **organizational chart**.

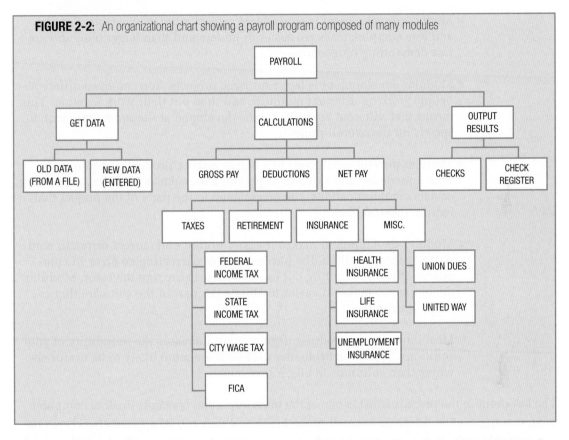

FIGURE 2-2: An organizational chart showing a payroll program composed of many modules

Organizational charts show the overall structure of separate units that have been organized to form a single complex entity. The chart shows how the upper levels are broken down into the parts at the lower levels, and conversely, how the parts at the lower levels are layered together to form the upper levels. Organizational charts are most commonly seen describing hierarchies of organizations, such as government agencies. In this case, you can see how the specific modules farther down the chart are combined to form the overall payroll program. A programmer, or a team of programmers working together, can create each of the modules as software methods, and then put them together to build the entire payroll program.

The process of top-down design leads to **modular development**, in which the parts, or modules, that make up a complete solution to a problem are developed individually and then combined to form that complete solution. Modular development of computer software has the following advantages, especially for larger projects:

- Modular development makes a large project more manageable. Smaller and less complex tasks are easier to understand than larger ones and are less demanding of resources.

- Modular development is faster for large projects. You can have different people work on different modules, and then put their work together. This means that different modules can be developed at the same time, which speeds up the overall project.

- Modular development leads to a higher quality product. Programmers with knowledge and skills in a specific area, such as graphics, accounting, or data communications, can be assigned to the parts of the project that require those skills.

- Modular development makes it easier to find and correct errors in computer programs. Often, the hardest part of correcting an error in computer software is finding out exactly what is causing the error. Modular development makes it easier to isolate the part of the software that is causing trouble.

- Most importantly, modular development increases the reusability of your solutions. Solutions to smaller problems are more likely to be useful elsewhere than solutions to bigger problems.

The last point in the preceding list is one of the most important concepts in all of computer programming. Saving solutions to small problems so that they can be applied elsewhere creates **reusable code**. In fact, most of the software on a computer system is filled with layers of reusable code because computer programs contain many small tasks that need to be repeated, such as getting a user's name and password before running a program. Everything, from the low-level parts of the operating system that directly control the hardware to the most complex user applications, is filled with layers of short programming modules that are constantly reused in different situations.

Reusable code makes programming easier because you need to develop the solution to a problem only once; then you can call up that code whenever you need it. You can also save the modules you have developed as part of one software development project, and then reuse them later as parts of other projects, modifying them if necessary to fit new situations. Over time, you can build libraries of software modules for different tasks.

Object-oriented programming, by its very nature, encourages such development of reusable code. Methods to perform simple tasks can be reused within an object to form more complicated methods, and entire classes of objects created for one project can be reused as needed for other projects.

Figure 2-3 shows part of the methods tab for the iceSkater from the lakeSkater world seen in Chapter 1. Methods to perform simple tasks, such as *spin*, *blinkEyes*, and *jump*, are reused as necessary to form the overall routine in this Alice world. The entire skater object itself can be reused in other worlds where different routines might be assembled from these simple methods. As you create Alice worlds, you should keep this concept in mind and try to write small reusable methods as much as possible. This approach to programming will serve you well in any language you use—Java, Visual Basic, C++, Python—and is one of the driving principles behind much of the modern object-oriented approach to programming. Good computer software is filled with reusable code, and Alice is no exception.

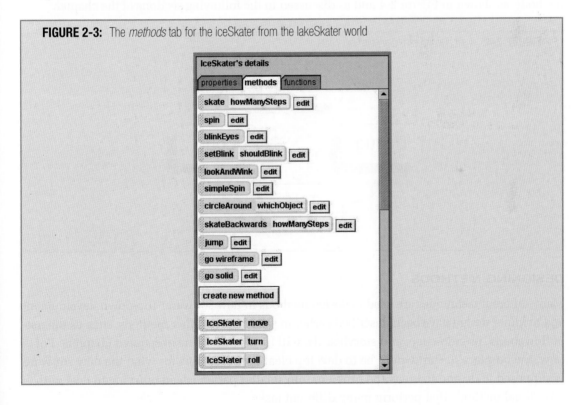

FIGURE 2-3: The *methods* tab for the iceSkater from the lakeSkater world

A PROGRAM DEVELOPMENT CYCLE

Traditional approaches to algorithm development, in which algorithms are developed and tested to see if they meet original specifications, led to the notion of a software development cycle in computer programming. The first step in the creation of software is to design the methods that will make up that software, that is, to plan what the methods will do. Once the methods have been designed, they can then be implemented.

The process of implementing a new method primarily involves entering instructions (and data) on the computer in a particular programming language. This process has traditionally been called **coding**. After each method has been coded, it needs to be tested to make sure that it works, and then edited as necessary. Whenever a method is edited, it needs to be compared to the original design to be sure that it still performs according to the original specifications. In all, programmers follow a **program development cycle**, in which they design, code, test, and debug methods, as shown in Figure 2-4 and as discussed in the following sections of the chapter.

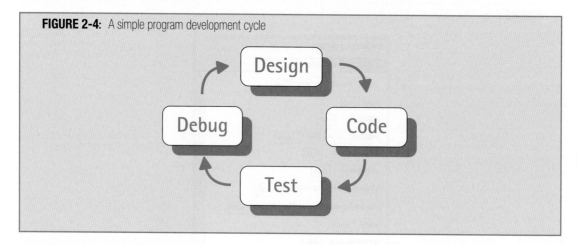

FIGURE 2-4: A simple program development cycle

DESIGNING METHODS

Many different techniques are used to design methods in new software. Top-down development and modular design have been described earlier in this chapter. Other methods, such as the use of flowcharts, pseudo-code, and storyboards, will be discussed in subsequent chapters. For now, a good place to start would be to develop clear specifications for what the new software is supposed to do and to break the problem into smaller parts instead of trying to deal with individual methods that perform many different tasks.

CODING METHODS IN ALICE

One of the unique features of Alice is its drag-and-drop interface, in which tiles containing existing instructions and logic and control structures are dragged into place to create a new method. You should recall from Chapter 1 that tiles for existing methods can be found on the methods tabs for various objects, while logic and control tiles can be found at the bottom of the Editor area, as shown in Figure 2-5.

In more traditional programming languages, such as Java, C++, or Visual Basic, the coding phase of software development includes translating a software design into a particular language, and then entering that language on the computer. Coding in Alice, however, is a little different. Dragging Alice's language tiles into place to create new methods eliminates the need for carefully translating and typing individual instructions. Programmers still need to be familiar with the features of the language and how to use them, but they do not need to be so concerned with details such as spelling and punctuation. There is still a need to be careful, but Alice programmers can focus their attention on the logic of how new methods will operate rather than on the syntax of the language.

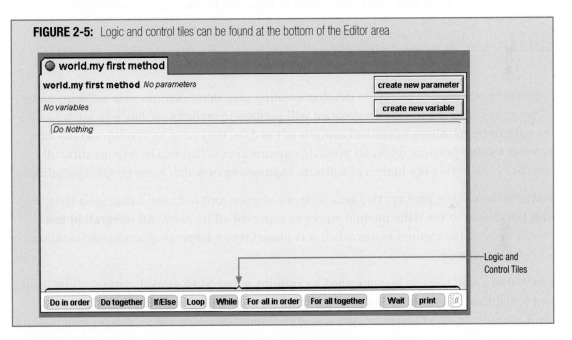

FIGURE 2-5: Logic and control tiles can be found at the bottom of the Editor area

TESTING AND DEBUGGING ALICE METHODS

The techniques that professional software developers use to test newly developed methods can be varied and complex, but generally they involve answering a few simple questions, such as the following:

- Most important, does the new method do what it is supposed to do? This is known as a **test for correctness**. Tests for correctness measure whether the program meets the original specifications.

■ Is the method reasonably efficient? How much time does it take for the method to complete its task, and how much space does it use? If a program takes two hours to sort a list that another program can sort in two seconds, then it is not a very time-efficient program. Similarly, one program could use more or less memory and disk space than another program, but typically time efficiency is more critical than space efficiency as computer memory chips and disk drives become larger and less expensive.

■ Does the method have any undesirable side effects? For example, if a method to print a long document also erases the hard disk drive, then that would be considered an undesirable side effect. Side effects are related to how methods change stored data, how one program affects the performance of another program, how one method affects another method, or even how two instructions in the same method affect each other.

NOTE □ □ □ | Here's a common example of a side effect: Alice methods to move and turn objects at the same time can occasionally produce unexpected results if the programmer failed to consider that the object's directions were changing as it turned.

Software testers need to be able to develop a testing plan that examines new software under all possible circumstances. If the program will perform operations on data sets, such as sorting a list or performing a numerical analysis of the data, they need to develop sample data sets that test the program under all possible circumstances. This can be a rather difficult task. Software testing is a branch of software engineering in which some people specialize.

Software developers perform two general types of tests: unit tests and integration tests. A **unit test** checks to see if the method works as expected all by itself. An **integration test** checks to see if the method works when it is placed into a larger program in combination with other methods.

Sometimes a unit test can be performed by running a newly developed method all by itself, and sometimes it is necessary to create another method, called a **testing shell**. A testing shell is a short method that simulates the environment in which a newly developed method will be used. This is especially important if the new method will be receiving values from other methods or passing values on to other methods. The testing shell can be written to pass known values into the method being tested, and then the output can be captured and examined for correctness.

Consider the method to calculate state tax in the payroll program mentioned earlier. That method receives values as input and sends values as output. A testing shell for the method to calculate state tax would pass it some known values, and then capture the method's output so that it could be examined, as seen in Figure 2-6. Passing in known values and examining the output to see if it is correct enables a software tester to determine if the method is performing the correct calculations.

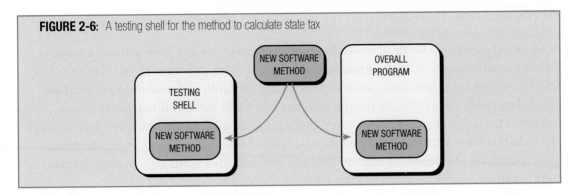

FIGURE 2-6: A testing shell for the method to calculate state tax

In the lakeSkater demonstration that you have already seen, the iceSkater's *spin* method could be tested without a testing shell. The method could be run all by itself, and the tester could observe the action to see if the method performs according to specifications.

Once a method has been unit tested and debugged, it can be integration tested. That is, it can then be put in position in the overall program, which can then be run to see if it works with the new methods in place.

This chapter only scratches the surface of testing and debugging, which can be quite complicated and detailed. For now, just try to keep the following questions in mind:

- Does the method do what it supposed to do according to the specifications? Does it work by itself? Does it work as a part of a larger program?

- Is it reasonably efficient? Is there any indication that something is taking too long or using up too much memory?

- Is anything unexpected happening when the program runs?

- Has the program been tested under all possible circumstances? This is especially important if the program has numeric input. For example, what happens if you tell a method to move forward a negative amount? What happens if you tell a method to turn a negative number of revolutions?

If any problems are discovered when the software is tested, then the cause of the problem needs to be isolated. Here unit tests are most helpful, especially when software has been developed as many smaller modules, rather than as a few larger modules. Once you know what is causing the error, you can develop a plan for fixing the problem, modify the necessary method or methods, and then test again.

TUTORIAL 2A—WORKING WITH PRIMITIVE METHODS IN ALICE

Alice objects have two kinds of methods—primitive methods and user-defined methods. Primitive methods are built-in, predefined methods that are part of each Alice object. They provide simple basic behaviors, such as move, turn, and roll, and cannot be edited. User-defined methods are written by people who use Alice and can be edited. Some of the objects in the Alice object galleries, such as the Penguin class of objects, have user-defined methods that were written by the people who created the object. These are in addition to the standard set of primitive methods. You can use primitive methods and user-defined methods to write new methods of your own.

Let's examine the methods for Penguin class objects:

1. Start Alice, click the **Templates** tab when the Welcome to Alice! dialog box appears, and begin an Alice world using the snow template.
2. Once the new world is open, click the large green **ADD OBJECTS** button in the lower-right corner of the World window to enter Scene Editor mode.
3. Now you can see the object galleries at the bottom of the screen. Click the **Animals gallery**, and then find and click the **Class Penguin** tile.

You should be able to see the Information window for the Penguin class of objects, as shown in Figure 2-7. It contains information about the designers who modeled and painted the Penguin class, tells us how much memory is required for an instance of the object, and lists user-created methods that the designers included with the object. Most Alice objects don't come with any user-created methods, only a standard set of primitive methods, but here we can see that the designers of the Penguin class included user-defined methods to give the penguin additional behaviors, such as flapping its wings, turning its head, and walking.

FIGURE 2-7: The Information window for the Penguin class of objects

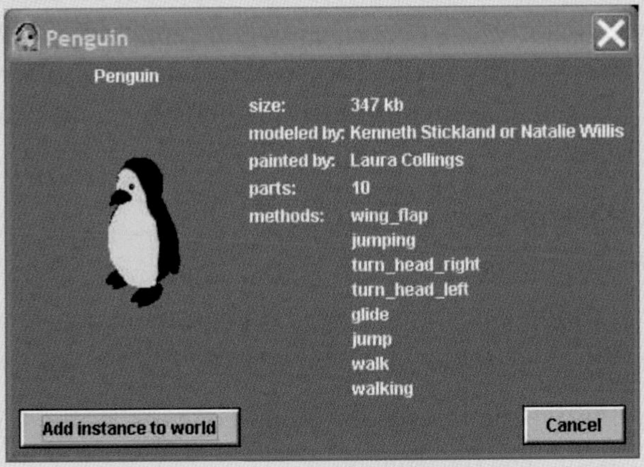

Let's add the penguin to the new world and then look at its methods tab.

1. Click the **Add instance to world** button, and then click the **DONE** button. This will return you to the standard Alice interface.

2. Click the **penguin** tile in the Object tree and the **methods** tab in the Details area. You can now see the *methods* tab for your instance of the Penguin class of objects, which is shown in Figure 2-8.

FIGURE 2-8: The *methods* tab for the Penguin class of objects

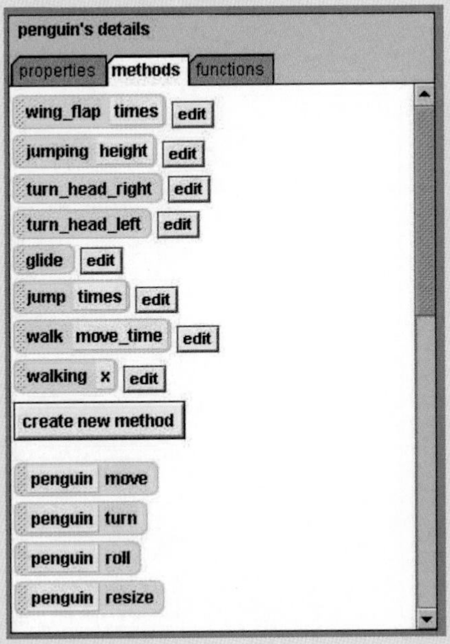

Tiles for the penguin's user-created methods appear above the *create new method* button and are each followed by an *edit* button. Notice that this set of methods matches the list in the Penguin's Information window. The tiles below the *create new method* button have no edit button. These are the primitive methods that come with each Alice object. You cannot edit them. In other words, they are **encapsulated methods**—you can use them, but you cannot access their inner workings.

RUNNING PRIMITIVE METHODS DIRECTLY

Primitive methods may be used to build more complex methods, or they may be run directly. You can run a primitive method directly by right-clicking an object or an object tile in the object tree, and then selecting the method you want to run from a list that appears.

One of the penguin's primitive methods is the turn to face method. Let's run this method directly to make the penguin face the camera.

1. Right-click the **penguin** tile in the Object tree, and then point to **methods** on the small menu that appears. Now you should see a list of the penguin's primitive methods, similar to Figure 2-9.

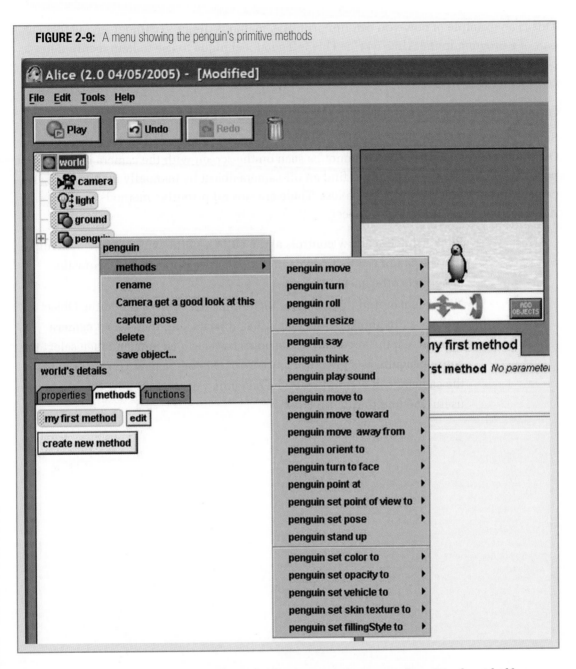

FIGURE 2-9: A menu showing the penguin's primitive methods

2. One of the methods in the list is *penguin turn to face*. It's about halfway down the menu. Point to **penguin turn to face**, and then click **camera** from the submenu that appears. On the screen you should see the penguin turn to face the camera.

This is an example of how you can run primitive methods directly, without saving them as part of a program in the Alice world. This is a good technique to use to help manipulate objects when setting the scene for an Alice world, or simply to experiment to learn how certain methods work.

USING PRIMITIVE CAMERA METHODS TO FIND A LOST OBJECT

Sometimes in Alice, an object is off-camera, and you're not sure exactly where the object is. **Off-camera** means that an object cannot be seen on the screen with the camera in its current position. Often it can be difficult to find an off-camera object by manually manipulating the camera, and the object appears to be lost. There are several primitive methods that you can run directly to help find the lost object.

1. First, using the arrow controls at the bottom of the window world, manipulate the camera so that you cannot see the penguin anymore. Now the penguin is off-camera.

2. Now you can find the penguin. Right-click the **camera** tile in the Object tree, select **methods** on the menu that appears, and then select **camera point at**. On the target menu that appears, select **penguin**, and then select **the entire penguin**, as shown in Figure 2-10. On your screen you will see that the camera is now pointing at the penguin. Can you see how this might be a useful method to run directly?

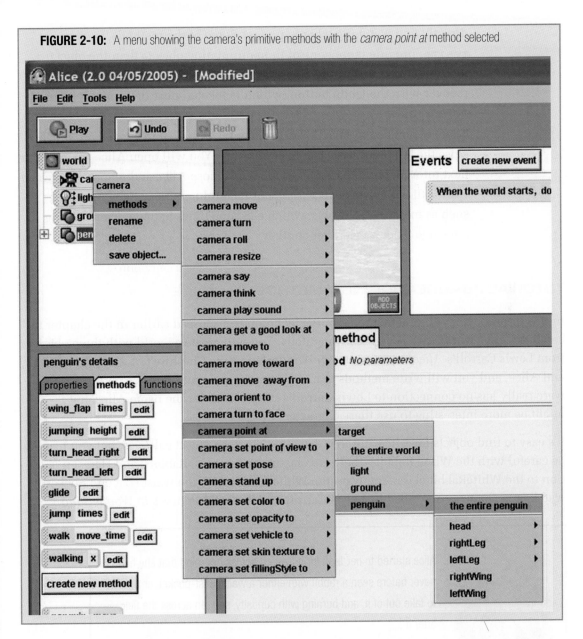

FIGURE 2-10: A menu showing the camera's primitive methods with the *camera point at* method selected

3. Using the arrows, move the camera again so that the penguin is off-camera.

4. This time, run the *camera get a good look at* method on **the entire penguin**. Do you see how this is a little different than the *camera point at* method?

5. Try experimenting by running a few more of the penguin's methods directly before moving on to the next tutorial. For example, can you determine the difference between the turn and roll methods by running them

directly and watching what happens? Some of the methods, such as `resize`, provide more control in manipulating objects than the object manipulation tools in the Scene Editor. If you run into trouble, you can recover with the Undo button, which is located near the upper-left corner of your screen.

6. There is no need to save this experimental world, so when you are finished, close the Alice software before continuing. You will open Alice again in the next tutorial, but often it is a good idea to close Alice and reopen it between worlds. It isn't always necessary, but it could help to avoid side effects, such as memory overflows, which can sometimes happen when loading one large Alice world after another.

TUTORIAL 2B—CREATING NEW METHODS IN ALICE

In this tutorial, you will practice some of the techniques discussed earlier in the chapter to create an Alice world with several new methods. You will create a world with three objects from Lewis Carroll's *Alice's Adventures in Wonderland*—the Cheshire Cat, the White Rabbit, and Alice, and you will write methods to make them jump up and down. The Alice software really has no connection to Lewis Carroll's story except for the name Alice, but it might be more interesting to use these characters in this exercise.

It's easy to find objects for Alice and the Cheshire Cat in the object galleries, but you need to be careful with the White Rabbit—there are classes for Bunnies, Rabbits, and Hares, in addition to the WhiteRabbit class. You want the White Rabbit with the waist coat and pocket watch on a chain, as described by Lewis Carroll in *Alice's Adventure's in Wonderland*.

Alice started to her feet, for it flashed across her mind that she had never before seen a rabbit with either a waistcoast-pocket, or a watch to take out of it, and burning with curiosity, she ran across the field after it …

—*Alice's Adventures in Wonderland*
by Lewis Carroll, 1865

SETTING THE SCENE

The first step in creating a new world is to set the scene by opening a template, adding necessary objects, and positioning things. In long programs, a naming convention is needed to make it easier to read the names of the many objects, methods, and variables used within the program. As you work with Alice, you will notice that the names of classes and objects in Alice follow a pattern called the CamelCase naming convention, which is used with most programming languages and is recommended by many software developers, such as Microsoft.

CamelCase is the practice of writing compound names without using blank spaces, but capitalizing the first letter of each name that forms the compound name, like the name CamelCase itself. In Lewis Carrol's *Alice in Wonderland,* the proper name of the character is "Cheshire Cat," while the name of the class of characters in the object gallery is "CheshireCat." You will also notice that the very first letter of object class names begin with capital letters, whereas the names of instances of a class begin with lowercase letters. The class name is CheshireCat, with a capital "C" at the beginning; the first instance of the class is named cheshireCat with a lowercase "c."

1. Start the Alice software, select the **grass** template from the Templates tab, and then click the **Open** button. Next, click the **ADD OBJECTS** button to enter Scene Editor mode.

2. You need to add the three characters to this Alice world and position them as seen in Figure 2-11. Start with the Cheshire Cat. Click **Local Gallery**, and then click **Animals**. Click the **CheshireCat** tile, and then click the **Add instance to world** button. A cheshireCat should appear near the center of the world window, and a cheshireCat tile should appear in the Object tree.

FIGURE 2-11: A world with three objects from *Alice in Wonderland*

3. Place the **cheshireCat** on the left, as seen by the camera, and have him face the camera. Drag the **cheshireCat** over to the left side of the World window.

4. Next, you will make the cat turn to face the camera. Right-click the **cheshireCat** tile in the Object tree, and then point to methods from the small menu that appears. Now you should see a list of the cheshireCat's primitive methods, similar to Figure 2-12.

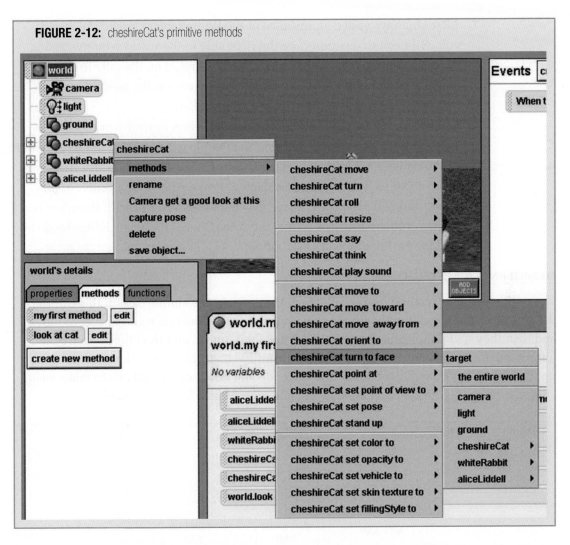

FIGURE 2-12: cheshireCat's primitive methods

5. About halfway down the list, find and point to the **cheshireCat turn to face** method, and then click **camera** as the target object. On the screen you should see the cheshireCat turn to face the camera.

6. The WhiteRabbit class is in the same animal gallery as the CheshireCat class. Note that you will have to scroll to the far right in the Animals gallery to see it. Add an instance of the WhiteRabbit class to your world.

7. After you have added an instance of the WhiteRabbit class to the world, you will need to position it on the right side of the world window, facing the camera, just as you positioned the cheshireCat on the left. To do this, drag the **whiteRabbit** over to the right, and then run the method to make it face the camera as you did with the cheshireCat.

8. Finally, add an instance of the AliceLiddell class to your world. The aliceLiddell object can be found in the People gallery. Alice Liddell was the young daughter of a friend of Lewis Carroll's for whom the story *Alice's Adventures in Wonderland* was named. Leave Alice in the center of the scene, and make her turn to face the camera, as you did with the other two objects. You are finished setting the scene, so exit the Scene Editor Mode by clicking the large green **DONE** button.

DESIGNING A METHOD

The design of a new method begins with specifications. In the simple case in this tutorial, the specifications are given: the three characters will first appear on a grass background, and then they will jump. Alice jumps, the whiteRabbit jumps, and then the cheshireCat jumps. Alice's programming language has no primitive instruction to make an object jump up and down, so you will need to use the move up and move down methods to make each character jump. Figure 2-13 contains the organizational chart for the program.

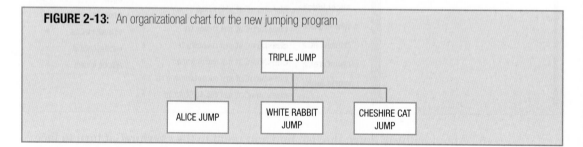

FIGURE 2-13: An organizational chart for the new jumping program

The outline for the program would resemble Figure 2-14.

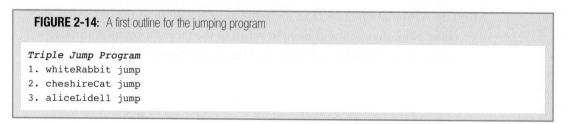

FIGURE 2-14: A first outline for the jumping program

```
Triple Jump Program
1. whiteRabbit jump
2. cheshireCat jump
3. aliceLidell jump
```

And finally, an expanded outline for the program would resemble Figure 2-15.

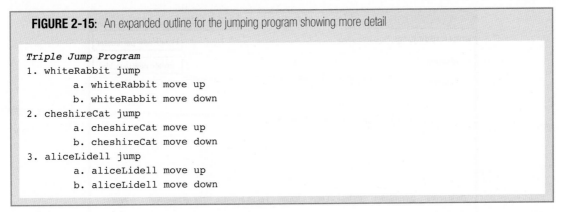

FIGURE 2-15: An expanded outline for the jumping program showing more detail

```
Triple Jump Program
1. whiteRabbit jump
        a. whiteRabbit move up
        b. whiteRabbit move down
2. cheshireCat jump
        a. cheshireCat move up
        b. cheshireCat move down
3. aliceLidell jump
        a. aliceLidell move up
        b. aliceLidell move down
```

Top-down design and modular development suggest that separate jump methods should be written for each object rather than placing all of the code into a single method. By using proper programming techniques as you begin to write short programs like this one, you will develop good habits that will help you when you write larger programs, whether in Alice, Java, Visual Basic, or some other language.

CODING THE JUMP METHODS

To make an object jump, you are simply going to move the character up one meter and then move the character down one meter.

1. Let's start by creating a jump method for the whiteRabbit. Click the **whiteRabbit** tile in the Object tree, and then the **methods** tab in the Details area.

2. Click the **create new method** button, and a small New Method dialog box will appear asking you to name the method. Type **jump** as the name for the new method, and then click the **OK** button. In the Editor area, a new tab appears for a blank method with the name whiteRabit.jump, as seen in Figure 2-16.

FIGURE 2-16: A new method tab with the name *whiteRabbit.jump*

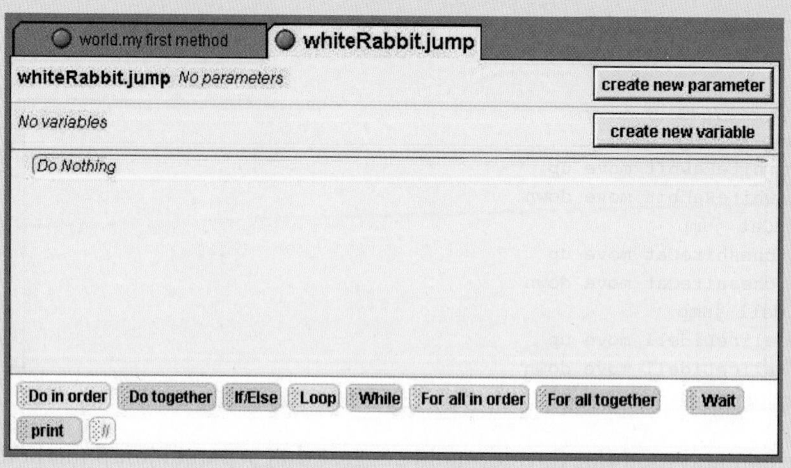

The new blank method in the Editor area has several components. You see the name of the method on a tab at the top of the method, and again on the method's first line of text, followed by the phrase *No parameters.* To the right of this you see a *create new parameter* button. On the next line of text you see the phrase *No variables,* with a *create new variable* button on the right. Your method will not have any variables or parameters, so for the moment, you can ignore these buttons. (You will learn more about variables and parameters in the next part of this chapter.) The lines of text at the top of the method can be considered a **header** for a method, which gives us information about how the method works. From the header information, you can see that you can run this method without any parameters, and that there are no variables in the method.

You can see a box with rounded corners containing the phrase *Do Nothing* below the header for the method. This part of your method is sometimes called the **instruction zone**. Right now there are no instructions in the method, so the zone has the text *Do Nothing.*

You now want your method to include an instruction to make the whiteRabbit move up one meter followed by an instruction to make the whiteRabbit move down one meter, as shown by the specifications back in Figure 2-15.

1. Drag the **whiteRabbit move** tile from the left side of the screen and drop it on the *Do Nothing* phrase. The tile will be surrounded by a red border as you drag it. The border will turn green when you reach the right place.

2. When you drop the tile into the instruction zone, a menu will appear asking you the direction in which you want to move the object. Select **up** for the direction, and then select **1 meter** for the amount. Direction and amount are two parameters, or pieces of information, that you must give a method whenever you want to use the method.

3. Next, drag another copy of the **whiteRabbit move** tile from the left into the instruction zone below your first instruction. This time set the direction to **down**, and the distance again to **1 meter**.

You are now finished with your method to make the whiteRabbit jump. Now you need to create a `jump` method for the cheshireCat, just as you did for the whiteRabbit.

1. Select the **cheshireCat** tile in the Object tree, and then click the **methods** tab in the Details area.

2. Click the **create new method** button, and then name the method **jump**.

3. Add an instruction to make the cheshireCat move up **1** meter.

4. Add an instruction to make the cheshireCat move down **1** meter.

5. Create a `jump` method for aliceLiddell in a similar manner.

CREATING THE MAIN METHOD

Now you need a method that calls all three jump methods in the order in which you want the characters to jump. This method will be your main method, at the top of the organizational chart. `World.my first method` is often used as this top-level method, which is what you will do here. This is a world-level method, associated with the world itself rather than with any particular object in the Alice world.

1. Start by clicking the **world** tile in the Object tree, and then click the **methods** tab, if necessary, to see the methods in the Details area. Things look a little different here than when you looked at an object's methods. There are no

primitive methods listed below the *create new method* button, but *my first method* already exists as a user-created method.

2. Click the **edit** button. This will open up the method for editing in the Editor area. It begins as a blank method with no parameters, variables, or instructions. Your plan calls for aliceLiddell to jump, followed by the whiteRabbit, and then the cheshireCat.

3. First you want aliceLiddell to jump. Click the **aliceLiddell** tile in the Object tree, and then click the **methods** tab, if necessary, in the Details area. Note that there will be a tile for the *jump* method above the *create new method* button because this is a user-created method that can be edited.

4. Click the **jump** tile and drag a copy of it into the instruction zone of *world.my first method*.

5. Next you need to add a `whiteRabbit.jump` method. Click the **whiteRabbit** in the Object tree and drag and drop the whiteRabbit's **jump** method into *world.my first method*. Make sure that you drop it just below the *aliceLiddell.jump* instructions in the desired sequence.

6. Finally, you need to add the `cheshireCat.jump` method by clicking the **cheshireCat** in the Object tree and then dragging and dropping its **jump** method below the *whiteRabbit.jump* instruction. Your screen should resemble Figure 2-17.

FIGURE 2-17: Adding the *cheshireCat.jump* method

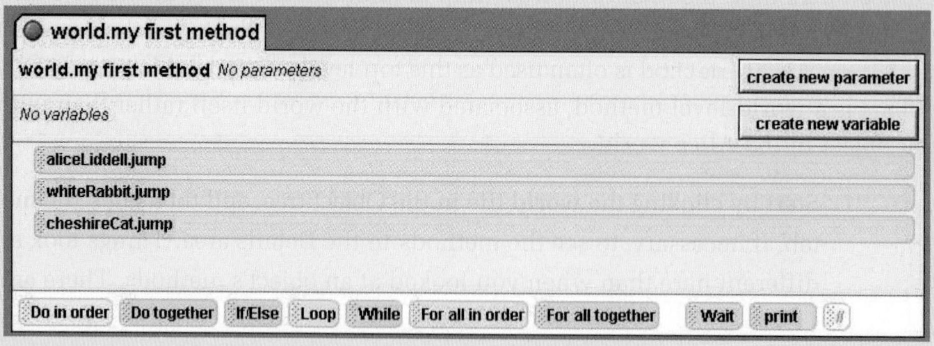

TESTING (AND DEBUGGING) YOUR FINISHED SOFTWARE

If you have done everything correctly, then your Alice world should be ready to go. Let's find out.

1. Click the **Play** button to play the Alice world.

2. Watch what happens. Did it perform according to your original specifications? Did Alice, then the whiteRabbit, and then the cheshireCat each jump up and down? If not, then you need to look at each of your methods, find the error, and fix it.

3. Before you move on to the next tutorial, you should save your Alice world as **triple jump**. (You can do this through the File menu, just as you can with most Windows programs.) Remember to pay attention to where the file is saved, as discussed in Chapter 1.

You can think of each method as performing a single task. If an object is doing something wrong, then you should ask which of your methods performs that task. If you have an error, then it could be in either the main method or one of the jump methods. If the three objects are jumping in the wrong order, then the main method is probably where you have an error. If one of the objects is not jumping properly, then that object's jump method is where you can expect the error to be. By writing small methods for each individual task, you not only have all the benefits of modularity listed earlier, but there is another benefit—it is much easier to debug software that is written as small modules, each performing an individual task.

TUTORIAL 2C—GENERIC METHODS AND PARAMETERS

In the previous tutorial, you created an Alice world with specific methods to make each of your three objects jump. You created an `aliceLiddell.jump` method, a `whiteRabbit.jump` method, and a `cheshireCat.jump` method. In this part of the chapter, you will create a generic jump method that will work for any object.

Your new method will have a variable parameter. A **variable** is a name for a memory location that temporarily stores a value while a method is running. Variables are a lot like the properties of objects. They have data types, just like properties, and they are stored in the memory of the computer, just like properties. However, properties are associated with an object, and their values are maintained as long as the object exists, whereas variables are associated with a particular method, and their values exist only inside the method. Once the method stops running, their values are gone, unless, of course, you had saved them somewhere else while the method was running.

A parameter is a variable whose value is passed from one method to another—just like a baton is passed from one runner to another in a relay race. Thus, a variable is a value that can change inside a method, and a parameter is a variable whose value is passed from one method to another. You had to tell the `cheshireCat.move` method that you used inside your `cheshireCat.jump` method in the last exercise the direction and amount you wanted the cheshireCat to move. These values are parameters for the primitive `cheshireCat.move` method. Your `cheshireCat.jump` method passed the values up (or down) and 1 meter to the `move` method when the `move` method was called to perform its task.

DESIGNING A GENERIC METHOD

Methods that are associated with a particular object are called **object-level** methods, or **class-level** methods if they work with any object in a particular class. Methods that are associated with the entire world are called **world-level** methods in Alice.

You can build a generic world-level method that will make any object jump, very similarly to the object-level jump methods you previously created. To do this, you need to use a variable. You can design a generic jump method, based on your `aliceLiddell.jump` method.

You want to create a method to do the same thing, but instead of moving the cheshireCat, you want to add a variable to your method that will allow any object to jump. However, how will the new method find out which object should jump each time the method is used? You want the user to specify which object will jump whenever this new method is called. Thus, the variable needs to be a parameter because its value needs to be passed from the calling method. Figure 2-18 shows what the new method will look like with a parameter in place to indicate who will jump.

FIGURE 2-18: New Alice code for a generic jump method

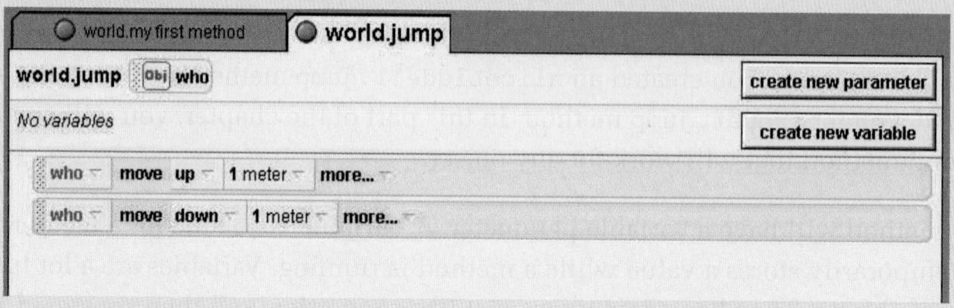

Now that you have a design in mind for the method, let's write the code.

CREATING A PARAMETER

As you work through this exercise, you'll see that it's the same thing you did to create a `cheshireCat.jump` method, except now you are creating a `jump` method for the world. You'll find that you need to give your parameter a name, and declare what data type the parameter will be. Remember that the computer stores different data types in different formats, so you need to tell the system what data type to use for this new parameter. The data type can be an Alice object, a number, a Boolean value (true or false), or any one of more than a dozen types built into Alice, such as a string of text, a color, a sound file, a direction, and so on.

1. First, start a blank Alice world with the **grass** template.

2. Next, select the **world** tile in the Object tree, and then the **methods** tab in the Details area below it. Click the **create new method** button, and a small New Method dialog box will appear asking you to name the method.

3. Type **jump** as the name for the new method, and then click the **OK** button. In the Editor area, a new tab appears for a blank method with the name *world.jump*.

4. You know that your method needs a parameter. Click the **create new parameter button** on the right side of the `jump` method's header information, and a Create New Parameter dialog box appears, as seen in Figure 2-19.

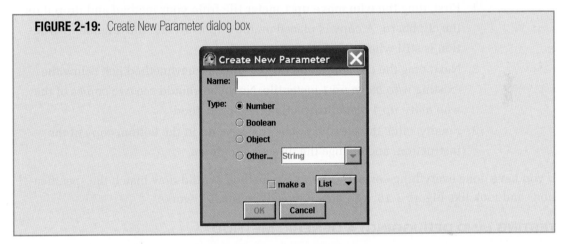

FIGURE 2-19: Create New Parameter dialog box

5. Type **who** as the name of your new parameter and select **object** as the data type. Make sure that the list box is not checked, and then click the **OK** button. Now you should see a tile appear after the name of the method showing you that this method has an object parameter. The *who* parameter may now be used like a variable within the method, and its value must be specified whenever this method is called from another method.

CODING A GENERIC INSTRUCTION

You need to use an object in your world to gain access to the primitive methods that are associated with individual objects. To do this, you are going to use the *ground* object.

1. Select the **ground** tile in the Object tree and then, if necessary, click the **methods** tab in the Details area.

3. First, drag and drop the ground's **move** method into your new method in the Editor area in place of *Do Nothing*. Select **up** for the direction and **1 meter** for the amount.

4. Next, drag the **who** tile from the method header and drop it to replace *ground* in the instruction you just added. If you drop it in the wrong place (which could happen), click the **Undo** button and try again.

COPYING AN INSTRUCTION

Instead of adding and modifying another instruction from the *ground* object, this time you're going to copy the *who move up 1 meter* tile, and change the direction to *down*. To copy an instruction, you can drag a copy of the instruction to the clipboard, found in the upper-right corner of the standard Alice interface, and then drag it to its new location.

1. First, drag the **who move up 1 meter** tile from your method and drop it on the clipboard. A copy is placed on the clipboard and the original instruction is still where it belongs.

2. Next, drag the **clipboard** and drop it in your new method just below the existing *who move up 1 meter* tile. Now you should see two copies of the *who move up 1 meter* instruction in your method.

3. Finally, click the parameter box that says **up** in the bottom copy of the instruction, and change the direction to **down**.

If you have done everything correctly, then your method should now match the specifications and look like Figure 2-18. You now are ready to see if it works.

TESTING (AND DEBUGGING) A GENERIC METHOD

To test your new generic method, you need to perform two steps. First, you need to see if the method makes an object move up and down as specified. Then, you need to make sure that the method works with a variety of objects.

1. You need to add a few objects to the new method so that you can use them to test your new generic method. First click the large green **ADD OBJECTS** button to enter Scene Editor mode, so that you can access the object galleries and tools to position the objects.

2. Add one instance each of the aliceLiddell, whiteRabbit, and cheshireCat classes, position them as you did at the start of Tutorial 2B, and then click the **DONE** button to return to the standard Alice interface.

3. Select the **world** tile in the Object tree and then the **methods** tab in the Details area.

4. In the Details area, you can see tiles for two methods that can be edited: *world.myfirst method* and *world.jump who*. Click the **edit** button to access *world.myfirst method* in the Editor area.

5. You next need to add your generic jump instruction to *world.myfirst method*. Drag and drop the tile for **jump who** from the Details area to replace *Do nothing* in the Editor area. When you do this, you will be asked to select a value for the who parameter from a list of all the objects in the current world. If you follow the same pattern as the last tutorial, then Alice should jump first, so select **aliceLiddell, the entire aliceLiddell**.

6. Before continuing, play the world to see what happens. Did it perform as expected? Did Alice jump up and then down? If not, it might be time for the debug step in the program development cycle—design, code, test, and debug.

7. Once the method works properly with alice.liddell, add instructions to *world.my first method* to make the whiteRabbit jump. You do this by adding a copy of the **world.jump method** after the instruction to make Alice jump, and then choosing **whiteRabbit** as the value of the who parameter.

8. Do the same actions for the **cheshireCat**, which should jump after the whiteRabbit jumps. When you are finished, *world.my first method* should look like Figure 2-20.

FIGURE 2-20: *world.my first method* with three generic jump instructions

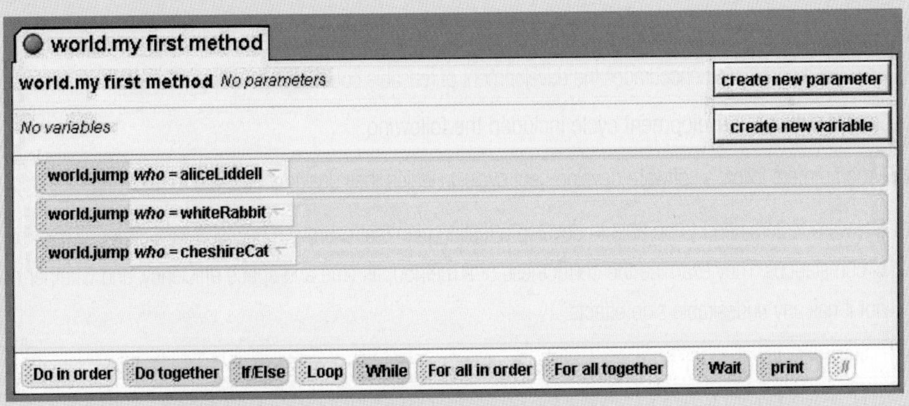

9. Now test your method again. If everything is correct, Alice should jump, then the whiteRabbit, and then the cheshireCat. When you play the world you should not be able to see the difference between a world with a generic jump method and one with three separate object-level jump methods.

10. This is a world that you should save for use in future tutorials. Save it with the name **generic triple jump** and remember where you saved it.

CHAPTER SUMMARY

This chapter consisted of discussions of top-down development, modular design, and a simple software development cycle, followed by three hands-on tutorials involving Alice methods. The discussion of top-down design and modular development included the following:

☐ The process of developing methods for objects is mostly a process of developing algorithms, because each method is an algorithm.

☐ Algorithm development has a long history in the world of mathematics, where algorithms are step-by-step solutions to well-defined mathematical problems.

☐ Good mathematicians often start solving a problem by trying to break a large algorithm into parts that are more manageable. This process is also known as top-down design or top-down development, starting at the top with one concept or big idea, and then breaking that down into several parts.

☐ The process of top-down design leads to modular development. In modular development, the parts, or modules, that make up a complete solution to a problem are developed individually and then combined to form that complete solution.

☐ Modular development makes a large project more manageable, is faster for large projects, leads to a higher quality product, makes it easier to find and correct errors, and increases the reusability of your solutions.

☐ Saving solutions to small problems so that they can be applied elsewhere creates reusable code. Object-oriented programming encourages the development of reusable code.

The discussion of a software development cycle included the following:

☐ Programmers follow a software development cycle, in which they design, code, test, and debug methods.

☐ Software testers need to be able to develop a testing plan that examines new software under all possible circumstances. They examine the correctness of a method, its time and space efficiency, and whether or not it has any undesirable side effects.

☐ Unit tests check to see if methods work as expected individually. Sometimes a method, called a testing shell, is used in unit testing to simulate the environment in which a method will operate.

☐ Integration tests check to see if larger methods work after newer methods are incorporated into them.

In Tutorial 2A, you explored the primitive methods that come with every Alice object. Sometimes it is desirable to run primitive methods directly, such as when positioning objects to set up a scene, or to find a lost object. You also saw that some methods come with user-created methods to provide them with additional behaviors, such as the walk method in the Penguin class.

In Tutorial 2B, you applied some of the methods discussed earlier in the chapter to create an Alice world with a top-level method and separate sub-level methods to make three characters from *Alice's Adventures in Wonderland* jump up and down on the screen.

In Tutorial 2C, you learned to create a generic method to make any object jump up and down. You learned that a parameter can be used to pass a value to a method when the method is called.

<u>REVIEW QUESTIONS</u>

1. **Define the following terms:**

   □ CamelCase   □ off-camera   □ testing shell

   □ coding   □ parameter   □ top-down design

   □ encapsulated methods   □ primitive methods   □ unit test

   □ integration test   □ program development cycle   □ user-defined methods

   □ method header   □ reusable code   □ variable

   □ modular development   □ test for correctness

2. **Describe the processes known as top-down design and modular development, and how they are used together.**

3. **How do organizational charts help with top-down design and modular development?**

4. **List and describe the advantages of using modular development.**

5. **How does the practice of object-oriented programming encourage the development of reusable code?**

6. **List and describe the steps in a simple program development cycle.**

7. **What is the difference between a unit test and an integration test? Why are they both used in software development?**

8. **What are the differences between primitive methods and user-defined methods in Alice? Which of these are encapsulated methods, and what does that mean?**

9. **Describe two different primitive methods that can be used to find objects that are off-camera. What are the differences between using these methods?**

10. **Describe what parameters are, and how they are used in Alice methods.**

<u>EXERCISES</u>

1. **Create an organizational chart showing a top-down, modular design for each of the following:**

   a. Baking a cake

   b. Traveling from your house to Buckingham Palace in London

   c. Sorting a list of names alphabetically by last name

   d. The plot of your favorite film or episode of a television show

   e. The solution to your favorite math problem

2. **Create a modified `jump` method, similar to the one you created in the generic triple jump world in Tutorial 2C, to include a parameter for how high the object should jump.**

3. Open an Alice world with a bunny in it. Create a `hop` method for the bunny that has the object move forward while jumping up and down. (*Hint*: Use the do together logic and control tile.) Create and test a generic hop method that has three parameters—`who`, `how high`, and `how far`.

4. Modify the generic triple jump world from Tutorial 2C, so that it functions as follows:
   a. The three characters appear on the screen in position as before.
   b. Alice says, "Simon says, Jump!"
   c. Alice jumps.
   d. The White Rabbit jumps.
   e. The Cheshire cat jumps.
   f. The Cheshire cat disappears, but his smile stays visible. (*Hint*:There is a property named `opacity`. Dragging a property into a method will create an instruction to set the property to a new value.)
   g. Alice and the White Rabbit both turn their heads to look at the Cheshire cat.

   Save your new world with a different name so that the generic triple jump word is preserved.

5. Begin a new Alice world and add instances of a chicken, a horse, and a cow to the world. Look at the Object tree. Can you see which object violates one of the naming conventions in Alice?

6. Some Alice method names do not follow the CamelCase naming convention. How should `world.my first method` be renamed so that it is in CamelCase? What about the names of user-created methods that are supplied with the Penguin class of objects?

7. Examine the code in the lakeSkater world that is provided with the Alice software as an example world and that was used in Chapter 1.
   a. Explain how the organization of the iceSkater's object-level methods are related to the concept of reusable code.
   b. While the world exhibits good modular design in many of its methods, the method `world.my first animation` could be improved. Create an organizational chart showing an improved design for `world.my first animation` that exhibits better modular design.

8. The American Film Institute's list of *The 100 Greatest Movie Quotes Of All Time* is on the Web at *http://www.afi.com/tvevents/100years/quotes.aspx#list*. Pick one of the quotes and create a short Alice world in which one of the characters uses the quote. Make sure that your world exhibits good modular design.

9. On the surface of the moon there is a crater, named al-Khwarizmi, which sounds a lot like algo-rithm. It was named after Abu Ja'far Muhammad ibn Musa al-Khwarizmi, who lived in the ninth century. See if you can find out why he is important enough in the history of mathematics to have a crater on the moon named after him. What does his work have to do with computer programming and with ancient Greek mathematicians?

10. Select one of the themed folders in the Alice galleries, such as the Japan, Egypt, or Old West fold-ers. Select several objects from the folder and develop an outline for a short story using those objects. Create an organizational chart that shows the modules in the story, and develop a list of the Alice methods that you would need to write to implement your story as an Alice world. Which of these methods do you think would be reusable for other stories? If you have high speed Internet access, you may want to look in the Web Gallery, which is more extensive than the Local Gallery.

3

EVENTS IN THREE-DIMENSIONAL SPACE

After finishing this chapter, you should be able to:

○ Provide a brief definition of each the following terms: absolute direction, BDE event format, Cartesian coordinates, command-driven interface, dimension, Euclidean 3-space, event handler, event listener, event trigger, event-driven programming, to frame an object, Graphical User Interface (GUI), object-relative direction, object-relative position, ordered pair, orientation, pan, point of view, quantification, side effects, tilt, and zoom

○ Describe what is meant by event-driven programming, including how event listeners, event triggers, and event handlers work together to make events function

○ Describe what is meant by an object's point of view, and list and describe the six object-relative directions and six object-relative positions in Euclidean 3-space

○ List and describe the nine event types available in Alice

○ Describe basic camera operations, including, move, pan, tilt, and zoom, and how to implement these in Alice

○ Create Alice events to allow the user to manipulate objects moving in three-dimensional space

> **NOTE** □ □ □ | There are two readings in this chapter. The first is relatively short, describing event-driven programming. The second, which is a bit longer, discusses the nature of three-dimensional space. They are combined in this chapter because events in Alice often are used to manipulate objects in three-dimensional space.

EVENT-DRIVEN PROGRAMMING

One of the most important places in the history of computer technology is the Xerox Palo Alto Research Center (Xerox PARC) in California. Xerox PARC was established as a research lab where some of the world's best computer scientists and designers could work to improve modern computer technology. We see their innovations almost every time we use a modern computer. Local area networks, the laser printer, and the **Graphical User Interface (GUI)** were all developed or refined at Xerox PARC.

A GUI has icons on the computer screen and a mouse to control a pointer that can be used to operate the computer. Most modern software, such as word processing, electronic spreadsheets, Internet browsers, and computer games, depends on the use of a GUI. Before GUIs existed, people had to control a computer by typing commands into what was called a **command-driven interface**. Often it was necessary to write or run a computer program to complete tasks that involved more than a few steps, such as formatting the output for a document.

It's no coincidence that the use of personal computers really took off after the introduction of the graphical user interface. The Apple Macintosh approach to computing and the Microsoft Windows operating system both incorporate a GUI based directly on developments at Xerox PARC.

> **NOTE** □ □ □ | For more information on XEROX PARC, see *www.parc.com*.

The use of a GUI on a computer system requires **event-driven programming**. An event occurs whenever an event listener detects an event trigger and responds by running a method called an event handler. An **event listener** is a combination of hardware and software that repeatedly checks the computer system for the event trigger. Modern operating systems contain facilities to let programmers set up event listeners in their software. An **event trigger** can be any activity or condition selected by the programmer, such as someone pressing the Enter key or a bank account balance going below zero. An **event handler** is a method that is activated when the event trigger occurs. Almost any method can serve as an event handler. When the event listener detects an event trigger, an event handler is called into action.

Events are often employed to provide user controls in computer software. In Alice, events can be used to manipulate objects moving in three-dimensional space. So, before beginning to work with events in Alice, let's explore the nature of three-dimensional space.

THREE-DIMENSIONAL SPACE

A dimension is a way of measuring something. The word dimension is a derivative of the ancient Latin word *demetiri*, meaning to measure out. It is an abstract idea, a concept invented by people to help us understand something. We create a dimension whenever we assign a value on a continuous scale to some property. This process is called **quantification**. For example, a survey might contain the question, "On a scale of 1 to 10, how much do you like chocolate ice cream?" Someone has created a scale to quantify the popularity of chocolate ice cream, making popularity a dimension of the chocolate ice cream.

If you wish to measure the location of a point on a straight line, then you only need one number. You could mark a starting point on the line, and then measure distance—how far a point is from the starting point. By using negative and positive numbers, you could also indicate which direction the distance spans. Figure 3-1 shows a line marked with a scale to help us quantify the location of each point on the line.

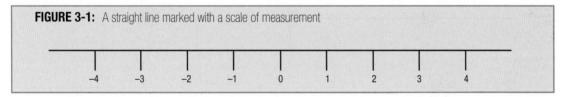

FIGURE 3-1: A straight line marked with a scale of measurement

In addition to the concepts of distance and direction, we also have the concept of **orientation**, which means the direction an object is facing. If an object is facing the positive direction on the line, toward higher numbers, its orientation would be forward. An object facing the negative direction, toward lower numbers, would be facing backward.

Location and orientation together are known as the **point of view** of an object. Figure 3-2 shows three people in a straight line with the point of view for each of them.

Actually, there are two ideas of direction. A direction can be in relation to a scale of measurement, called **absolute direction,** or from the point of view of another object, called **object-relative direction**. In Figure 3-2, the absolute direction of the boy on the bicycle is backward, but the direction he is facing in relation to Alice is forward. Object-relative position can also be considered. From the coach's point of view, Alice is behind the boy, while the coach is in front of the boy. In front of and behind are two object-relative positions.

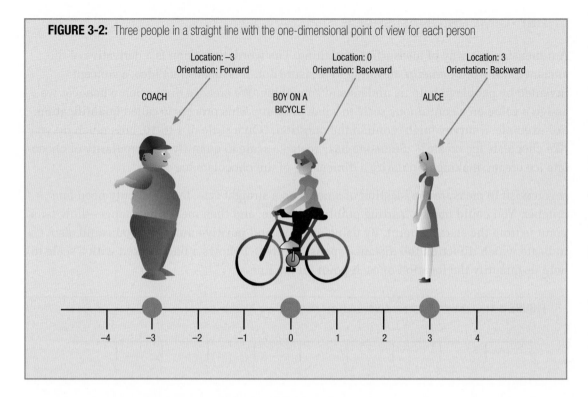

FIGURE 3-2: Three people in a straight line with the one-dimensional point of view for each person

On a flat surface, like a sheet of paper, you need two values to specify an object's position. That is, you need two scales of measurement, each called an axis. The first would measure the object's position along a straight line, and the second how far it is from that straight line along a second straight line. A flat surface is two-dimensional. Such a flat two-dimensional surface is called a plane.

The French mathematician René Descartes developed a system of quantification for two dimensions called **Cartesian coordinates**. Cartesian coordinates have an X-axis and a Y-axis. The location of each point is referenced by an ordered pair of the form (x, y), in which x represents the point's location along the X-axis, and y represents its location along the Y-axis. An ordered pair is any pair in which one dimension is always listed first, and another dimension is always listed second. For example, a set of numbers showing the temperature at various times throughout the day might be given in the form of ordered pairs with the format (time, temperature). The data set would look something like this: (8:00 am, 54°), (9:00 am, 56°), (10:00 am, 59°), (11:00 am, 61°), and so on. In Cartesian coordinates, the X-axis value is always listed first. Figure 3-3 shows several points marked on a Cartesian plane.

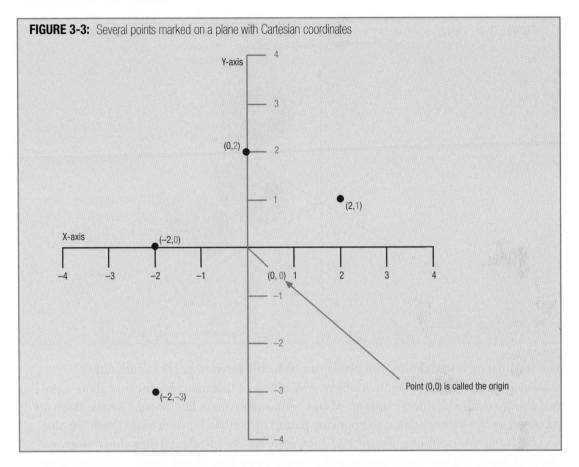

FIGURE 3-3: Several points marked on a plane with Cartesian coordinates

Moving up or down off a flat plane requires a third axis and a third number to indicate how far a point is above or below the plane. In other words, a third dimension is needed. Thus, instead of an ordered pair to indicate location, an ordered **triplet** is used, with three values. Each point has x, y, and z coordinates. Figure 3-4 shows three buildings with an x-axis, a y-axis, and a z-axis for orientation in three-dimensional space. You can think of the x-axis as running east and west, the y-axis as running north and south, and the z-axis as running up and down.

The physical world around us is a three-dimensional space. Mathematicians sometimes call such a space a **Euclidean 3-space** after the ancient Greek mathematician, Euclid. Around the year 300 B.C., Euclid wrote one of the most popular textbooks of all time, *The Elements*, about geometry on flat surfaces and in a corresponding three-dimensional space. Today we also have non-Euclidean geometries, such as hyperbolic geometry and parabolic geometry, to describe location, distance, etc., on curved surfaces, but the virtual world of Alice is a simple Euclidean 3-space.

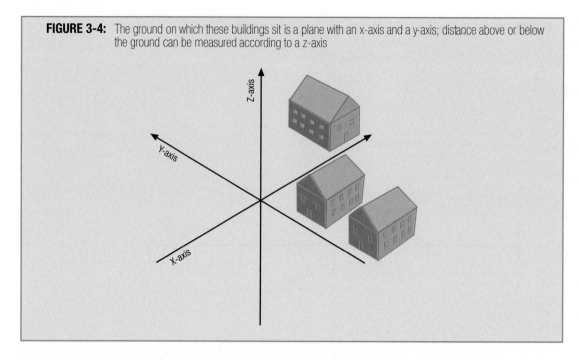

FIGURE 3-4: The ground on which these buildings sit is a plane with an x-axis and a y-axis; distance above or below the ground can be measured according to a z-axis

You saw that on a straight line, an object can be facing forward or backward, either absolutely or in relation to another object. You also saw that on a straight line, there were the two object-relative positions: in front of and behind. In Alice's Euclidean 3-space, there are six object-relative directions, one opposing pair of directions for each axis. There are also six object-relative positions. Figure 3-5a shows the six object-relative directions—forward and backward, left and right, and up and down. Figure 3-5b shows the six object-relative positions—in front of and behind, to the left of and to the right of, and above and below.

Is there a real four-dimensional space? Albert Einstein pointed out that time is a dimension, and suggested what he called a four-dimensional space-time continuum. Many important developments in the field of physics during the past 100 years have been based on Einstein's work. So, you see, the simple of idea of quantification, of applying a system of measurement to something such as the location of a point in space, can lead to some very sophisticated results. In fact, almost all of modern science is based on dimensioning—quantifying the properties of objects, and then studying how those quantities change and affect one another.

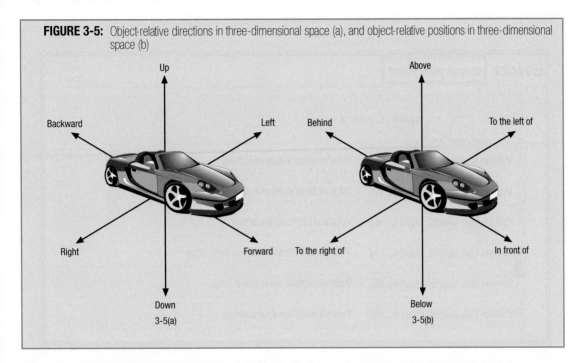

FIGURE 3-5: Object-relative directions in three-dimensional space (a), and object-relative positions in three-dimensional space (b)

The goal of this chapter is to learn about computer programming in the three-dimensional space of Alice. Even though the text refers to direction and movement, the text does so without getting too caught up in the mathematics, so that instead, you can focus on concepts of computer programming and algorithm development.

TUTORIAL 3A—EVENTS IN ALICE

In this tutorial, you will explore events in Alice and create several simple events. Before starting, you should understand the nature of event-driven programming, as discussed in the first reading earlier, especially the terms event trigger and event handler. You should also have an understanding of methods, as discussed in Chapter 2.

EXPLORING EVENTS

In this tutorial, you will explore event types in Alice.

> 1. Start the Alice software and open the **amusementPark** example world. In the Events area of the Alice interface, you see seven event tiles, as shown in Figure 3-6.

FIGURE 3-6: The seven event tiles in the amusementPark example world

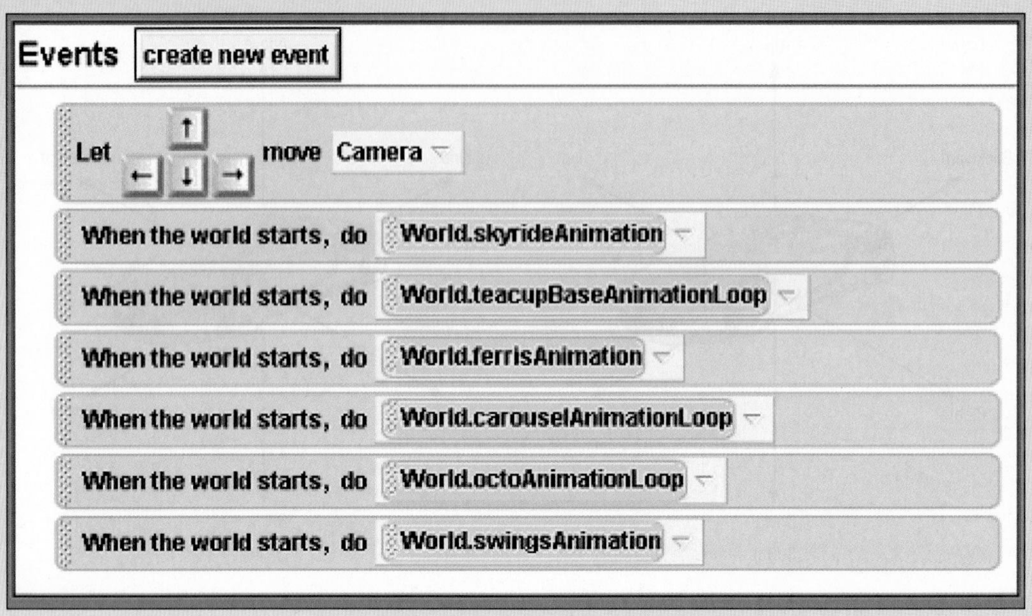

Events [create new event]

Let [↑ ← ↓ →] move Camera ▽

When the world starts, do World.skyrideAnimation ▽

When the world starts, do World.teacupBaseAnimationLoop ▽

When the world starts, do World.ferrisAnimation ▽

When the world starts, do World.carouselAnimationLoop ▽

When the world starts, do World.octoAnimationLoop ▽

When the world starts, do World.swingsAnimation ▽

NOTE □ □ □ | If you cannot see all seven events at once, then it might be necessary to adjust the size of the areas in your Alice interface. You can do this by clicking the background space between areas and dragging the pointer to resize the areas. To lengthen the Events area, click between the Events area and the Editor area and drag the pointer down the screen.

2. The first tile contains an event to let the user move the camera with the four arrow keys on the keyboard. The other six event tiles are of the form *When the world starts do <event handler>*. These events run programs to animate the amusement park rides when the world starts.

3. Play the world and use the arrow keys to move the camera around to look at the various parts of the amusement park. You can see the effects of the six events that animate the amusement park rides. Also notice that the camera moves down slightly when it moves forward, and up slightly when it moves backward. This is because the original camera position was tilted slightly downward. Take a few minutes to look around the amusement park before continuing. If you restart the world, the camera will move back to its original position.

CREATING A SAMPLE WORLD FOR EVENT EXPLORATION

You are going to start a new Alice world with two objects, a blue ballerina and a pink ballerina, to explore the different Alice events types.

1. Exit Alice and restart the Alice software with a blank world using the **grass**
    template. The amusementPark world uses a lot of memory, and exiting and
    restarting Alice is a good way to be sure that it is cleared from the memory
    before continuing.
2. You are going to build a world with two objects, a blueBallerina and a
    pinkBallerina, similar to Figure 3-7. Click the green **ADD OBJECTS** button
    and add a **blueBallerina** and a **pinkBallerina** to the world from the People
    folder in the Local Gallery.

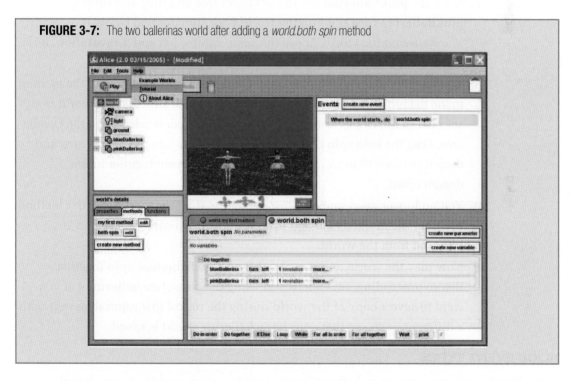

FIGURE 3-7: The two ballerinas world after adding a *world.both spin* method

3. Move the ballerinas apart from each other and turn them to face the camera,
    as seen in Figure 3-7. When you are finished setting up this simple world,
    click the **DONE** button to exit Scene Editor mode and return to the standard
    Alice interface.
4. Next, you are going to create a world-level method to make both ballerinas
    spin at once. Click the **world** tile in the Object tree, and then click the

methods tab in the Details area. Now click the **create new method** button, and when the dialog box appears, name the method **both spin** and click **OK**.

5. You now need to add instructions to the *both spin* method to make the two ballerinas spin. The code in the Editor area in Figure 3-7 shows what this will look like when you are done. First click and drag a **do together** tile from the bottom of the Editor area into the instruction zone to replace the phrase *Do Nothing* in the *world.both spin* method.

6. Click the **blueBallerina** tile in the Object tree and then the **methods** tab in the Details area. Drag and drop a **blueBallerina turn** method tile from the Details area into the *do together* tile in the *world.both spin* method. Choose **left** and **1 revolution** as values for the direction and amount parameters.

7. Click the **pinkBallerina** tile in the Object tree and drag and drop a **pinkBallerina turn** tile into the *world.both spin* method below the *blueBallerina turn* tile. Choose the same values, **left** and **1 revolution**, for the direction and amount parameters.

8. You are finished creating your new method and now need to add the method to the default event tile as the event handler. Make sure that the world is selected in the Object tree and that the methods tab is selected in the Details area. Drag the **both spin** tile from the methods tab into the Events area and drop it in place of *world.my first method* as the event handler in the default event.

9. You no longer need *world.my first method*, so drag the **world.my first method** tile from the methods tab and drop it in the trash can; the method is removed from the world.

10. Now play the world and you should see both ballerinas spin together. Before proceeding, save the world using the name **two ballerinas**. If you want to save a copy of the world during the rest of this tutorial, save it with a different name, so that your basic ballerina world is saved.

ALICE EVENT TYPES

In the Events area, you can see only the *When the world starts, do world.both spin* default event. Whenever the *create new event* button is clicked, a list of the nine event types in Alice appears, as shown in Figure 3-8.

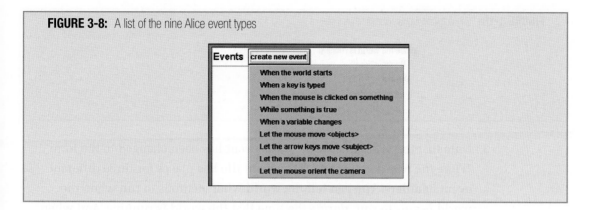

FIGURE 3-8: A list of the nine Alice event types

You are next going to look at several of the nine event types and experiment with a few of them. Remember, your goal is to learn something about events and building object controls with events, not to learn everything there is to know about events in Alice. You'll begin with *When the world starts*.

1. Click the **create new event** button, and then click **When the world starts**. A new event tile of that form will appear in the Events area.

2. This event functions the same as the default event, as shown in Figure 3-9. It will cause a method to run whenever the world starts. You can change the form of the *When the world starts* event to make a method run continuously while the world is playing. To do so, right-click the new event tile. (Make sure you click the blue background of the tile itself, and not a parameter within the tile.) On the menu, three items will appear: *delete*, *change to*, and *disable*. The *delete* option will remove an event from your world. The *disable* option will keep the event, but it will not function until you again right-click the event and enable it. You need to change the form of the event, so click **change to**, and then click **While the world is running**. Now you can see a more sophisticated version of an event handler, as shown in Figure 3-10.

FIGURE 3-9: *When the world starts* event tile

When the world starts, do world.my first method

FIGURE 3-10: *While the world is running* event tile

```
While the world is running
    Begin: <None> ▽
   During: <None> ▽
      End: <None> ▽
```

3. Note that the *When the world starts* event has been changed to the form *While the world is running*. This event tile has places for three different event handlers. You can tell the world what methods to run when the world *begins* to run, *during* the time that the world is running, and when the world *ends* running. This format for an event in Alice is called the **BDE** format, for **Before**, **During**, and **E**. There are BDE formats for several different events. What you see in Figure 3-10 is only one of several event types with the BDE format. You are going to make the pink ballerina spin to her right while the world is running.

4. Click the **pinkBallerina** tile in the Object tree, drag a **pinkBallerina turn** tile from the methods tab, and drop it into the event tile in place of *None* following the phrase *During:*. Choose the values **left** and **1 revolution** for the direction and amount parameters.

5. Now play the world again. Notice two things—first, the pink ballerina continues to spin while the world is running, and second, when the world starts, she spins more quickly. Restart the world, and you will see this happen. Why does she spin more quickly when the world starts? This is a side effect of two event handlers running at the same time. The default event handler causes the pink ballerina to spin left. Combined with the spin from the new event you just added, she spins twice as fast the first time around.

6. Change the direction of the spin to **right** in the *while the world is running* method and then run the world again. Now what happens? The pink ballerina doesn't spin at all the first time, because the two methods triggered by the two events cancel out each other. After the first method stops, she spins to her right. Two events or methods that overlap might sometimes cause unintended results known as **side effects**. Professionals who test computer software routinely check for such side effects.

THE *WHEN A KEY IS TYPED* EVENT

Alice has a *When a key is typed* event that can be used to add controls or user interaction to a world. The event trigger will be the press of a key, and the event handler can be almost anything that can be coded in an Alice method.

1. Click the **create new event** button again, and this time click **When a key is typed** from the menu that appears. This event type will cause a method to run whenever a key is pressed. It takes two parameters: the first is the key that will trigger the event, and the second is the method that will serve as the event handler. The event tile is shown in Figure 3-11.

FIGURE 3-11: *When a key is typed* event tile

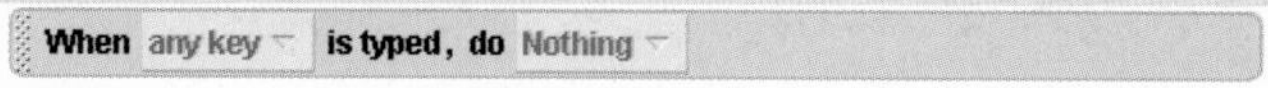

When any key ▽ **is typed, do** Nothing ▽

2. Let's set up an event and give it a try. Click the **any key** box and you will be allowed to select a key from a drop-down menu. The menu contains a list of several control keys, such as *space* for the spacebar and *enter* for the enter key, followed by the words *letters* and *numbers* with small arrow-heads after them. These small arrowheads show us that these menu items lead to sub-menus, with the various letter and number keys listed on the sub-menus.

3. Select **letter** from the menu and then the letter **B** for blue as the trigger key for this event. Click the **blueBallerina** tile in the Object tree and then click the **methods** tab in the Details area. Drag a **blueBallerina turn** method tile from the Details area and drop it into the event tile in place of *Nothing*; choose **right** and **1 revolution** as values for the *direction* and *amount* parameters.

4. Now play the Alice world. Wait at least one second until the opening move is complete, then try the **B** key a few times. Each time you press it, the blue ballerina spins to her right. If you hold down the **B** key, notice that she will *not* continue to spin. Note that Alice event triggers are not case sensitive—this event will be triggered by a capital *B* or a lowercase *b*. Stop the world when you are finished experimenting.

THE *WHILE A KEY IS PRESSED* EVENT

You can change the form of the *When a key is typed* event to make a method run continuously as long as the triggering key is held down.

1. Right-click the **When B is pressed** event tile's blue background, select **change to**, and then click **While a key is pressed**. Now you can see a more sophisticated version of an event handler, as shown in Figure 3-12.

FIGURE 3-12: *While a key is pressed* event tile

```
While  B  ▽   is pressed
    Begin:  <None> ▽
   During:  <None> ▽
      End:  <None> ▽
```

2. Notice that the B key is still in place as the trigger, but that the three event handlers are now all empty. Drag and drop a **blueBallerina turn** tile into place after *During:*, as you did before, with the values **right** and **1 revolution** as parameters.

3. Now play the world again, and, after the opening move is complete, try pressing and holding down the **B** key a few times for different durations. Notice that even though the method calls for the ballerina to turn one complete revolution; when you let go of the key, the method stops, even if the ballerina is in mid turn.

THE *WHEN THE MOUSE IS CLICKED ON ANYTHING* EVENT

Alice has an event type that will cause a method to run whenever the mouse is clicked on an object. Let's experiment with it.

1. Click the **create new event** button, and select **When the mouse is clicked on something** from the menu that appears. A new tile of this type will be added to the Events area, as shown in Figure 3-13. New events are added to the bottom of the Events area, so it might be necessary to scroll down in the Events area to find the new event.

FIGURE 3-13: *When the mouse is clicked on anything* event tile

2. You're going to create an event to make the blueBallerina roll one revolution whenever the mouse is clicked on her. First, click the word **anything** in the new event tile, and a menu of the objects in this Alice world will appear. Select **blueBallerina, the entire blueBallerina** as the target object. Next, make sure that the **blueBallerina** is selected in the Object tree, and that the **methods** tab is selected in the Details area. Drag the **blueBallerina roll** tile from the methods tab and drop it to replace *Nothing* in the event tile. Choose the values **right** and **1 revolution** for the direction and amount parameters.

3. Now play the world and try the new method. After the opening move, click the blue ballerina and watch her roll. The B key event is still active, so you can try that also. Experiment a little. What happens if you click the blue ballerina while holding down the B key to make her turn? The two methods combine to cause unexpected results. If things get really messed up, you can restart the world and try again.

ADDITIONAL NOTES ABOUT MOUSE EVENTS

Sometimes it is very difficult to click an object while it is moving, so it is best to choose a stationary object as the target object. For example, you could put a tree into the world and make the ballerina spin while the mouse is pressed on the tree. In the interest of time, you will skip that for now, but you might want to try it on your own sometime.

You can change the *When the mouse is clicked on something* event to be *While the mouse is pressed on something*, with the BDE format. This change will be similar to what you did with the *When a key is typed* and *While a key is pressed* event types.

Alice also has an event type to let users change the position of an object while a world is running. This event type is *Let the mouse move <objects>*. However, this event type requires the use of a data structure called a list, which isn't covered until Chapter 8, so we'll look at it when we get there.

TUTORIAL 3B—BUILDING CAMERA CONTROLS WITH EVENTS

In this tutorial, you are going to build controls to allow the user to manipulate the camera while a world is running. The tutorial will be brief because Alice has several event types with built-in event handlers for camera control.

OPEN AN EXISTING WORLD

You are going to add some camera controls to the lakeSkaterDemoStart world that is included with the Alice software.

1. First, start the Alice software. If it is already open, then close it and open it again to make sure that the old Alice world has been cleared from the computer's memory. When the Welcome to Alice! dialog box appears, open the **lakeSkaterDemoStart** world from the Examples tab. Be careful—this is not the same lakeSkater world that you saw in Chapter 1, but is a similar world named lakeSkaterDemoStart. lakeSkaterDemoStart is a nice world to use for experimenting with camera controls because it contains some interesting winter scenery with a frozen lake, hills, and trees.

2. Note that once the world loads, you can see the world window with three sets of blue arrows below it to manipulate the camera, as shown in Figure 3-14.

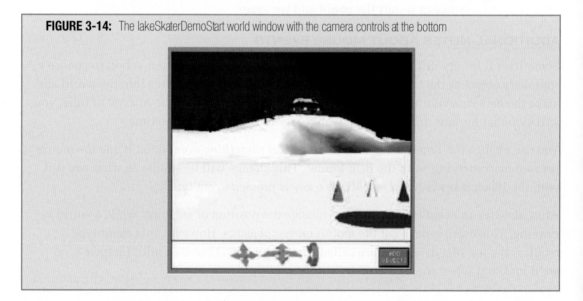

FIGURE 3-14: The lakeSkaterDemoStart world window with the camera controls at the bottom

The curved arrow on the right is the camera's **tilt control**. It is used to tilt the camera up or down, similarly to the way that you might tilt your head up or down. The center control is a mixed control, to **zoom** and **pan** the camera. A camera can zoom in and zoom out, and pan

left and pan right. Zooming in means the camera is moved in closer to get a tighter shot of something, so that it fills more of the screen. Zooming out means the camera is moved out farther to get a longer shot of something, so that it becomes smaller on the screen. Panning means to turn the camera left or right without moving the position of the camera, although it is possible that you could pan and move at the same time.

Most cameras have a lens that will allow the photographer to zoom in and zoom out without moving the camera. In Alice, you zoom in and zoom out by actually moving the camera forward and backward.

Remember, an object in 3-D space can move in six different directions: forward, backward, left, right, up, and down. The left set of arrows at the bottom of the world window is the **move control**, which provides controls to move the camera left and right, and up and down, while the vertical arrows in the center set move the camera forward and backward.

Take a few minutes to experiment with the camera controls and explore the landscape in this Alice world. Try to see if you understand the concepts of tilt, zoom, pan, and move. Pick an object, such as a particular tree, and see if you can frame it in the world window. **To frame an object** means to position the camera so that it fills the screen. You could frame an individual object, a group of objects, or a particular scene.

The blue arrows can be used to control the Alice camera before a world starts, but they don't work once a world is running. There are three Alice events designed to let us manipulate the camera once a world is running:

> n *Let the mouse orient the camera*

> n *Let the mouse move the camera*

> n *Let the arrow keys move the camera*

We'll look at each one individually.

THE *LET THE MOUSE ORIENT THE CAMERA* EVENT

1. Click the **create new event** button, and you can now see a list of the nine event types in Alice, as shown earlier in Figure 3-8. Select **Let the mouse orient the camera,** the last item in the list. You should see a new event of this type appear in the Events area, as shown in Figure 3-15.

FIGURE 3-15: *Let the mouse orient the camera* event tile

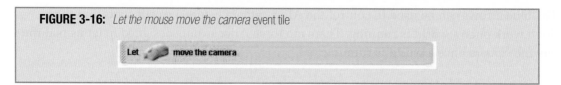

Let   orient the camera

2. This event calls a special hidden event handler that will let the user pan the camera with the mouse when an Alice world is running. You cannot tilt or zoom the camera with this event; you can only pan left and right.

3. Play the world and try panning left and right by dragging the mouse. After you are finished experimenting, stop the Alice world.

THE *LET THE MOUSE MOVE THE CAMERA* EVENT

Alice has an event to allow the user to move the camera by clicking and dragging the mouse around the window for the playing world.

1. Click the **create new event** button, and this time click the second-to-last item in the list, **Let the mouse move the camera**. As before, you should see a new event of this type appear in the Events area, as shown in Figure 3-16.

FIGURE 3-16: *Let the mouse move the camera* event tile

Let   move the camera

2. Note that this event is only slightly different from the *Let the mouse orient the camera* event. It allows the user to pan the camera left and right (not move the camera as the name implies), and move the camera backward and forward.

3. Play the world and then test the new event by dragging the mouse. Do you see how this is different from *Let the mouse orient the camera*? When you are finished, stop the world before continuing.

THE *LET THE ARROW KEYS MOVE THE CAMERA* EVENT

A separate event in Alice allows the user to move the camera while the world is running by using the arrow keys, as shown in Figure 3-17.

FIGURE 3-17: An event tile to let the arrow keys move the camera

Let's take a look at this event.

1. Click the **create new event** button, and look at the list that appears.

2. Notice that there is no method named *Let the arrow keys move the camera.* However, the third item up from the bottom of the list says *Let the arrow keys move <subject>.* Select this item, and a new event of this type appears in the Events area. The last two events you saw had no parameters, but this one does. The default value for the subject is the camera, so it's easy to use this event to move the camera with the arrow keys.

3. Unfortunately, like the last event, it only allows you to move the camera forward and backward, and to pan left and right. This was the event used to let the user control the camera in the amusementPark world in Tutorial 3A. Try it now in this world, and then you are finished with this tutorial. It is not necessary to save your work.

TUTORIAL 3C—BUILDING A FLYING MACHINE IN ALICE

In this tutorial, we are going to create a flying machine—an object that can move around in three-dimensional space under the control of a user. The purpose of the exercise is to learn to build user controls for moving objects.

NOTE □ □ □ | Before you start, you should have finished Tutorial 3A so that you are somewhat familiar with events in Alice.

SOFTWARE SPECIFICATIONS

Let's start with some specifications for the flying machine. The first step in creating software is to make sure that you as the programmer know what the program is supposed to do. Software specifications provide that information. The specifications usually come from the client—the person requesting that the software be written. They need to be refined by the programmer to more specifically reflect the features of a particular programming language or development system.

In this part of the tutorial, you will review and refine the specifications but not actually create the code. Remember the program development cycle discussed in the last chapter—design, code, test, and debug? The development of clear specifications is part of the design process that should occur before coding begins.

In this case, the following specification will be given as a starting point for the flying machine world:

1. It should contain a flying machine in a somewhat realistic environment.
2. The flying machine should be able to move in three-dimensional space.
3. There should be user controls to turn the object up, down, left, and right while the flying machine is in motion.
4. The user should be able to find the flying machine if it moves off camera.

REFINING SPECIFICATIONS

Let's refine each of these specifications by adding more precise details. First, you need to find objects in the Alice object galleries that could serve as a flying machine and then pick one of them.

1. Start the Alice software and open a blank world with the **grass** template. Next, click the **ADD OBJECTS** button to look at the Alice galleries. The Vehicles folder seems like a good place to start, so let's look there. Scroll through it, and you will see object class tiles for a Biplane, a Blimp, a Helicopter, a Jet, a NavyJet, and a Seaplane, as shown in Figure 3-18. Don't add anything to the world yet; you are just looking through the galleries for ideas to help refine the specifications.

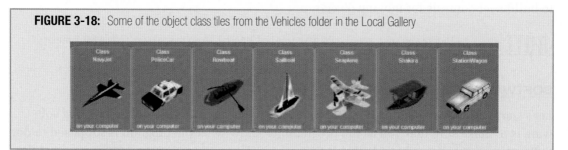

FIGURE 3-18: Some of the object class tiles from the Vehicles folder in the Local Gallery

2. So far, you have worked with the grass template, so for this world, let's pick the **seaplane** and start with the **water** template. Right now you're just putting together the specifications, so close the object gallery and note the revision to the first specification, as follows:

   1. Create a water world with a seaplane in it.

3. The specifications call for the world to look somewhat realistic, so let's add a few items to the water world to make it look better. The vehicle gallery contains a sailboat, and the environment gallery contains two different islands. You can use these. The revised first specification looks like this:

   1. *Create a water world with a seaplane in it:*
      a. *Select the water template.*
      b. *Add a seaplane to the world.*
      c. *Add a few more items—perhaps an island or two, and a sailboat.*

4. Our second specification says that the object should be able to move in three-dimensional space. To do this you will create an event to keep the seaplane moving while the world is playing. The primitive move method has parameters for distance and amount. Our refined specifications will call for the seaplane to move forward, with 1 meter as the amount. This event will keep happening while the world is running—as soon as the seaplane finishes moving forward 1 meter, it will move forward another meter, and so on, for as long as the world runs. Our revised second specification is:

   2. *Create an event—while the world is running, do seaplane move forward one meter.*

5. The primitive move method has additional parameters that are not often used. We can get to them by clicking the word **more** in the turn method and then selecting **style** from the list that appears. Four styles are available, as seen in Figure 3-19: *gently, begin gently, end gently,* and *abruptly*. Gently means that our movement will begin and end gently. Abruptly means that the movement will be at a constant speed. If we choose abruptly, then the motion of our seaplane will look more even.

FIGURE 3-19: The *move* and *turn* events have four style parameters

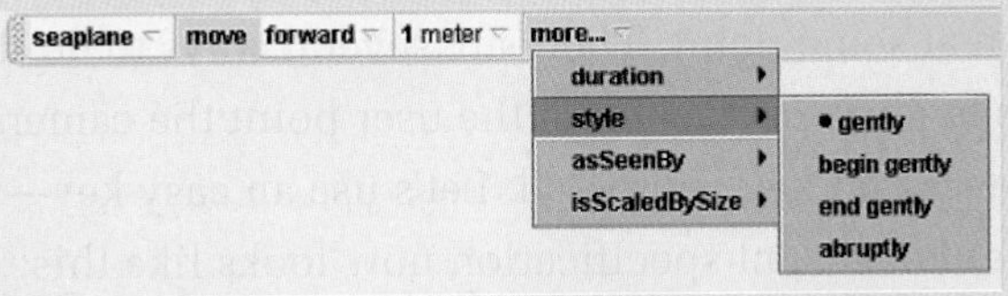

So, now, our specification should say:

2. *Create an event—while the world is running do: seaplane move forward one meter, style = abruptly.*

6. The specifications don't call for us to be able to modify the seaplane's speed, so for now we will assume the speed to be constant. When we set up and then test the world, we can change the speed by changing the distance parameter for each move from 1 meter to a larger or smaller amount.

We need user controls to make the seaplane turn up, down, left, and right. The built-in method for controlling an object with the keyboard lets us move objects, but not turn them. We need to build the own controls—left arrow to turn left, right arrow to turn right, down arrow to turn down, and up arrow to turn up. The turn method has two commonly used parameters—direction and amount.

Left and right are easy, but the turn method does not have parameters up and down, it has parameters forward and backward. Is turning up the same as turning forward or backward? Try this: stand or sit facing straight ahead. Tilt your head backward. Did your face move up or down? We can see that turning backward makes an object's orientation turn up, and, conversely, turning forward makes an object's orientation turn down.

We also need to decide how much the seaplane will turn each time we press one of the arrow keys. Try one-eighth of a revolution. That's equivalent to 45 degrees. So, all together, we have the following control event specifications:

3. *Create four turn control events:*
    a. *When the left arrow key is pressed, turn left 1/8 revolution.*
    b. *When the right arrow key is pressed, turn right 1/8 revolution.*
    c. *When the up arrow key is pressed, turn backward 1/8 revolution.*
    d. *When the down arrow key is pressed, turn forward 1/8 revolution.*

7. Finally, the fourth specification says that the user needs to be able to find the flying machine if it moves off camera, which we can probably expect to happen at some point. There are several ways to do this, but one simple way is to choose a key to let the user point the camera at the seaplane whenever that key is pressed. Let's use an easy key—the spacebar. The *find the seaplane* event specification now looks like this:

4. *Create an event: When the spacebar is pressed, point the camera at the seaplane.*

Let's list all of the more detailed specifications together:

1. *Create a world with a seaplane in it:*
   a. *Select the water template.*
   b. *Add a seaplane to the world.*
   c. *Add and position a few more items—an island or two, and a sailboat.*
2. *Create an event—while the world is running do: seaplane move forward 1 meter, style = abruptly.*
3. *Create four turn control events:*
   a. *When the left arrow key is pressed, turn left 1/8 revolution.*
   b. *When the right arrow key is pressed, turn right 1/8 revolution.*
   c. *When the up arrow key is pressed, turn backward 1/8 revolution.*
   d. *When the down arrow key is pressed, turn forward 1/8 revolution.*
4. *Create an event: When the spacebar is pressed, point the camera at the seaplane.*

CODE THE WORLD—SPECIFICATION 1, CREATE A WORLD WITH A SEAPLANE

Now you are ready to create the world. Following the specifications, you need to create a water world with a seaplane in it. Note that this specification is a bit subjective. What looks somewhat realistic to one person might not look so to another.

1. First, start the Alice software. If it is already open, close it and restart Alice.
2. When the Welcome to Alice! dialog box appears, select the **water** world from the Templates tab.
3. Once the blank water world opens, click the **ADD OBJECTS** button, and add a **seaplane** to the world from the Vehicles folder in the Local Gallery. Also add a **sailboat** from this gallery and position it somewhere on the water away from the seaplane.
4. Next, add an **island** or two from the Environment gallery and position the island(s) in the world.
5. When you are finished setting up the world, click the **DONE** button.

CODE THE WORLD—SPECIFICATION 2, ANIMATE THE SEAPLANE

An event is needed to make the seaplane move continuously. Almost everything is spelled out in the second revised specification—*while the world is running do: seaplane move forward 1 meter, style = abruptly.*

1. Click the **create new event** button and choose **When the world starts** for the event type.

2. When the new event appears in the Events area, right click it. From the menu that appears, select **change to**, and then **While the world is running**.

3. Next, make sure that the **seaplane** is selected in the Object tree and that the **methods** tab is selected. Drag and drop a **seaplane move** tile into the event in place of *None* following the phrase *During:*.

4. Choose the values **forward** and **1 meter** for the direction and amount parameters. Also, click the word **more**, and then select **style** from the menu that appears, similar to Figure 3-19, and change the style to **abruptly** so that the seaplane will move more smoothly. If the seaplane moves too slowly when the world is tested, remember that we can change the speed by changing the distance parameter for this event.

CODE THE WORLD—SPECIFICATION 3, ADD TURN CONTROLS

Next, four control events are needed to add controls to turn the seaplane, one for each of the four arrow keys.

1. Click the **create new event** button, and select **When any key is typed** as the event type. A new event tile of the form *When any key is typed* will appear in the Events area.

2. Change the *any key* parameter to be the **left arrow key**.

3. Make sure that the seaplane is selected in the Object tree and that the methods tab is selected in the Details area. Drag and drop a **seaplane turn** method tile into the new event in place of *Nothing* following the word *Do*, and choose the value **left** for the direction parameter. For the *amount* parameter, select **other** from the amount parameter list. A calculator style keypad will appear. Type **1/8** (as individual characters) and then click **Okay**.

4. Now the world has a control to turn left. In a similar manner, create three more events to provide controls to turn right, up, and down.

CODE THE WORLD—SPECIFICATION 4, ADD A FIND CONTROL

We can expect that the seaplane will move off camera while the world is running, so the specifications call for us to create a method to point the camera at the seaplane when the spacebar is pressed.

1. Start by clicking the **create new event** button, and select **When a key is typed** as the event type.

2. When the new event appears, click the **any key** parameter and select **space** from the menu that appears, similar to what you did earlier to create arrow key controls.

3. Next, make sure that the **camera** is selected in the Object tree and that the **methods** tab is selected in the Details area. Drag and drop a **camera point at** method tile into your new event in place of *Nothing*, and select **seaplane, the entire seaplane** when the menu of possible target objects appears.

4. When this step is finished, you should be done coding your seaplane world. Save the world with the name **seaplane** before continuing.

TEST THE WORLD

Once you are finished coding the world, try it to see if it works properly—that is, according to the specifications. A test plan is often used in professional software development. Such a plan often includes a series of questions based on the specifications. You need to determine if this world meets each of the original specifications, so your test plan might include the following questions:

1. Does the flying machine look like a flying machine in a somewhat realistic environment? (This is a fairly subjective requirement, with a loose standard for what looks realistic.)

2. Is it able to move in three-dimensional space?

3. Are there user controls to turn the object up, down, left, and right while the object is in motion? Do each of these work properly?

4. Can the user find the flying machine if it moves off camera?

To see if the world meets the specifications, play it several times, answering the questions from the test plan as you go along. It might also be good to let someone else, such as a fellow student or your instructor, do so as well. We want to see if it meets the specifications, and if there are any obvious problems or side effects in the finished world.

DEBUG THE WORLD

This might be the hardest part of the entire exercise. If the world does not meet one of the specifications, see if you can isolate the problem and fix it. Usually the problem lies in the code related to the failed specification, but not always—sometimes it is a side effect of other code.

Remember that software development is a cycle. If we find any errors, we need to repeat the steps in the cycle to review the design specifications, code any changes, test, and debug.

CHAPTER SUMMARY

This chapter consisted of discussions of events and three-dimensional space, followed by hands-on tutorials involving events, camera controls, and construction of a flying machine in Alice.

The discussion of events included the following:

o A modern personal computer requires event-driven programming for its graphical user interface (GUI), which has icons on the computer screen and a mouse to control a pointer that can be used to operate the computer.

o An event occurs when an event listener detects an event trigger and responds by running an event handler.

o An event listener is a combination of hardware and software that repeatedly checks the computer system for the event trigger.

o An event trigger can be any activity or condition that causes an event to occur.

o An event handler is a method that is activated when the event trigger occurs. Almost any method can serve as an event handler.

o When the event listener detects an event trigger, an event handler is called into action.

The discussion of three-dimensional (3D) space included the following:

o A dimension is a way of measuring something. It is an abstract idea invented by people to help us understand something.

o Only one dimension is needed to measure the location of a point on a straight line; on a flat plane, two dimensions are needed; and in real physical space, three dimensions are needed.

o A three-dimensional space, like the physical world around us, is sometimes referred to as Euclidean 3-space. The 3D worlds of Alice are Euclidean 3-spaces.

o The concepts of distance and direction together make up an object's point of view.

o A direction or position in relation to a scale of measurement is called absolute, and from the point of view of a specific object, it is called object-relative.

o In Alice's Euclidean 3-space, there are six object-relative directions—forward, backward, left, right, up, and down. There are also six object-relative positions—in front of, behind, to the left of, to the right of, above, and below.

In Tutorial 3A you explored events in Alice and saw some of Alice's nine different event types that can be used to provide mouse and keyboard controls. You also saw that some events have a BDE format.

In Tutorial 3B you experimented with events to create camera controls. You saw that a camera can move, pan, tilt, and zoom.

In Tutorial 3C you created a flying machine in Alice. You applied what you had learned about events and the ideas from Chapter 2 about a program development cycle to design the world before coding it.

REVIEW QUESTIONS

1. **Define each of the following terms:**
   - absolute direction
   - BDE event format
   - Cartesian coordinates
   - command-driven interface
   - dimension
   - Euclidean 3-space
   - event handler
   - event listener
   - event trigger
   - event-driven programming
   - frame (verb)
   - Graphical User Interface (GUI)
   - object-relative direction
   - object-relative position
   - ordered pair
   - orientation
   - pan
   - point of view
   - quantification
   - side effects
   - tilt
   - zoom

2. **Describe the difference between the terms object-relative position and object-relative direction.**

3. **Create a drawing of a number line and with three objects at different points on the number line. For each object, list the following:**
   a. The point of view of each object.
   b. The distance and absolute direction from each object to each other object.
   c. The object-relative direction from that object to each of the other two objects.

4. **Describe the function of each of the blue arrows that appears below the world window in the standard Alice interface.**

5. **Does the cabin in Alice's lakeSkaterDemoStart world have a back door? To answer this question, you will need to open the world and manipulate the camera using the camera controls below the world window so that you can see the back of the cabin.**

6. **Describe an Alice event of the BDE format that will make a ballerina jump up when a key is pressed, spin around for as long as the key is held down, and return to the ground when the user lets go of the key.**

7. **Individual keyboard events can be created to control the camera. As such, do the following:**
   a. Describe a set of two keyboard events to allow the user to pan the camera.
   b. Describe a set of two keyboard events to allow the user to tilt the camera.
   c. Describe a set of two keyboard events to allow the user to zoom the camera in and out.

8. **List and describe each of the four style parameters that can be used for move, turn, and roll methods. Why is the abruptly style used in the following event?**

   While the world is running, move seaplane forward 1 meter style = abruptly.

9. **Why wasn't Alice's built-in event for moving an object with the arrow keys used in the seaplane world in Tutorial 3C?**

10. **Look up the aviation terms pitch, roll, and yaw in a dictionary, or find a Web site on basic aeronautics, and read about them. How are they related to our seaplane controls?**

EXERCISES

1. Create a simple Alice world to let a user drive a vehicle, such as a car, around on the ground. The Vehicles folder in the Local Gallery has a Zamboni machine, which could be driven around the lakeSkaterDemoStart world.

2. Create your own set of camera controls to allow the user to pan, tilt, zoom, and move the camera. The built-in controls do not allow for all of these options. Remember, in Alice we simulate zooming in and out by moving the camera closer or farther away.

3. Alice has a Take Picture button to capture the image from the world window while a world is playing. Open the amusementPark world and, for each element in the following list, use the camera control arrows to frame the object or group of objects before playing the world. Then play the world and take the indicated picture.
   a. The octopus ride
   b. The Alice fountain
   c. The roller coaster and carousel together
   d. One of the teacups in the teacup ride
   e. Most of the amusement park, shown from slightly up in the air

4. Modify the seaplane world to include a barrel roll control. This would make the plane roll one complete revolution whenever a chosen key is pressed.

5. Modify the seaplane world to make the seaplane's propeller spin while the world is running. Does the propeller need to turn or roll to make this work?

6. Modify the seaplane world to make the turn events work more smoothly. To do this, we can change the form of each of the turn control events to *While the arrow key is pressed* instead of *When the arrow key is typed*, and change each turn's style to *abruptly*. You might also want to experiment with the turn at speed primitive method in place of the turn method.

7. Try to create a speed control for the seaplane world. This is a little harder than it looks. Here are some ideas:
   a. You might want to create an object variable for the seaplane called speed.
   b. Set the initial value of the speed to zero.
   c. Pass the speed variable as the amount parameter to the seaplane's movement method instead of a fixed amount.
   d. Create two controls—one to increase the speed and one to decrease it. You can use a math expression to do this.

8. Create a simple Alice world to fly a pterodactyl instead of a plane. There is a pterodactyl in the Animals folder in the Local Gallery. You could build a method to flap its wings, and then use this as an event handler for an event while the world is in motion. Do the wings need to turn or roll? Should they go up and then down, or down and then up? How far should they move?

9. Find a book or a Web site with information on how to make films or videos so that you can learn more about camera movements, angles, etc. to improve your Alice worlds. Write a short report on your findings for your fellow students.

10. The people folder in the local Alice gallery has hebuilder and shebuilder classes to let you create your own Alice characters. These characters will have built-in methods to stand, walk, and show different moods. Experiment with the hebuilder or shebuilder in a simple Alice world to build a character of your own, and then create several events to show what the character can do. For example, create a method to make the character walk when the "W" key is pressed, or show confusion when the "C" key is pressed.

4 THE LOGICAL STRUCTURE OF ALGORITHMS

After finishing this chapter, you should be able to:

☐ Provide a brief definition of the following terms: binary branching, binary bypass, binary choice, branch, concurrency, control variable, count-controlled loop, flowchart, linear sequence, loop, multiple branching, parallel algorithm, post-test loop, pre-test loop, pseudo-code, repetition sequence, selection sequence, sentinel loop, and thread

☐ List and describe the three major elements of logical structure found in algorithms and describe how they relate to one another

☐ List several criteria that should be met by each linear sequence

☐ Describe how binary bypass and binary choice branching routines work, create simple flowchart segments and pseudo-code for each, and implement each in at least one Alice method

☐ Describe how count-controlled and sentinel loops work, create simple flowchart segments and pseudo-code for each, and implement each in at least one Alice method

☐ Describe what is meant by concurrent execution of instructions in an algorithm, and how to implement concurrent execution in Alice

This chapter includes readings about the logical structure of algorithms—including linear sequences, selection sequences, repetition sequences, and concurrent execution of instructions in an algorithm—followed by four tutorials that will provide you with experience implementing these in Alice.

ELEMENTS OF LOGICAL STRUCTURE

Algorithms contain the steps necessary to complete a particular task or solve a particular problem. A recipe for baking a cake will have a list of all the ingredients needed, as well as step-by-step instructions on what to do with those ingredients. In other words, the recipe provides an algorithm for baking a cake.

When young children learn to perform long division, they are learning an algorithm. Professionals, such as engineers, architects, and doctors, apply many different algorithms in the course of their daily work. Some algorithms are simple; some can be quite long and complex. The Holtrop and Mennen Algorithm, which can be used by naval architects to design the optimum propellers for an oceangoing ship, involves several thousand steps and must be run on a computer.

Algorithms are sequential in nature. There are examples where several instructions in an algorithm are executed at the same time, but generally, we can think of the instructions in an algorithm as being executed one at time. They form a kind of sequential logic. Modern approaches to developing software recognize that this is only part of the story, but programmers still need to be able to design, manipulate, and implement sequential algorithms. They need to understand sequential logic.

There are certain patterns that exist in the design of sequential logic. These patterns fall into categories that can be understood as elements of logical structure, which can be combined in myriad ways to form the logical structure of algorithms in modern computer software. A programmer who is familiar with the design patterns of logical structure can more easily create and edit software.

Think about how a programmer's work compares to the work of a plumber or an electrician. A person who wants to design a plumbing system for a building, such as a residential home, has a selection of existing parts from which to choose. We can see these parts in a hardware store or building supply warehouse—elbow joints, T-joints, certain kinds of valves, and so on. Despite the differences from one home to another, the plumbing systems will be composed of many of the same parts, which we might think of as the elements of structure for a plumbing system. The architects who design the system need to know how the parts work and how they fit together. The plumbers who build or repair the system need to know how to work with each of the parts.

The same concept is true for an electrical system. The electrical engineers and electricians who design and build such systems need to be familiar with the parts that are available, how they work, and how they fit together. Switches, wires, outlets, junction boxes, circuit breakers, and so on can be thought of as the building blocks of the system.

Now consider this concept in terms of the elements of the logical structure in an algorithm. They form the building blocks of the algorithm's sequential logic. Each element of logical structure is a set of instructions that forms part of an algorithm. However, there are only a handful of basic elements of logical structure that programmers need to learn, not hundreds or even thousands of different parts, as in plumbing and electrical systems. In the 1960s, two Italian mathematicians, Corrado Böhm and Giuseppe Jacopini, showed that algorithms are composed of three major structures: linear sequences, branching routines, and loops. Modern computer programming focuses on these three elements of logical structure.

FLOWCHARTS

Böhm and Jacopini used a system they called flow diagrams to describe their work. In Figure 4-1, you can see part of their manuscript showing some of their flow diagrams, which soon became known as flowcharts. A **flowchart** is a diagram showing us the structure of an algorithm. They weren't the first to use such diagrams, but they formalized them and used them in their work on algorithms.

FIGURE 4-1: A portion of Böhm and Jacopini's original manuscript as it appeared in the *Communications of the ACM*, Volume 9, Number 5, May 1966

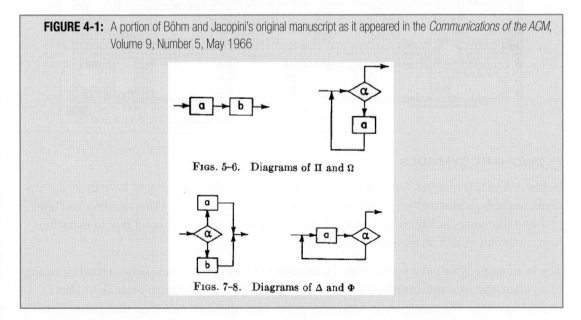

FIGS. 5–6.   Diagrams of II and Ω

FIGS. 7–8.   Diagrams of Δ and Φ

Böhm and Jacopini used a simple system of flowcharting with two symbols: rectangles to show each step in an algorithm, and diamond-shaped boxes to show what they called a logical predicative. More commonly, the diamond symbol for a logical predicative is called a decision diamond, a decision box, or a conditional.

To say that one thing is "predicated" on another means that one thing is determined by another. In other words, there is some condition that will determine what happens next. In an algorithm, these conditions will be either true or false. If the condition is true, one thing happens; if the condition is false, then something else happens. The path through an algorithm each time it is executed is determined by the state of the true or false conditions in that algorithm at that time. Flowcharts are designed to show the possible paths through an algorithm.

FLOWCHARTING TEMPLATE

Böhm and Jacopini's notion of flow diagrams was relatively simple, but, in practice, flowcharts quickly became complicated as people continued to add more shapes. Figure 4-2 shows a flowcharting template first introduced by IBM in 1969. It was accompanied by a 40-page manual showing the proper way to use all of the symbols.

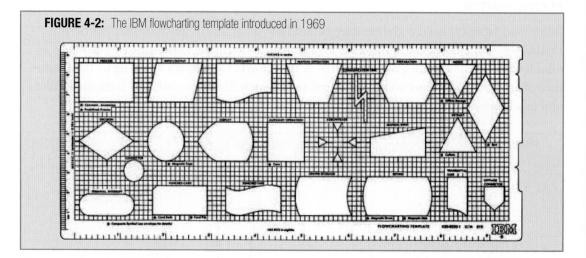

FIGURE 4-2: The IBM flowcharting template introduced in 1969

FLOWCHART SYMBOLS

In the rest of this chapter, we will use a simple version of flowcharting to help describe the elements of logical structure found in algorithms. We will use only three symbols: rectangles and diamonds as Böhm and Jacopini did, along with an oval-shaped box to mark the beginning and end of an algorithm, as shown in Figure 4-3.

The oval shape is called a terminator. There should be only one terminator at the beginning of an algorithm and one terminator at the end of an algorithm, because each algorithm should have one beginning, called an entry point, and one end, called an exit point. Usually they are labeled with the words "start" and "stop," or sometimes "begin" and "end."

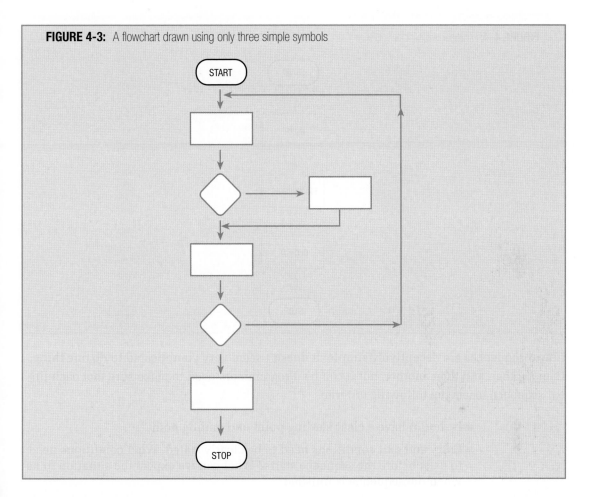

FIGURE 4-3: A flowchart drawn using only three simple symbols

LINEAR SEQUENCES

The simplest element of logical structure in an algorithm is a **linear sequence**, in which one instruction follows another as if in a straight line. The most notable characteristic of a linear sequence is that it has no branching or looping routines—there is only one path of logic through the sequence, which doesn't divide into separate paths, and nothing is repeated.

On a flowchart, this would appear as a single path of logic, which would always be executed one step after another, as shown in Figure 4-4.

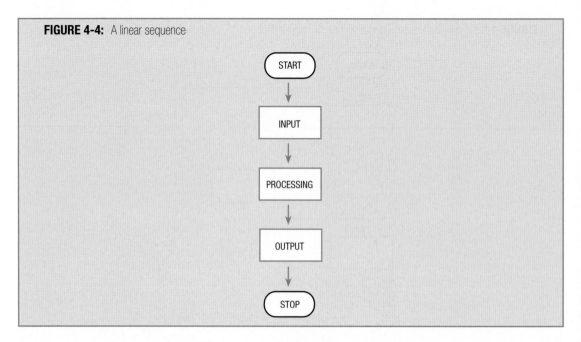

FIGURE 4-4: A linear sequence

Linear sequences are deceptively simple. It doesn't seem very complicated to do one thing, then another, and then another, but it can be. Programmers need to make sure that each linear sequence meets the following criteria:

- It should have a clear starting point and ending point.
- Entry and exit conditions need to be clearly stated. What conditions need to exist before the sequence starts? What can we expect the situation to be when the sequence is finished?
- The sequence of instructions needs to be complete. Programmers need to be sure not to leave out any necessary steps. (This is harder than it sounds. See Exercise 2 at the end of this chapter for an example.)
- The sequence of instructions needs to be in the proper order.
- Each instruction in the sequence needs to be correct. If one step in an algorithm is wrong, then the whole algorithm is wrong.

In short, linear sequences must have clearly stated entry and exit conditions, and they need to be complete, correct, and in the proper order.

SELECTION SEQUENCES—BRANCHING ROUTINES

Sometimes an algorithm reaches a point where the path through the algorithm can go one way or another. That is, the code can execute a selection sequence. Consider this example of a student who has chemistry lab at 2:00 p.m. on Fridays only:

```
Start
IF (Today is Friday)
THEN (Get to chemistry lab by 2:00 p.m.)
Stop
```

Diagrammed as part of flowchart, it would look like Figure 4-5.

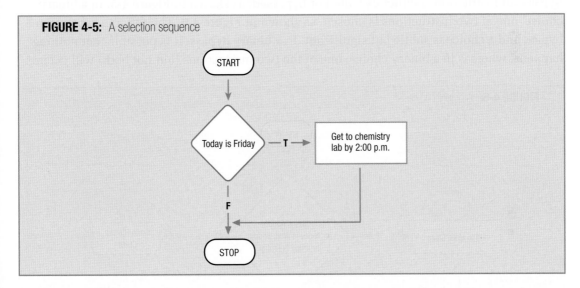

FIGURE 4-5: A selection sequence

This is an example of a branching routine. A **branching routine** occurs whenever the path or flow of sequential logic in an algorithm splits into two or more paths. Each path is called a **branch**. Branching routines are also known as **selection sequences** or selection structures.

BINARY AND MULTIPLE BRANCHING

If there are two possible paths, then the routine is known as **binary branching**. If there are more than two paths, then it is called **multiple branching**. "Would you like vanilla ice cream?" is a binary question—it has two possible answers, yes and no. "What flavor ice cream would you like?" is a question with many possible answers, not just yes or no. Binary branching is similar to the first question; multiple branching is similar to the second.

It is possible to rewrite each multiple branching routine as a collection of binary branching routines. Consider an ice cream parlor with 28 flavors of ice cream. Instead of asking the multiple question, "What flavor ice cream would you like?", a series of binary questions could be asked, for example: "Would you like vanilla ice cream?" "Would you like choco-late ice cream?" "Would you like strawberry ice cream?" In a similar manner, every multi-ple branching routine in an algorithm can be rewritten as a series of binary branching routines.

The Alice exercises later in this chapter focus on binary branching, not multiple branching. In fact, Alice does not have an instruction for multiple branching.

BINARY BYPASS AND BINARY CHOICE ROUTINES

There are two kinds of binary branching: a **binary bypass** and a **binary choice**. In a binary bypass, an instruction is either executed or bypassed, as shown in Figure 4-5. In a binary choice, one of two instructions is chosen, as shown in Figure 4-6. The difference between a bypass and a choice is subtle but significant. In a binary bypass, it is possible that nothing happens, whereas in a binary choice, one of the two instructions (but not both) will occur.

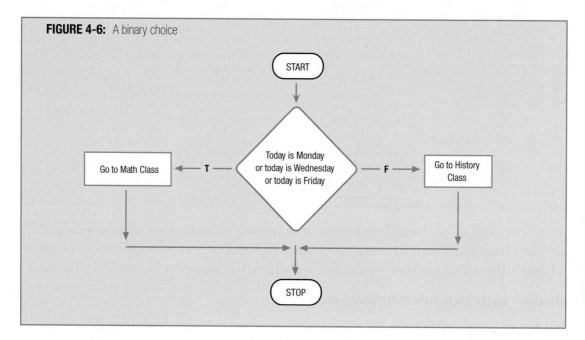

FIGURE 4-6: A binary choice

PSEUDO-CODE

Sometimes computer programmers use a more formal language, called **structured language** or **pseudo-code,** to describe algorithms. The term pseudo-code comes from the fact that it looks something like the code in a computer programming language, but not quite. It's like code, but it's only a tool to help describe and understand algorithms, just as flowcharts are.

In pseudo-code, a bypass is equivalent to an IF/THEN instruction of the form IF (*condition*) THEN (*instruction*). If the condition is true, then the instruction is executed; if the condition is not true, then the instruction is ignored, and the computer will move on to the next step in the algorithm. The chemistry lab example prior to Figure 4-5 shows a binary bypass.

A binary choice is equivalent to an IF (*condition*) THEN (*instruction A*) ELSE (*instruction B*). If the condition is true, then instruction A is executed; if the condition is not true, then instruction B is executed. Either instruction A or instruction B will be executed, but not both. One of the two always happens, as seen in the example in Figure 4-6, in which a student has Math class on Monday, Wednesday, and Friday, and History class on Tuesday and Thursday. We will assume the student only needs to consider weekdays and not weekends. The pseudo-code showing an algorithm for the student's day might include the following:

```
IF (today is Monday, or today is Wednesday, or today is Friday)
THEN (go to math class)
ELSE (go to history class)
```

A set of instructions, called a block of instructions or block of code, could take the place of a single instruction anywhere in an algorithm, including in binary branching routines. In the preceding example, go to math class could be a whole series of instructions.

One thing is common to all binary branching routines and to all repetition sequences as well—there must be a condition to determine what to do. These conditions will be either true or false when the algorithm is executed. They are a form of conditional logic known as Boolean logic, which will be discussed in the next chapter.

REPETITION SEQUENCES—LOOPING

In the branching routines that you saw earlier in the chapter, the algorithms split into different paths that all moved forward; nothing was repeated. Whenever we branch backward to a previous instruction, and then repeat part of an algorithm, we have what is known as a **repetition sequence**. A repetition sequence forms a **loop** in an algorithm, which can be seen on a flowchart, as shown in Figure 4-7. This figure shows both the pseudo-code and a flowchart for the algorithm for printing numbers from 1 to 10.

In this algorithm, the word "WHILE" is used for looping instead of the word "IF" that was used for branching. In pseudo-code, as in many programming languages, this usage tells the computer to loop back to the conditional expression when the block of code following the WHILE instruction is finished. Each time the condition is true, the computer will execute the block of code, and then come back to the condition again. When the condition is no longer true, the block of code will be ignored, much like a binary bypass, and the computer will move on to whatever comes next in the algorithm.

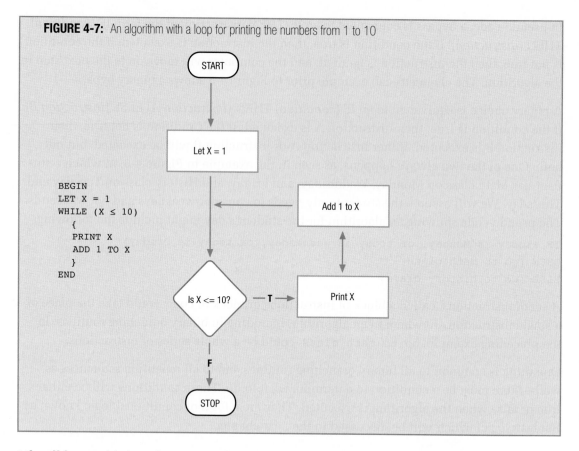

FIGURE 4-7: An algorithm with a loop for printing the numbers from 1 to 10

Like all loops, this loop has a control variable in its condition. A **variable** holds a value that can change, much like a variable from algebra, which stands for a number that could change. A **control variable** is a variable whose value controls whether or not a selection sequence will be executed. In this loop, the variable X stands for a number that is used to keep track of how many times to go through the loop. X starts at 1, the WHILE instruction tests to see if X is still less than or equal to 10, and 1 is added to X each time the loop is executed. The loop is executed while the control variable X is less than or equal to 10. The last value that is printed is 10. When the value of the control variable reaches 11, the loop is no longer executed.

PRE-TEST AND POST-TEST LOOPS

The loop in Figure 4-7 is a **pre-test loop,** meaning that the test to determine whether or not to go though the loop comes before the block of code to be executed. Traditionally, there are four parts to every pre-test loop:

- Initialization: an instruction that sets the first value of the control variable
- Test: the instruction that looks at the control variable to see if the loop should be executed

- Processing: instructions defining the process to be repeated
- Update: an instruction that changes the value of the control variable

Figure 4-8 shows the example again, this time using COUNT instead of X and highlighting the four parts of the loop.

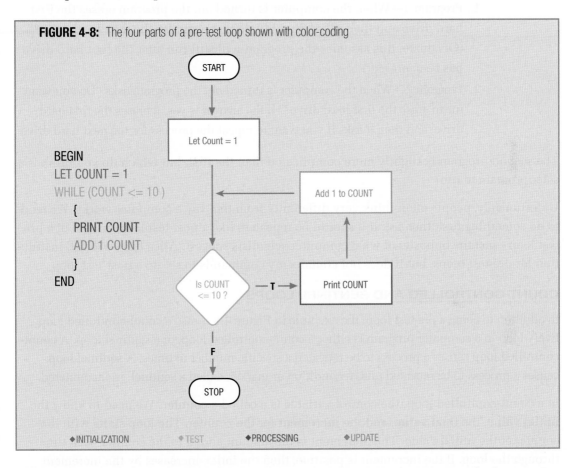

FIGURE 4-8: The four parts of a pre-test loop shown with color-coding

In a pre-test loop, the test to determine whether or not to continue executing the loop comes before any other instructions that are to be repeated. It is also possible to set up a **post-test loop**, with the test to determine whether or not to repeat a loop coming after the instructions that are to be repeated. Figure 4-1, near the beginning of this chapter, shows diagrams of four different logical structures from Böhm and Jacopini's original manuscript. Look closely at both the upper-right diagram and the lower-right diagram. In both cases, the condition in the diamond-shaped box is labeled with the Greek letter "α" (alpha), and the rectangular box representing an instruction to be repeated is labeled with the letter "a." Notice that the upper structure is a pre-test loop with the decision diamond before the instruction to be repeated, and the lower structure is a post-test loop, with the decision diamond after the instruction to be repeated.

Some computer programming languages contain a REPEAT (*instruction*) UNTIL (*condition*) structure to set up a post-test loop, yet many computer scientists suggest that only pre-test loops should be used in programming. To see why they suggest this, consider the following two programs:

1. Program 1—When the computer is turned on, the program erases the first hard drive and then asks "Should I do that again for the next hard drive?" (Of course, this assumes the program will still run after the first hard drive has been erased.)

2. Program 2—When the computer is turned on, the program asks "Do you want me to erase the first hard drive?" If the answer is yes, it erases the first hard drive, and then it asks if you want to repeat the process for the next hard drive.

The second program is slightly more complicated than the first, but which do you think is a safer program to run?

Unfortunately, people often think very differently from the way a computer works. We tend to do something first, then ask if it should be repeated, like a post-test loop instead of a pre-test loop—just the opposite of what computer scientists suggest. Alice has a WHILE instruction for pre-test loops, but it does not contain any commands to set up a post-test loop.

COUNT-CONTROLLED AND SENTINEL LOOPS

In addition to being a pre-test loop, the example in Figure 4-8 is also a count-controlled loop. Every loop in a computer program is either a count-controlled loop, or a sentinel loop. A **count-controlled loop** causes a process to be repeated a specific number of times. A **sentinel loop** causes a process to be repeated until a condition or marker, called a **sentinel**, is encountered.

In a count-controlled loop, the control variable is a called a **counter**. We need to know the **initial value**, the **final value**, and the **increment** for the counter. The loop starts with the counter at the initial value. The increment is the amount added to the counter each time through the loop. If the increment is positive, then the index increases by the increment each time through the loop. If the increment is negative, then the index decreases by the increment each time through the loop. The final value is the last value processed by the loop. In Figure 4-8, the initial value is 1, the increment is 1, and the final value is 10.

It's important to make sure that the initial value, the final value, and the increment all match each other. If a computer were programmed to start the counter at 100, and then increase it by 1 each time through the loop until it reached 0, we would probably get some unexpected results. If the increment is positive, then the final value should be higher than the initial value. If the increment is negative, then the final value should be lower than the initial value.

Alice handles count-controlled loops with a special Loop instruction; thus, most of the time, counters and increments will be handled for you automatically in Alice. However, Alice's loop instruction does not let us use a negative increment. That is, you could not use the loop instruction to add a negative number to the counter each time through the loop, or, effectively, subtract a number from the counter. If you wanted to start at 100 and count backward until you reached zero, such as for the countdown for launching the space shuttle, then you would need to set up your own count-controlled loop using the While instruction instead of the special Loop instruction.

NOTE▫ ▫ ▫ | A count-controlled loop is a special case of a sentinel loop, in which the sentinel involves a counter, but the term "sentinel loop" is generally used to refer only to loops that are not count-controlled.

As an example of such loops, imagine a machine that tests a car door. The machine, which is controlled by a computer program, opens the door, and then closes the door. The machine could be programmed to repeat this a certain number of times with a count-controlled loop, but it could also be programmed to repeat the process until the door falls off, as shown in the following pseudo-code:

```
BEGIN
LET counter = 0
WHILE (door is still on the car)
    {
    open the door
    close the door
    increment counter by 1
    }
PRINT "The door fell off after opening and closing this many times:"
PRINT counter
END
```

This loop has a counter, but the counter does not control when the loop stops running, so this would not be a count-controlled loop, but a sentinel loop. It is the sentinel condition, the door falling off, that controls when the loop will stop.

In summary, when code in a computer program is repeated, the algorithm contains a repetition structure, which is also called a loop. Algorithms can contain count-controlled loops or sentinel loops that are not count-controlled. Each loop is also a pre-test loop or a post-test loop. Alice has a WHILE instruction for pre-test loops and does not allow post-test loops. Alice also has a special LOOP instruction for count-controlled loops.

NOTE▫ ▫ ▫ | There are two methods of programming that are often more appropriate than loops in many situations—event-driven programming and recursion. You already know enough about events in Alice to ask yourself if it might be more appropriate to prepare an event to handle the situation whenever you are considering the use of a loop. The seaplane world in Chapter 3 is an example where this occurs. Recursion, a powerful programming tool in which a method calls itself, will be covered in Chapter 7. Events and recursion are sometimes a little harder to use than loops, but in the long run, they often work better than loops.

CONCURRENCY IN ALGORITHMS

It is possible for one computer, or several computers working together, to work on several parts of an algorithm at the same time. Each path of logic that is being executed is called a **thread** of sequential logic, and algorithms that run multiple threads at the same time are called **parallel algorithms**. The process of running multiple threads is called concurrent execution, or **concurrency**.

Parallel algorithms can be quite powerful, but they can be difficult to design and use. Many problems arise, such as the different threads interfering with each other. It might be easier to run a restaurant kitchen with four chefs instead of one, but if things aren't carefully coordinated, then chaos could ensue.

Concurrency is mentioned here for two reasons: first, it is becoming more common, even in simple programs, and second, concurrency is important in Alice. For instance, you need it when an object should move and turn at the same time, or when two objects should move at the same time.

 You have already seen a simple version of concurrency in Alice. In Chapter 3, you used the *Do together* logical structure, which causes concurrent execution of separate instructions. Alice also has a *For all together* instruction that can be used with lists, which will be covered in Chapter 8.

TUTORIAL 4A—BRANCHING IN ALICE METHODS

In this exercise, you will modify the generic triple jump world from Chapter 2 to include user input and branching. The world contains three objects, each a character from *Alice's Adventures in Wonderland*. The existing version of the world contains a method to make all three characters jump, one at a time. The algorithm in `world.my first method` is simply a linear sequence. You will modify it to include user input and `If…Then` instructions. The new program will ask the user questions about which character should jump, then have one of the three characters jump, depending on the answers to those questions.

Alice has a world-level function to ask the user a yes or no question. You are going to add two questions to `world.my first method`. First, the method will ask if the user wants Alice to jump. If the answer is yes, then Alice will jump. If the answer is no, then the method will ask if the user wants the White Rabbit to jump. If the second answer is yes, then the White Rabbit will jump: if the answer is no, then the Cheshire Cat will jump. The pseudo-code and flowchart in Figure 4-9 describe this algorithm.

FIGURE 4-9: Psuedo-code and a flowchart specifying the program to be created in Tutorial 4A

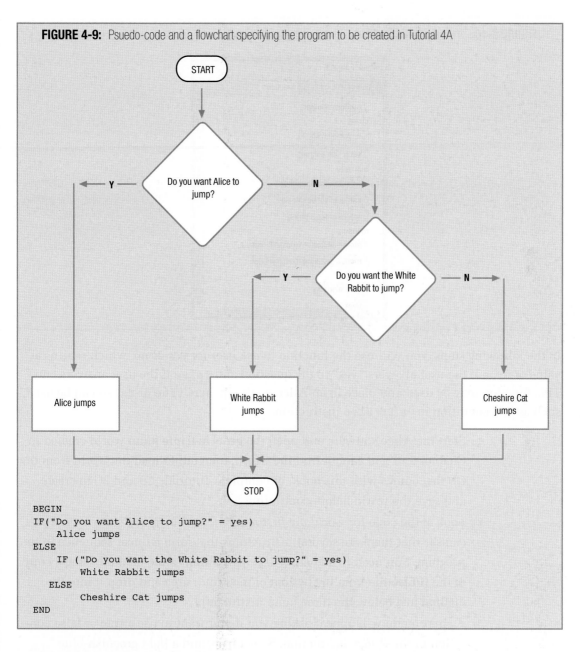

```
BEGIN
IF("Do you want Alice to jump?" = yes)
    Alice jumps
ELSE
    IF ("Do you want the White Rabbit to jump?" = yes)
        White Rabbit jumps
    ELSE
        Cheshire Cat jumps
END
```

USER FUNCTIONS IN ALICE

Before you start, you need more information about the user input functions in Alice. There are three world-level functions in Alice to ask the user a question: *ask user for a number*, *ask user for yes or no*, and *ask user for a string*. Figure 4-10 shows the tiles for these three functions on the functions tab in the Details area for the world.

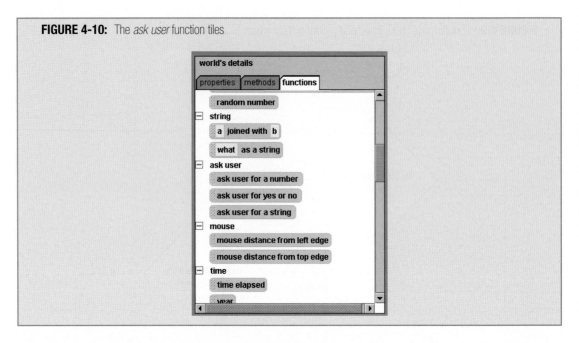

FIGURE 4-10: The *ask user* function tiles

In the following steps, you will use the function to *ask user for yes or no,* which returns a value of `true` if the user answers "yes" to the question and `false` if the user answers "no." This function may be used any place in an Alice method where `true` or `false` can be used, such as in a condition in an `If/Else` instruction.

1. Start the Alice software and open the **generic triple jump** world created in Chapter 2. If you cannot find the world, then either load the world from the CD that comes with this book, or complete Tutorials 2B and 2C to create and save the world before continuing.

2. Look at the code for *world.my first method*, as shown in Figure 4-11. You can see that there are several instructions that form a linear sequence in the program. You need to add an *If/Else* instruction to the method. Drag a copy of the **If/Else** tile from the bottom of the Editor area and drop it into the method just below the three jump instructions.

3. A short menu will appear asking you if you want to use a true or false condition in the *If/Else* instruction. Select **true**, and a light greenish-blue *If/Else* tile will appear in your method, as shown in Figure 4-12.

FIGURE 4-11: The generic triple jump world's *world.my first method*

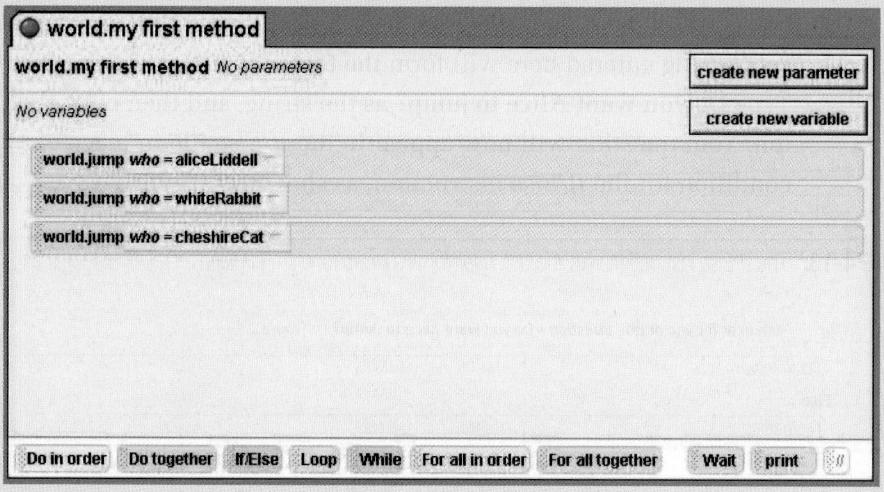

● **world.my first method**

world.my first method *No parameters*	create new parameter
No variables	create new variable

> world.jump *who* = aliceLiddell
> world.jump *who* = whiteRabbit
> world.jump *who* = cheshireCat

Do in order   Do together   If/Else   Loop   While   For all in order   For all together   Wait   print   //

FIGURE 4-12: The generic triple jump method with an added *If/Else* instruction tile

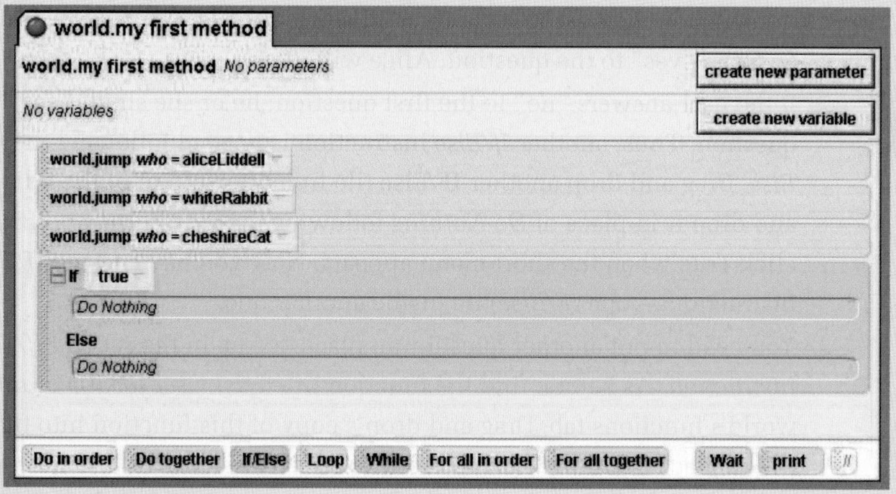

● **world.my first method**

world.my first method *No parameters*	create new parameter
No variables	create new variable

> world.jump *who* = aliceLiddell
> world.jump *who* = whiteRabbit
> world.jump *who* = cheshireCat

⊟ **If** true
> Do Nothing

Else
> Do Nothing

Do in order   Do together   If/Else   Loop   While   For all in order   For all together   Wait   print   //

---

4. Next, you need to replace *true* as the condition for the *If/Else* instruction with the function to *ask user yes or no*. Select the **world** tile in the Object tree, and then click the **functions** tab in the Details area. Scroll through the list of functions and find the function titled *ask user for yes or no*. Drag and drop a copy of this function into the *If/Else* tile in place of *true* following the word *If*.

5. A short menu will appear with the options *Yes or No?* and *other....* This menu is asking you how you want to word the question that the user will see. Click **other ...**, and the Enter a string dialog box will appear. The character string entered here will form the text of the question the user will see. Type **Do you want Alice to jump?** as the string, and then click the **OK** button. Your question will now appear in the *If/Else* tile in place of *true* as the condition for the *If/Else* instruction, as shown in Figure 4-13.

FIGURE 4-13: The *If/Else* instruction with the *ask user for yes or no* function in place

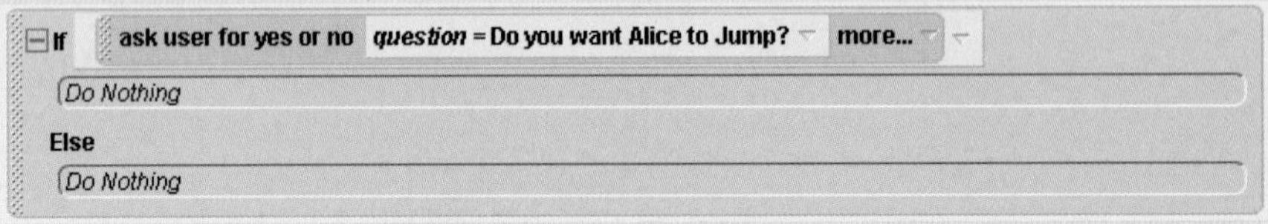

6. Drag the **Alice jump** tile from its place in the linear sequence above the *If/Else* tile, and drop it into the *If/Else instruction* in place of *Do Nothing* immediately below the *If* clause, and above the word *Else*. Now if the user answers "yes" to the question, Alice will jump.

7. If the user answers "no" to the first question, he or she should see a second question. Thus, another *If/Else* instruction is needed following the word *Else*. Drag and drop another **IF/Else** tile from the bottom of the Editor area and drop it in place of *Do Nothing* following the word *Else*, and then click **True** when the short menu appears. Now you have nested *If/Else* instructions—one *IF/Else* tile inside another one.

8. You need to put another question in place of true in the second *If/Else* instruction. As before, find the function titled *ask user for yes or no* on the world's functions tab. Drag and drop a copy of this function into the *If/Else* tile in place of *true* following the word *If* in the second *If/Else instruction*.

9. A short menu will appear. Click **other ...**, and the Enter a string dialog box will appear. Type **Do you want the White Rabbit to jump?** as the string and click the **OK** button. Your second question will now appear in the *If/Else* tile in place of *true* as the condition for the *If/Else instruction*.

10. If the user answers "yes," the whiteRabbit should jump. Drag the **whiteRabbit jump** tile and drop it in the instruction in place of *Do Nothing* below the *If* clause and above the word *Else*.

11. Drag the **cheshireCat jump** tile, and drop it in the instruction in place of *Do Nothing* below the word *Else*.

12. Your method should now match the specifications as shown in Figure 4-9, and should look like the code shown in Figure 4-14. You are now ready to test the new program, but first you should save your work. Save the world with the name **jump user choice**.

FIGURE 4-14: The completed *world.my first method* in the jump user choice world

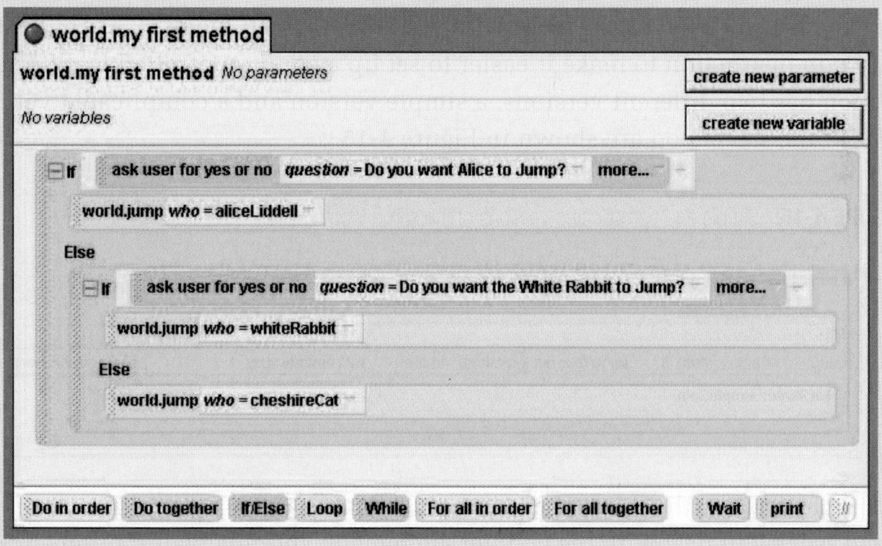

It's now time to test the world. It's a good idea to test the world under all possible circumstances, which in this case means trying the world with all possible combinations of user input. This calls for a testing plan.

The specifications back in Figure 4-9 show that there are three possible paths for the logic in the program. The answer to the first question could be yes or no. If it's yes, then Alice should jump and the program is done. If it's no, then the second question appears. If the answer to the second question is yes, then the White Rabbit jumps, and the program ends. If the answer to the second question is no, then the Cheshire Cat jumps, and the program ends. The testing plan must include three trials, one for each possibility, as follows:

- Trial 1—first answer "yes"
  Expected outcome—Alice jumps

- Trial 2—first answer "no," second answer "yes"
  Expected outcome—White Rabbit jumps

■ Trial 3—first answer "no," second answer "no"
Expected outcome—Cheshire Cat jumps

Test your program according to the testing plan, and see if it works as expected. If it does, you're done; if not, then it's time to debug. Remember to save your world again if you make any significant changes.

TUTORIAL 4B—A SIMPLE COUNT-CONTROLLED LOOP

In this exercise, you will experiment with count-controlled loops in Alice. Alice has a special *Loop* instruction to make it easier to set up a count-controlled loop. The *Loop* instruction has two different versions: a simple version and a complicated version. Both versions of the same loop are shown in Figure 4-15.

FIGURE 4-15: Simple and complicated versions of the same loop

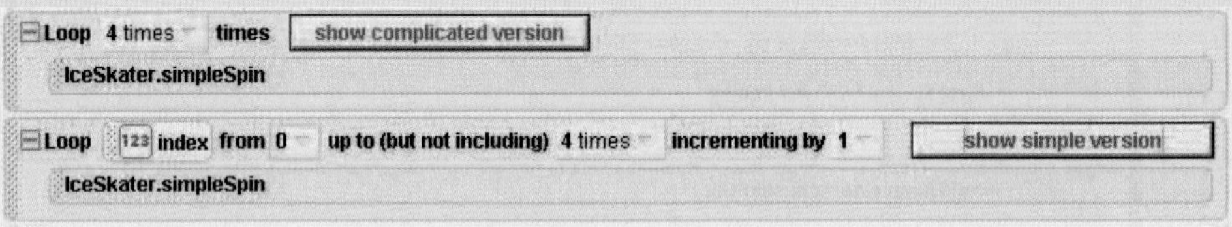

In the simple version, the programmer simply tells Alice how many times to repeat the loop, and Alice will deal with the counter, increment, and final value automatically to stop the loop when it has been executed the specified number of times. In the complicated version, the programmer has access to the initial value, final value, and increment.

In the next several steps, you will modify the generic triple jump world created in Chapter 2 using the simple versions of Alice's loop instruction to make the characters jump a specified number of times.

1. Open the **generic triple jump** world created in Chapter 2, or create it again as described in Tutorials 2B and 2C in Chapter 2. A copy of the finished world is on the CD accompanying this book.

2. In this program, all three characters will jump at the same time. Drag a **Do together** tile from the bottom of the Editor area and place it in your method after the three jump instructions.

3. Drag each of the **jump** instructions into the middle of the *Do together* tile, as shown in Figure 4-16. This is an example of concurrency in an algorithm.

4. Save the world first with the name **triple jump loop,** and then play the world. If all three characters jump at the same time, then move on to the next step. If not, then find and fix the error.

FIGURE 4-16: Concurrent execution of the jump instructions

5. Next, you will add a simple count-controlled loop to the program to make the three characters jump a certain number of times. Drag a **Loop** tile from the bottom of the Editor area and drop a copy of it into the method just below the *Do together* tile. When you do this, a short menu will appear asking you how many times you want to repeat the loop. Select **5 times**.

6. Drag the **Do together** tile into the *Loop* tile. Your method is complete and should now look like Figure 4-17.

FIGURE 4-17: A simple count-controlled loop to make the characters jump five times

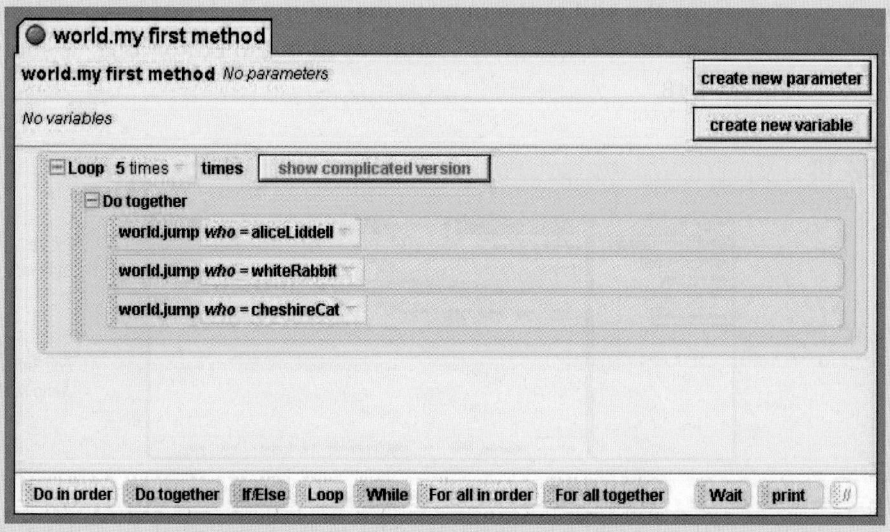

7. You can now test the world again, to make sure that the characters jump together five times. Save the world first, and then play it to see if it works.

This world demonstrates the use of the simple version of a loop instruction. All of the characters should jump together five times. If the program doesn't work properly, review your work to find the error in your program, and then fix it. Once it works, you are finished with this exercise.

TUTORIAL 4C—A MORE COMPLICATED COUNT-CONTROLLED LOOP

In this exercise, you are going to modify the triple jump loop world created in Tutorial 4B. You will work with the more complicated version of the *Loop* instruction, using the loop's control variable to determine how high the Cheshire Cat jumps. First, you will modify the jump method *world.jump [who]* to include a height parameter. Next, you will use the new method to make the characters each jump a different height—Alice will continue to jump one meter, the White Rabbit will jump two meters, and the Cheshire Cat's jump height will depend on the value of the counter in the loop. Let's start by adding a parameter to the jump method.

1. Open the **triple jump loop** world from Tutorial 4B.
2. Click **File** on the menu bar, and then click **Save World As** to save a copy of the world with the name **triple jump loop 2** so that the changes you make will not alter the original triple jump loop world.
3. Select the **world** tile in the Object tree and the **methods** tab in the Details area. Click the **edit** button next to the *jump [who]* tile on the methods tab, and the method *world.jump* should open in the Editor area, as shown in Figure 4-18.

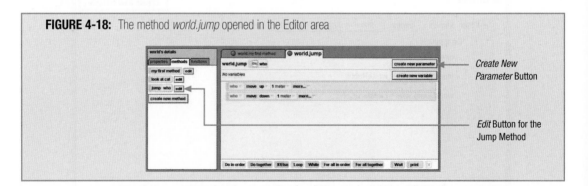

FIGURE 4-18: The method *world.jump* opened in the Editor area

4. You will now add a height parameter to the jump method. Click the **create new parameter** button on the right side of the top of the method, as identified in Figure 4-18. A dialog box will appear asking you for the name and type of the new parameter. Type **height** as the name, select **Number** as

the type, and then click the **OK** button. Now the method has two parameters—*who*, which is an object parameter, and *height*, the number parameter that you just added.

5. Next, you will modify the *move up* and *move down* instructions in the method to use the *height* parameter as the amount to jump instead of *1 meter*. Drag the **height parameter** tile from the top of the method and drop a copy of it into the *move up* instruction tile in place of the value *1 meter*. Do the same thing for the *move down* instruction. Now, instead of jumping up and down one meter each time the `generic jump` method is used, the object will jump up and down the amount specified by the *height* parameter. Figure 4-19 shows the two move instructions.

FIGURE 4-19: The two jump instructions with the *height* parameter added

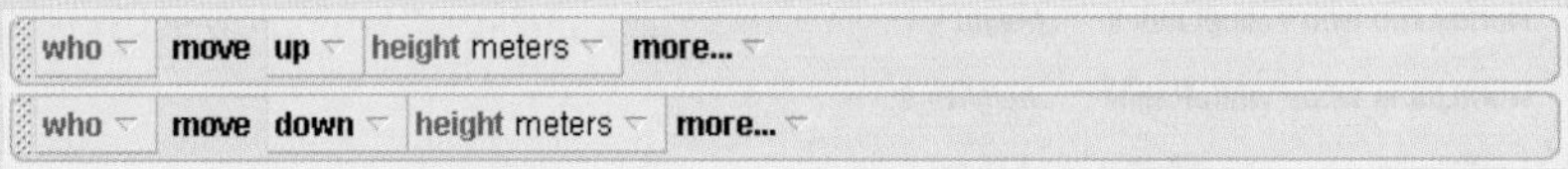

Now that a *height* parameter has been added to the *jump* method, you should be able to modify how high each character jumps in the program that calls the `jump` method. In this world, the method *world.my first method* calls the *jump* method for each of our three characters. You need to change the amount passed to the `jump` method from *world.my first method*.

1. Click the **edit** button next to the *my first method* tile in the Details area, and you will now see *world.my first method* in the Editor area. Notice that a *height* parameter has been added to each jump instruction with the default value 1.

2. The rabbit should be able to jump higher than Alice, so click the **height** parameter in the *world.jump who= whiteRabbit* tile in the middle of the method, and change the value to **2**.

3. Save and play your world. The White Rabbit should be jumping twice as high as Alice and the Cheshire Cat. If not, find and fix your error.

Each time through a loop is called an iteration of the loop. The loop control variable, named *index*, starts at zero, and increases by one with each iteration, as follows: 0, 1, 2, 3, and 4. The loop starts counting at zero and stops *before* reaching five. Thus, even though the loop executes five times, the first value of the index is 0, and the last value is 4.

You will now make the amount each time the Cheshire Cat jumps equal to the value of the index—0 the first time through the loop, 1 the second time, and so on. To do this, first you need to be able to see the complicated version of the loop instruction.

1. The *Loop* tile contains a *show complicated version* button. Click this button now, and you will see the complicated version of the loop, as shown in Figure 4-20.

2. Drag a copy of the *index* tile from the Loop instruction and drop it into the *world.jump who= cheshireCat* tile in place of the value *1* as the height parameter. Your code should now look like Figure 4-20.

FIGURE 4-20: A complicated version of a count-controlled loop, using *index* in an instruction within the loop

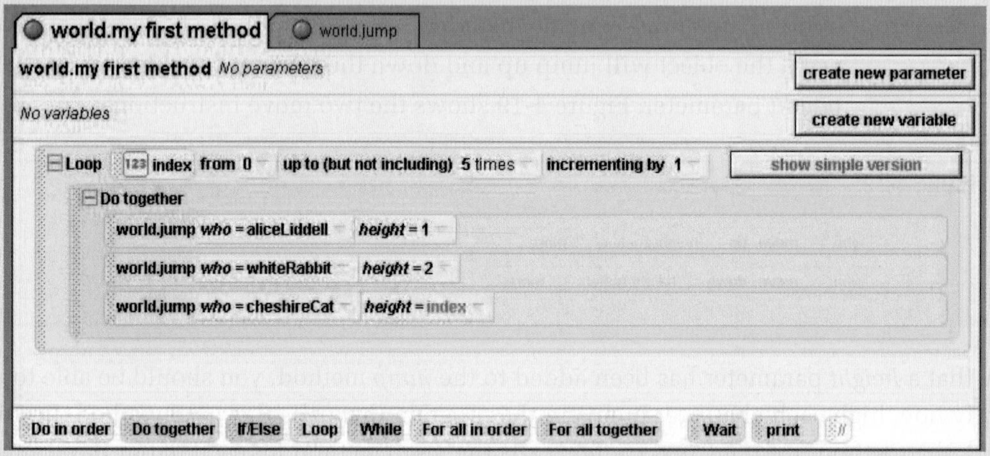

3. Save the world and test it. The amount the Cheshire Cat jumps should be equal to the index for the loop, which starts at 0 and increments by 1 each time, stopping before 5 is reached. The Cheshire Cat should first jump 0 meters, then 1 meter, 2 meters, 3 meters, and 4 meters. The Cheshire Cat might be jumping off the screen the last few times.

NOTE □ □ □ | The loop instruction in Alice is really intended to be used only in situations where the programmer wants to make something happen a certain number of times, such as jumping five times. Remember that a count-controlled loop is just a special case of a sentinel loop. Whenever a more sophisticated loop is called for, such as one that counts backward, it is best to create your own version of a count-controlled loop with a While instruction.

TUTORIAL 4D—USING THE WHILE INSTRUCTION

In this tutorial, you are going to use the `While` instruction to duplicate the effect of the `Loop` instruction used in Tutorial 4B. Remember that a sentinel loop has a value or condition that tells a loop when to stop executing. A count-controlled loop is just a special case of a sentinel loop.

You will use the triple jump loop world from Tutorial 4B as your base world, modifying it to use the `While` instruction instead of the `Loop` instruction, but the new world should function in a way very similar to the old world. Figure 4-21 shows the algorithm for a simple count-controlled loop alongside the new algorithm for the `While` loop you will create. Notice that the `Loop` instruction handles the initialization, test, and update automatically, whereas the programmer must include instructions to deal with these steps in the `While` loop.

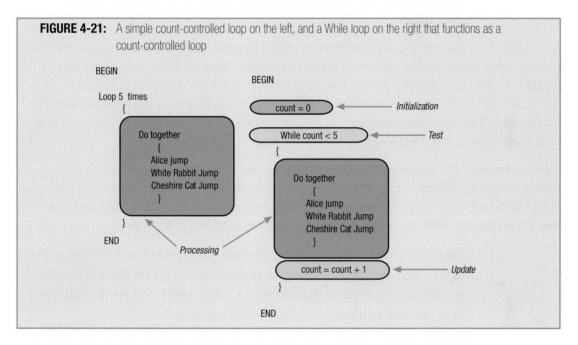

FIGURE 4-21: A simple count-controlled loop on the left, and a While loop on the right that functions as a count-controlled loop

You will need to add a variable to `world.my first method` to function as the control variable, add a `While` loop to the method, and delete the `Loop` instruction.

1. Open the **triple jump loop** world that you saved in Tutorial 4B. If you cannot find the world, then either load the world from the CD that comes with this book or redo Tutorial 4B to create and save the world before continuing.

2. Select the **world** tile in the Object tree and the **methods** tab in the Details area. Click the **edit** button next to the *my first method* tile on the methods tab; the method *world.my first method* should open in the Editor area.

3. You need to create a new control variable for the *While* loop that you will add to the program. Click the **create new variable** button, and a dialog box will appear asking you for the name and type of the new variable. Type **count** for the name, select **Number** as the type, and then click the **OK** button.

4. The variable tile at the top of the method shows that the count is initialized to 1. Click the **1** and change the value to **0**.

5. Drag a **While** instruction tile from the bottom of the Editor area and drop it in the method below the *Loop* tile. Select **true** from the short menu that appears.

6. Next, drag the **Do together** tile with the three jump instructions from the *Loop* tile and drop it in the *While* tile.

7. Now the *Loop* tile is no longer needed. Right-click the **Loop** tile and click **delete**.

Remember from the reading at the beginning of this chapter that there are four parts to every pre-test loop: initialization, test, processing, and update. Each of these parts of the loop needs to be properly in place for the loop to function as desired. Count is initialized to 0 in the count variable tile at the top of the method, so this will suffice as the initialization step for the loop. The three jump instructions are the processing in the middle of the loop. You only need to modify the test and add the update step.

The condition in the While instruction will be the test to see if the loop needs to be repeated. The algorithm in Figure 4-21 shows that the loop should continue while the count is less than 5. It also shows that 1 should be added to count at the end of the loop. You need to modify the code in world.my first method to match this.

1. Drag a copy of the **count** variable tile and drop it into the *While* tile in place of the value *true*. When the menu appears with different choices for the conditional expression, choose **count <** , then **other**, and set the value to **5**. Now the loop will repeat while *count* is less than *5*.

2. Drag the **count** variable tile from the top of the method and drop a copy in the *While* tile after the three jump instructions. When you do this, a short menu will appear asking you how you want to set the value of count. Choose **set value**, choose **expressions**, and then click **count**.

3. Now the tile says *count set value to count.* You need to build a math expression so that the tile will say *count set value to count +1.* Click the second word **count**, and select **math** from the menu that appears. Then select **count +** and then **1**. Now *world.my first method* should match the specifications as shown in Figure 4-21, and should look like Figure 4-22.

FIGURE 4-22: The completed *world.my first method* with the *While* loop

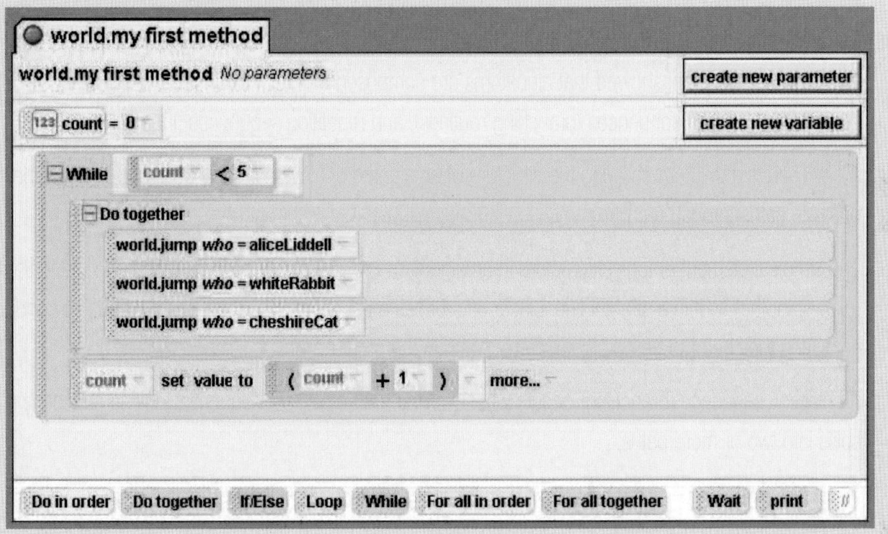

4. You need to save and test the world. Save the world with the name **triple jump while loop**, then play the world to make sure that the characters jump together five times, just as they did with the simple count-controlled loop in Tutorial 4B. If the program doesn't work properly, review your work to find the error in your program, and then fix it. Once it works, you are finished with this tutorial.

CHAPTER SUMMARY

This chapter consisted of several readings about the logical structure of algorithms—including linear sequences, selection sequences, repetition sequences, and concurrent execution of instructions in an algorithm—followed by four hands-on tutorials.

The readings discussed the following:

☐ Algorithms are sequential in nature; we can think of the instructions in an algorithm as being executed one at a time.

☐ Each element of logical structure is a set of instructions that forms part of an algorithm. Corrado Böhm and Giuseppe Jacopini showed that algorithms are composed of three major structures: linear sequences, selection sequences (branching routines), and repetition sequences (loops).

☐ A flowchart is a diagram showing the structure of an algorithm. Flowcharts are designed to show the possible paths through an algorithm.

☐ The simplest element of logical structure in an algorithm is a linear sequence, in which one instruction follows another as if in a straight line. Linear sequences must have clearly stated entry and exit conditions, and they need to be complete, correct, and in the proper order.

☐ A selection sequence (branching) occurs whenever the path or flow of sequential logic in an algorithm splits into two or more paths.

☐ There are two kinds of binary branching in algorithms: a binary bypass and a binary choice. In a binary bypass, an instruction is either executed or bypassed. In a binary choice, one of two instructions is chosen.

☐ Whenever we branch backward to a previous instruction, and then repeat part of an algorithm, we have what is known as a repetition sequence (loop).

☐ A control variable is a variable whose value controls whether or not a repetition sequence will be executed.

☐ In a pre-test loop, the test to determine whether or not to continue executing the loop comes before any other instructions that are to be repeated. In a post-test loop, it comes afterward. Many computer scientists recommend that only pre-test loops be used.

☐ There are four parts to every pre-test loop: initialization, test, processing, and update.

☐ Every loop in a computer program is either a count-controlled loop or a sentinel loop. A count-controlled loop causes a process to be repeated a specific number of times. A sentinel loop causes a process to be repeated until a condition or marker, called a sentinel, is encountered. Actually, a count-controlled loop is a special case of a sentinel loop.

☐ It is possible for a computer to execute several instructions from the same algorithm at the same time. This is called concurrency, and algorithms that include concurrency are called parallel algorithms.

In Tutorial 4A, you learned how to use the `If/Else` instruction to include binary branching in an Alice method, and to use the `ask user a yes or no question` function.

In Tutorial 4B, you learned how to include a simple count-controlled loop in Alice with the `Loop` instruction, and used the `Do together` instruction to perform concurrent execution of several methods.

In Tutorial 4C, you learned how to use the complicated version of the `Loop` instruction, and to use the loop index variable within an instruction in the loop.

In Tutorial 4D, you learned how to create a properly structured `While` loop.

REVIEW QUESTIONS

1. **Define the following terms:**

    - binary branching
    - binary bypass
    - binary choice
    - branch
    - concurrency
    - control variable
    - count-controlled loop

    - flowchart
    - linear sequence
    - loop
    - multiple branching
    - parallel algorithm
    - post-test loop
    - pre-test loop

    - pseudo-code
    - repetition sequence
    - selection sequence
    - sentinel loop
    - thread

2. **Create a set of instructions for a simple everyday process that contains a linear seqeuence of steps, such as making a cup of coffee or getting from your school to where you live. Exchange directions with another student, and critique each other's work. In particular, are the linear sequences in your algorithm complete, correct, and in the proper order?**

3. **Compare the structures created by using an If/Else instruction and a While instruction in pseudo-code. How are they the same? How are they different? What would each look like on a flowchart?**

4. **To add two fractions, such as 1/2 and 1/3, the fractions must have a common denominator. Using both pseudo-code and a flowchart, describe a general algorithm for adding two fractions.**

5. **What is meant by the term "nested" If/Else instructions? Give at least one example of nested If/Else instructions using pseudo-code and flowcharts to describe you answer.**

6. **List and describe the four parts of every pre-test sentinel loop.**

7. **The following algorithm was intended to result in the numbers from 10 to 1 being printed. What will it actually do? What is wrong with it, and how can it be corrected?**

```
BEGIN
count = 10
While count > 0
    {
    Print count
    Count = count +1
    }
Print "The countdown is finished."
END
```

8. Tutorial 4B shows how to set up a count-controlled loop using the Loop instruction. Tutorial 4D shows how to do the same thing using a While instruction. Figure 4-20 shows the two algorithms side-by-side. What are the advantages to using the Loop instruction to set up a count controlled loop? What are the advantages in using the While instruction to set up a count controlled loop?

9. Describe the difference between a pre-test loop and a post-test loop. Which is generally safer to use in a computer program, and why?

10. A data file for a payroll program consists of a set of records. There is one record for each employee, containing the employee's ID number, first name, last name, and hours worked. The last record contains "0000" as the employee number. Using pseudo-code and a flowchart, describe an algorithm that will read in and print each record no matter how many records are in the file when the algorithm is executed.

EXERCISES

1. Alice contains a world-level function that will `ask the user for a number`. Create an Alice world with a character of your choice that will ask the user for a number, cause the character to jump up, use a loop to spin around the number of times specified, and then come back down. Think about how variables will be used as you design the algorithm.

2. Modify the triple jump loop world so that Alice jumps if the index is equal to 1, the White Rabbit jumps if the index is equal to 2, the Cheshire Cat jumps if the index is equal to 3, and all three characters jump if the index is equal to 4.

3. Add a tree to the triple jump while loop world. Make the sentinel to be the tree's height, rather than the number 5, so that the loop will execute when the distance is less than or equal to the tree's height, but stop when the distance passes its height. To do this, you can use the character-level function that returns an object's height.

4. Modify the triple jump loop2 world from Tutorial 4C to make the height the Cheshire Cat jumps increase by .5 meters each time through the loop.

5. Make the height in the triple jump loop2 start at a higher number and decrease each time until it is less than or equal to a smaller value. For example, the initial value could be 5, the increment could be –1, and the final value could be 1.

6. Modify the triple jump loop2 world to make the height the White Rabbit jumps increase each time through the loop, and have the height the Cheshire Cat jumps decrease at the same time. Consider the following: what happens to (5 – x) as x increases from 0 to 4?

7. Modify the finished triple jump While loop world from Tutorial 4D to use the `increment` instruction instead of the instruction that says `count set value to count +1`. To do this, delete the old set value instruction, drag the count variable tile, drop it into the code for the method, and **select** increment count by 1 **instead of** set value.

8. Alice contains Hebuilder and Shebuilder class tiles in the People folder of the Local Gallery. You can create your own character objects in Alice using these. The new character will have a method to walk. Create an Alice world with a character of your own creation as an object in the world. Using the walk, move, and turn methods, create an Alice method with a loop to make the character walk around in a complete circle. (You can approximate a circle with a polygon, such as an octagon.)

9. The Animals object gallery contains a pterodactyl. The CD that comes with this book contains a world named "flapping pterodactyl" with a character-level method named `flap` that will cause the pterodactyl to flap its wings. Do each of the following:

    a. Create a method called `pterodactyl fly` that will make the pterodactyl move forward while flapping its wings, and then create a loop in `world.my first method` to make the pterodactyl fly away.

    b. Modify the world to use an event instead of a loop to make the pterodactyl fly while the world is running. You might need to refer back to Chapter 3, which covers events.

    c. Add controls to your pterodactyl world so that the user can steer the pterodactyl.

    d. Add a user control to point the camera at the pterodactyl when the spacebar is pressed.

10. In Exercise 9, why is it better to use an event instead of a loop to make the Pterodactyl continue flying while the world is running?

6. Alice contains Hebuilder and Shebuilder class files in the People folder of the Local Gallery. You can create your own characters/objects in Alice using these. The new character will have a method to walk. Create an Alice world with a character of your own creation as an object in the world. Usually the walk, move, and turn methods; create an Alice method with a loop to make the character walk around in a complete circle. (You can approximate a circle with a polygon, such as an octagon.)

8. The Amusuta object gallery contains a pterodactyl. The CD that comes with this book contains a world named "flapping pterodactyl" with a character-level method named Fly that will cause the pterodactyl to flap its wings. Do each of the following:

a. Create a method called pterodactyl.Fly that will make the pterodactyl move forward while flapping its wings, then create a loop in your worldmy .character method to make the pterodactyl to fly away.

b. Modify the world to use an event instead of a loop to make the world is dynamic. You might need to alter part a of Chapter 8, which creates events.

c. Add controls to your interactive world so that the user can steer the pterodactyl.

d. Allow the user to speed up and slow the movement of the pterodactyl as it moves.

10. In Exercise 9, why is it better to use an event instead of a loop to make the Pterodactyl Creature flying while the world is running?

5

BOOLEAN LOGIC IN PROGRAMMING

After finishing this chapter, you should be able to:

☐ Provide a brief definition of each the following terms: American Standard Code for Information Interchange (ASCII), AND, Boolean algebra, Boolean function, Boolean logic, collate, collating sequence, logical comparison operators, NOT, OR, proximity function, and Unicode

☐ Describe the function of the Boolean operations AND, OR, and NOT, and show how they are used in Alice branching and looping instructions

☐ List and describe the function of the six logical comparison operators, and show how they are used to form Boolean conditions in Alice

☐ Describe what a Boolean function is and how such functions are used in Alice

☐ Create new methods in Alice that use Boolean conditions, Boolean functions, and method parameters

BOOLEAN LOGIC

Branching and looping routines both contain conditions that are either true or false. In 1854, George Boole, the first Professor of Mathematics at Queen's College in Cork, Ireland, published a book titled *An investigation into the Laws of Thought, on which are founded the Mathematical Theories of Logic and Probabilities.* In that book, Boole outlined a system of logic and a corresponding algebraic language dealing with true and false values. Today that type of logic is called **Boolean logic,** and his language is called **Boolean algebra.** The conditions that exist in branching and looping routines are a form of Boolean logic.

ПOTE □ □ □   Boolean Logic is the basis for all modern digital electronic technology. The *howstuffworks.com* Web site has an article about how computers implement Boolean logic at *http://computer.howstuffworks.com/boolean.htm.* In 1858, Boole's original book was republished as *An Investigation of the Laws of Thought.* Copies of the 1973 reprint of this edition can still be found in many bookstores and online. The complete text of an 1848 paper by Boole titled the "Calculus of Logic," is available on the Web at: *http://www.maths.tcd.ie/pub/ HistMath/People/Boole/CalcLogic.* The site is maintained by the University of Dublin's Trinity College School of Mathematics. The school also maintains links to information about George Boole at *http://www.maths.tcd.ie/pub/HistMath/People/Boole.*

Boolean logic is a form of mathematics in which the only values used are true and false. There are three basic operations in Boolean logic—AND, OR, and NOT, as described in Figure 5-1.

FIGURE 5-1: The Boolean AND, OR, and NOT operations

AND	OR	NOT
true *and* true = true	true *or* true = true	*not* true = false
true *and* false = false	true *or* false = true	*not* false = true
false *and* true = false	false *or* true = true	
false *and* false= false	false *or* false = false	

The AND and OR operations are binary operations, meaning that they need two operands. Basically, when two values are combined in the **AND** operation, the result is true only if both values are true. Otherwise, the result is false. In the **OR** operation, if either value is true, then the result is true.

The **NOT** operation is a unary operation, which means that it works on only one operand. It simply reverses the true or false value of its operand. In other words, NOT true yields false; NOT false yields true.

The use of AND, OR, and NOT should be common sense. A statement like "today is Monday AND this is March" can be evaluated for its true or false value; yet people sometimes run into trouble converting the informality of human language into the formality needed for algorithms. Consider the following conversation:

> **BOSS:** Give me a list of all our offices in Pennsylvania and New Jersey.
>
> **PROGRAMMER:** Let me get this straight—you want a list of our offices located in either Pennsylvania or located in New Jersey, right?
>
> **BOSS:** Yes, isn't that what I just said?

The programmer, who has experience converting the informality of human language into a formalized computer programming language, knows what would happen if the condition (state = "PA" AND state = "NJ") were used to create the list. If each office is located in only one state, then both conditions can not possibly be true. What should the programmer do, give the boss a blank sheet of paper? Tell the boss the request is nonsense according to the rules of Boolean logic? No, neither response would be acceptable. However, the programmer's response clarified the boss's request in an appropriate manner.

Boolean expressions can become long and complex with many nested AND, OR, and NOT clauses layered together. Professional programmers often use Boolean algebra and other formal tools when dealing with the layered complexities of Boolean logic. For the purpose of this book, it won't be necessary to learn Boolean algebra, which is usually included in courses with titles like "Discrete Mathematics" or "Computer Math and Logic." However, do note that computer science students are usually required to complete several such courses during their academic careers.

COMPARING VALUES

Often the Boolean conditions in branching and looping routines are based on expressions that compare values. Consider the following warning message, which might be found in the documentation for a modern automobile:

The passenger-side air bag may cause injury to children who are under the age of 12 or who weigh less than 48 pounds. They should not sit in the front passenger seat of this car.

The condition in this warning might be expressed in pseudo-code like this:

```
IF (age < 12 OR weight < 48)
THEN do not sit in the front passenger seat
```

Two items, each with a true or false value, are joined by the OR operation. The two items are each comparisons of values. The condition "age < 12" is either true or false, as is the condition "weight < 48." When the algorithm is executed, the true or false value of each of these conditions is determined, then the overall true or false value is determined using the rules for the OR operation.

The symbol "<" in the above example stands for "is less than." There are six such **logical comparison operators** used in Boolean logic: **equals**, **is not equal to**, **is less than**, **is greater than**, **is less than or equal to**, and **is greater than or equal to**. Figure 5-2 shows the symbols most commonly used for these operators.

FIGURE 5-2: The six logical comparison operators

Condition	In Mathematics	In Computer Programming
A equals B	A = B	A = B or A == B
A is not equal to B	A ≠ B	A <> B or A ! = B
A is less than B	A < B	A < B
A is greater than B	A > B	A > B
A is less than or equal to B	A ≤ B	A < = B
A is greater than or equal to B	A ≥ B	A > = B

Notice that several of the computer programming symbols, such as "<>" for "not equals," are composed of two characters. This doubling of characters is required because modern computer keyboards do not include a single symbol for these comparison operators; this is in contrast to standard algebra, in which the symbol "≠"is often used.

STRING COMPARISONS

It's clear that numbers can be compared according to their value, but what about other data types? Well, other data types, such as character strings, each have their own rules for logical comparisons. Character strings, for example, are compared according to the place in a collating sequence for each character of the string.

Let's see what all this means. To **collate** means to put a set of items in order. A **collating sequence** is a list that shows the correct order to be used when collating a set of items. The English language alphabet is a collating sequence. It shows us that when putting things in alphabetic order, A comes before B, B comes before C, and so on. Modern computers most often use one of two codes to represent characters in the computer—either the **American Standard Code for Information Interchange (ASCII)** or a newer code called **Unicode**. There are other, older codes, but today they are rarely used. These codes can also be used as collating sequences for character string values, just as the English language alphabet can.

NOTE □ □ □ The ASCII code is a set of characters used in computer programming based on the English language. It includes letters, numeric digits, and some "hidden" characters, such as the Enter key and the Esc key. Each character is given a numeric value, and the binary equivalents of those numeric values are used to store characters in the computer. Unicode is a much larger code, which includes characters for other alphabets, such as Greek, Hebrew, Arabic, and the Cyrillic alphabet used for Russian and Eastern European languages. The ASCII code is now actually a subset of the longer Unicode. For more information on the ASCII code, see *www.webopedia.com/TERM/A/ASCII.html*. For more information on Unicode, see *http://www.unicode.org/standard/WhatIsUnicode.html*.

Both ASCII and Unicode are similar to the English language alphabet, except for two characteristics. First, they include characters, like the dollar sign, the decimal point, and the digits 0 through 9, which are not part of the English language alphabet; second, in both codes, all of the capital letters come before the lowercase letters. In English, the words *apple*, *Ball*, and *cherry* are in alphabetic order. According to the ASCII code, the order would be *Ball*, *apple*, and *cherry* because a capital B comes before a small A. Figure 5-3 shows a portion of the ASCII collating sequence.

FIGURE 5-3: A portion of the ASCII code

```
! " # $ % & ' ( ) * + , - . / 0 1 2 3 4 5 6 7 8 9 : ; < = > ? @

A B C D E F G H I J K L M N O P Q R S T U V W X Y Z [ \ ] ^ _

a b c d e f g h i j k l m n o p q r s t u v w x y z { } | ~
```

Comparisons using character strings are often used when searching and sorting data stored on a computer. While this is very important in data processing and database management, comparisons using character strings in Alice are rare.

BOOLEAN FUNCTIONS

The true and false values in computer programming can also come from Boolean functions. A **Boolean function** is a function that returns a true or false value instead of a numeric value. The *ask a user a yes or no question* function used in the last chapter and shown in Figure 5-4 is an example of a Boolean function. When a method using the function is played, a question will appear on the screen. If the user answers yes, then the function returns the value *true*. If the user answers no, then the function returns the value *false*.

FIGURE 5-4: A Boolean function to ask the user a yes or no question

Figure 5-5 shows some spatial relation functions on a seaplane's *functions* tab in Alice. Each of these functions is a Boolean function that returns a true or false value.

FIGURE 5-5: Spatial relation Boolean functions

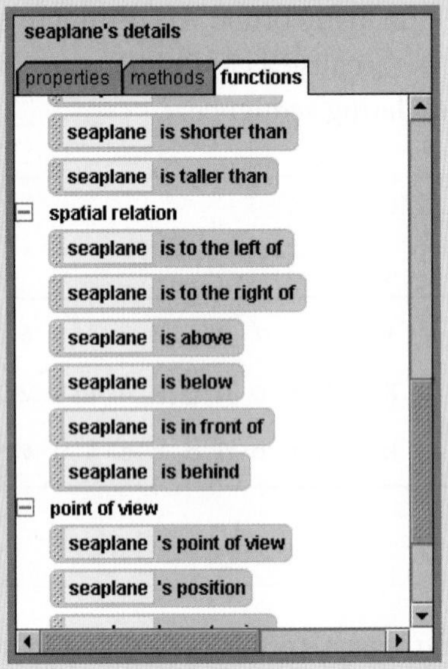

These and other Boolean functions can be used in any place that a true or false value can be used, such as in an *If* instruction or a *While* instruction, as shown in the *seaplane.fly* method in Figure 5-6. The *seaplane is above water* function in the *While* instruction in this example will return a value of *true,* and the loop will be executed as long as the seaplane is above the water. Within the loop, there is an *If* instruction to cause the seaplane to wave its wings whenever it is close to the island. This instruction uses a Boolean function that will return a value of *true* if the seaplane is within 10 meters of the island.

FIGURE 5-6: The *seaplane.fly* method, which uses two Boolean functions

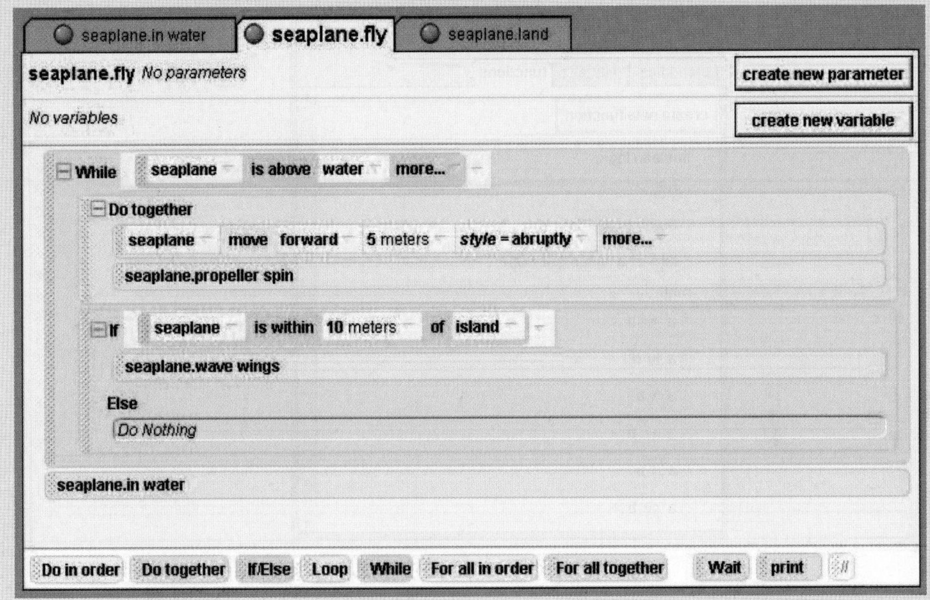

Alice also has comparison functions that can be found on the world's functions tab; in addition, with the proper presentation, the AND, OR, and NOT functions can be used to build more complex Boolean expressions. Both concepts are shown in Figure 5-7.

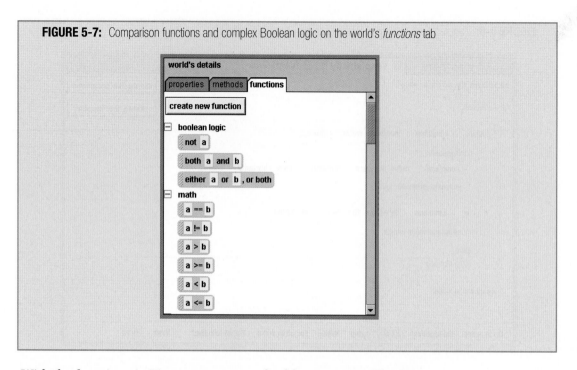

FIGURE 5-7: Comparison functions and complex Boolean logic on the world's *functions* tab

With the functions in Figure 5-7, you can build expressions like these:

- `If (age < 12 OR height <= 54)`

- `While (aliceLiddel distance to whiteRabbit <=10)`

- `While NOT (target = windmill) OR NOT (target = gazebo)`

- `If NOT (seaplane is in front of camera) AND ( (time < 10) OR (time > 30) )`

- `While numberOfGuesses <= log(range)`

The following tutorials will each provide experience with simple uses of Boolean functions in Alice.

TUTORIAL 5A—BRANCHING WITH RANDOM NUMBERS

In this exercise, you will modify the jump user choice world from Tutorial 4A to have the computer randomly select who will jump instead of asking for user input. Alice has a world level function that will return a random number in a specified range. The numbers that it returns are six-digit numbers, greater than or equal to the lowest number specified and less than the highest number specified. In this exercise, for example, you will ask Alice to return a number between 0 and 3. Alice will return numbers such as 1.83475, 0.41257, 2.89175, and so on. All of the numbers it returns will be greater than or equal to 0, but less than 3.

In this exercise, if the random number is less than 1, Alice will jump. If it is greater than or equal to 1 but less than 2, then the White Rabbit will jump. If it is greater than or equal to 2 but less than 3, then the Cheshire Cat will jump. Figure 5-8 shows the expected results of the program. The logic is very similar to the user input program in Tutorial 4A, with nested *If/Else* instructions to determine which character will jump.

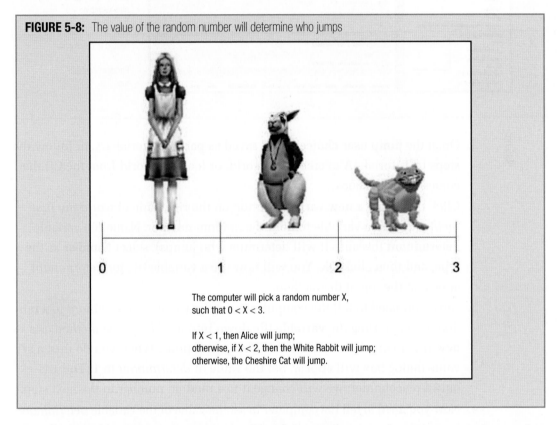

FIGURE 5-8: The value of the random number will determine who jumps

The computer will pick a random number X, such that 0 < X < 3.

If X < 1, then Alice will jump; otherwise, if X < 2, then the White Rabbit will jump; otherwise, the Cheshire Cat will jump.

You will add a variable to the program to hold the random number. Figure 5-9 shows what the code for the method will look like after you do this. You can refer to this image to guide you through the next several steps.

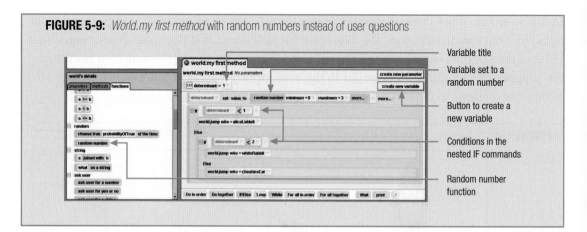

FIGURE 5-9: *World.my first method* with random numbers instead of user questions

1. Open the **jump user choice** world saved as part of Tutorial 4A, or follow the steps in Tutorial 4A to create the world, or load the world from the CD that comes with this book.

2. Click the **create a new variable** button on the right side of *world.my first method* to add a variable to hold the random number. Name the variable **determinant** (because it will determine who jumps), select **Number** as the type, and then click **OK**. You will now see a variable tile for *determinant* appear at the top of the method.

3. Next, you need to tell the computer to set the value of *determinant* to a random number. Drag the **variable** tile down into *world.my first method* as a new first instruction before the *If/Else* instructions. When you do this, a set value dialog box will appear. Set the value of *determinant* to **1**. The 1 is only a placeholder; we will change it to a random number in the next step.

4. Now you need to tell the computer to set the value of the variable *determinant* to a random number instead of a 1. To do this, select the **world** tile in the Object tree, and then click the **functions** tab in the Details area. Scroll through the list of functions and find the function titled *random number*. Drag and drop a copy of this function into the *set value* tile in place of the number 1.

5. You now need to tell the computer what range of values to use when picking a random number. To do so, click **more** in the blue *random number* tile, and set the *minimum* value to **0**. Click **more** again, and this time set the *maximum* value to **3**. The *set value* tile should now look like the *determinant set value to random number* tile near the top of the method shown in Figure 5-9.

6. The nested *If/Else* instructions still contain conditions based on the user question. You need to replace these conditions following the word *If* in each of the nested *If/Else* instructions with conditions based on the random number. To do so, drag the **determinant** variable tile from the top of the method down into the first *If/Else* instruction in place of the blue *ask user yes or no* condition tile. When you do this, a short menu will appear. Select **determinant <** and **1** as the value. Now the first *If/Else* instruction tile should look like it does in Figure 5-9.

7. Do the same thing for the second *If/Else* instruction, but this time, choose **2** as the value. When you are done, the second *If/Else* instruction should be *if determinant < 2*.

8. The method should now be ready to select a random number and make one of the three characters jump based on the value of the random number. Save the world as **triple jump random,** and you are ready to test the world.

You need a testing plan for your modified Alice world. If things work correctly, then one of the three characters should jump each time the world is run. Which character jumps depends on the value of the random number that the computer picks for the variable you named *determinant*.

To test the program properly, you would need to run it several hundred or several thousand times, and keep track of how many times each character jumps. Over a long period of time, we would expect each character to jump about one-third of the time the program runs. This will be left as an exercise at the end of the chapter. For now, test the program to make sure that the same character does not jump all the time, and that each of the three characters jumps at least part of the time. Play the world, and then use the restart button several times to replay the world. Because the numbers are random and not part of a pattern, the same character might jump several times in a row, but over a larger number of trial runs, each of the characters should jump at least once.

TUTORIAL 5B—THE NERVOUS PENGUIN

In this exercise, you will create a world with two penguins. The first penguin will be controlled by the user and may move around freely in the world. The second penguin, the nervous penguin, will flap its wings and jump up and down whenever the first penguin gets close to it. A Boolean **proximity function** returns a value based on the distance from one object to another. In this tutorial, a proximity function will be used to cause the nervous penguin to react.

NOTE □ □ □ | A proximity function returns a value of true or false, but a numeric proximity function returns the distance between two objects.

1. Start a new Alice world using the **snow** template.
2. Click the green **ADD OBJECTS** button to enter Scene Editor mode, and then add a **penguin** to the world from the Animals folder in the Local Gallery.
3. Move the **penguin** to the left side of the screen and push it back away from the viewer.
4. Add a second **penguin** to the world. Alice will give it the name *penguin2*. Right-click the **penguin2** tile in the Object tree and rename it as **nervousPenguin**.
5. Move **nervousPenguin** to the right side of the world window. The two penguins should now be positioned something like those in Figure 5-10.

FIGURE 5-10: The initial scene for the nervous penguin world

6. Now the scene is ready. Click the large green **DONE** button to exit, and save the world with the name **nervous penguin**.

The world will need one method and several events. The method will be the nervous penguin's reaction to the other penguin getting too close. Figure 5-11 shows the method you will need to create.

FIGURE 5-11: The *react* method for the nervous penguin world

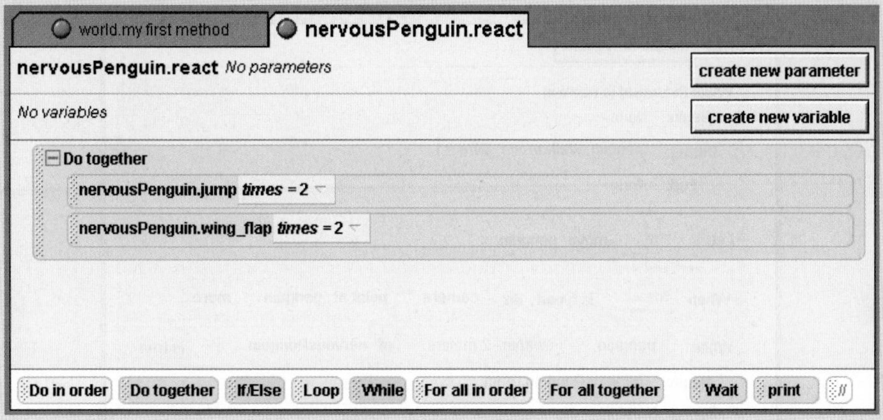

○ world.my first method	● **nervousPenguin.react**

nervousPenguin.react *No parameters*   `create new parameter`

No variables   `create new variable`

⊟ **Do together**
     nervousPenguin.jump *times* = 2 ⌄
     nervousPenguin.wing_flap *times* = 2 ⌄

`Do in order` `Do together` `If/Else` `Loop` `While` `For all in order` `For all together`   `Wait` `print` `//`

1. *World.my first method* will not be used further, so delete it as this time. Then, select the **nervousPenguin** tile in the Object tree and the **methods** tab in the Details area.

2. Click the **create new method** button. When the create new method window appears, type the name **react**, and then click the **OK** button.

3. The nervous penguin should jump up and down and flap its wings when the other penguin gets too close. These two actions—jumping and flapping—should happen at the same time. Drag a **Do together** tile from the bottom of the Editor area and drop it in the new method in place of *Do Nothing.*

4. Drag a **nervousPenguin jump times** tile from the methods tab and drop it in the *Do together* instruction in place of *Do Nothing.* When the short menu appears, select **2** as the number of times.

5. Drag a **wing_flap times** tile from the methods tab and drop it in the *Do together* instruction below the *nervousPenguin jump times = 2* instruction. When the short menu appears, select **2** as the number of times. The new method is now complete and should resemble Figure 5-11.

Now it's time to create several simple events that will be needed for this world. You will create methods to provide user controls for the moving penguin, to animate the moving penguin, and to cause the nervous penguin to react when the other penguin is near. It would also probably be a good idea to create a method to let the user point the camera at the moving penguin in case it moves off camera. Figures 5-12 shows these new events.

FIGURE 5-12: Several events for the nervousPenguin world

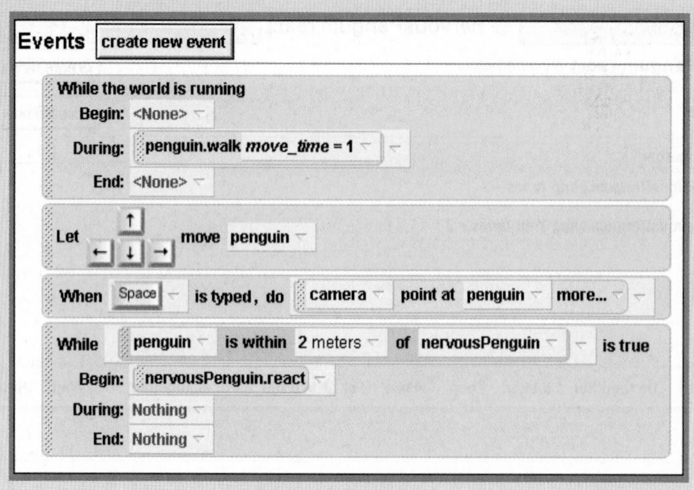

Events | create new event

While the world is running
  Begin: <None>
  During: penguin.walk *move_time* = 1
  End: <None>

Let ↑ ← ↓ → move penguin

When Space is typed, do camera point at penguin more...

While penguin is within 2 meters of nervousPenguin is true
  Begin: nervousPenguin.react
  During: Nothing
  End: Nothing

A built-in event can be used to provide control of the moving penguin. A second event can be created to use the *penguin walk move_time* method to animate the penguin. The default event can be modified to serve as this second event.

1. Click the **create new event** button in the Events area. When the menu appears, select **Let the arrow keys move <subject>** as the event type.

2. A new arrow key event will appear in the Events area, as shown in Figure 5-13. Click **camera** in the event tile and select **penguin**, **the entire penguin**. The event is now set to let the user move the penguin with the arrow keys.

FIGURE 5-13: The arrow key control event

Let ↑ ← ↓ → move penguin

3. Right-click the **When the world starts, do world.myfirst method** default event. When the short menu appears, select **change to**, **While the world is running**.

4. Select the **penguin** tile in the Object tree and the **methods** tab in the Details area. Drag a copy of the **walk move_time** method and drop it in place of *None* following *During:* in the new event. Select **1** from the short *move_time* menu that appears. The event should resemble Figure 5-14. The penguin will now shuffle its feet and waddle even when standing in place.

FIGURE 5-14: The event to animate the penguin

> While the world is running
> Begin: <None> ▽
> During: penguin.walk *move_time* = 1 ▽   ▽
> End: <None> ▽

The first two events are complete. The user can now move the penguin with the arrow keys, and the penguin will waddle and move its feet while the world is running, even when standing in place.

Next, you will add an event to allow the user to point the camera at the penguin in case it moves off camera.

1. Click the **create new event** button in the Events area. When the menu appears, select **When a key is typed** as the event type. A new *When any key is typed do Nothing* event tile will appear in the Events area.

2. Click **any key** and select **Space** from the menu that appears. Your actions will make the spacebar the trigger key for this event.

3. Select the **camera** tile in the Object tree and the **methods** tab in the Details area. Drag a copy of the **camera point at** method tile from the methods tab and drop it in place of *Nothing* in the new event. Select **penguin, the entire penguin** from the menu that appears. The event to allow the user to point the camera at the moving penguin is now complete, as shown in Figure 5-15.

FIGURE 5-15: The event to allow the user to point the camera at the moving penguin

> When Space ▽ is typed, do   camera ▽   point at penguin ▽   more... ▽   ▽

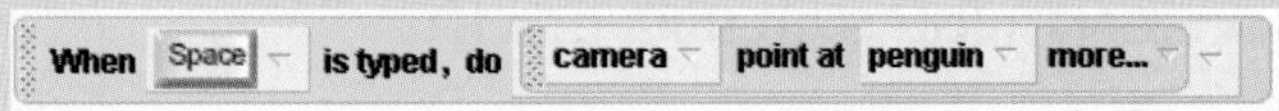

The last event that is needed is the event to cause the nervous penguin to react whenever the moving penguin gets too close. The event trigger will have a Boolean function that will return a value of *true* if the first penguin is within two meters of the nervous penguin. The event handler will be the *nervousPenguin.react* method. Figure 5-16 shows what the finished event will look like.

FIGURE 5-16: The event to cause the nervous penguin to react

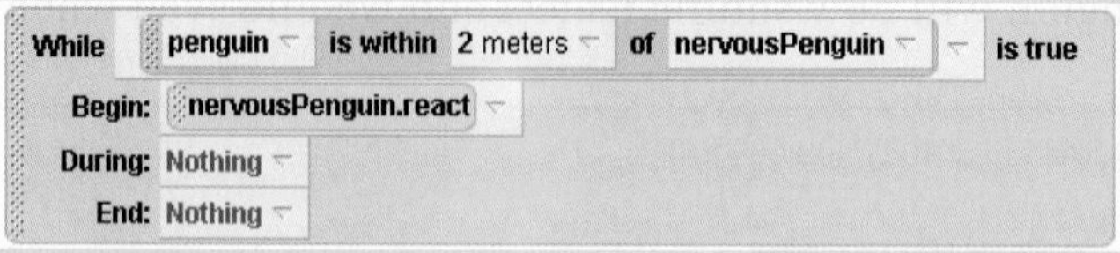

> While   penguin   is within   2 meters   of   nervousPenguin   —   is true
> Begin: nervousPenguin.react
> During: Nothing
> End: Nothing

1. Click the **create new event** button in the Events area. When the menu appears, select **When something is true** as the event type. A new *When None is true* event tile will appear in the Events area.

2. Select the **penguin** tile in the Object tree and the **functions** tab in the Details area.

3. Find the *penguin is within threshold of object* tile, as shown in Figure 5-16. Click and drag the **penguin is within threshold of object** tile and drop a copy of it in the new event in place of *None* following the word *When.* Select **2 meters**, **nervousPenguin**, and **entire nervousPenguin** from the menus that appear. The trigger for the event is now complete.

4. Select the **nervousPenguin** tile in the Object tree and the **methods** tab in the Details area; drag a copy of the **react** method and drop it in place of *Nothing* following *Begin:* in the new event.

5. The final event is in place. Save the world again before continuing.

The nervous penguin world is complete and ready for testing. You should be able to move the penguin around using the arrow keys. Be careful—it moves rather quickly. You should be able to point the camera at the penguin using the spacebar. The nervous penguin should jump up and down and flap its wings whenever the first penguin gets within two meters of it.

TUTORIAL 5C—A SENTINEL SAILING LOOP

In this exercise, you will create a world with a sailboat and several objects. When the world starts, you will be able to click an object, and the sailboat will sail to that object. You will create a *sail to* method that uses a sentinel loop to make the sailboat sail toward the island.

The method will use a Boolean condition with a method parameter in the condition. The loop will have the following logic:

```
WHILE (NOT (the sailboat is within 5 meters of the [object]))
    {
    turn to face [object]
    move forward 1 meter
    }
```

The brackets "{" and "}" are used to mark the beginning and end of the block of code within the loop. When this code is executed, the sailboat will turn to face a target object, then move one meter toward the object. It will continue to do so until it is within five meters of the object. You will write a `sail to` method that will work with any object and that will accept the target object as an input parameter, much like the way the primitive `move` method accepts direction and amount as parameters.

You will create your world in two steps. First, you will place an island in the world and hardcode the island as the target for the *sail to* method. (To **hardcode** a value in a program means that the programmer puts a specific value in a program instead of a variable or parameter.) Once this method works, you will add an object parameter called `target` and put it in the method in place of `island`.

THE SAIL TO ISLAND WORLD

Let's start by setting the scene for the new Alice world. First, you will need a water world with a sailboat in it, and it will be necessary to adjust the camera.

1. Start a new Alice world with a **water** template.

2. Click the green **ADD OBJECTS** button to enter Scene Editor mode, and then add a **sailboat** to the world from the Vehicles folder in the Local Gallery. Your screen should resemble the left side of Figure 5-17.

3. The camera is too close to the sailboat, creating a tight shot in which the boat fills most of the frame. Using the blue camera control arrows at the bottom of the world window, move the camera back from the sailboat and up a little bit so that the world window looks more like the image on the right side of Figure 5-17. You might also want to move the sailboat a little toward the side of the window.

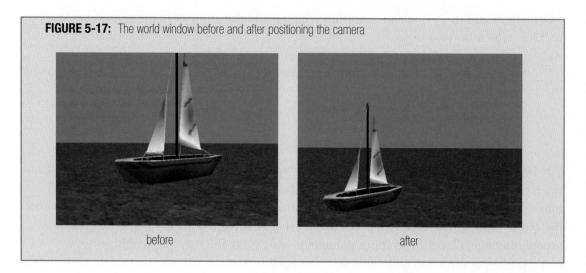

FIGURE 5-17: The world window before and after positioning the camera

before   after

Next, you need to add an island to the world. It's up to you where to put the island, but it should not be too close to the sailboat, and it should not be directly in front of the sailboat.

1. Add an **island** to the world from the Environments Gallery.
2. Position the island so that it is away from the sailboat and not directly in front of it. You can use Figure 5-18 as a guide.

FIGURE 5-18: An island has been added and positioned in the water world

3. Now click the large green **DONE** button to exit Scene Editor mode, and save the world with the name **sail to island**.

You are ready to create the new method. In this first version of the world, the sailboat will sail to the island when the world starts. You will need to create a method that is invoked by an event with `When the world starts` as its trigger. The default event does this, but it uses the method `world.my first method` as its event handler. The new method for the default event will be `sailboat.sail to`. Notice that it will be a method for the `sailboat` object and not a world-level method as is `world.my first method`. You can create the new method, change the event handler in the default event, and then delete `world.my first method`. You can delete this method because it won't be used further in your world.

1. Select the **sailboat** tile in the Object tree and the **methods** tab in the Details area.
2. Click the **create new method** button. When the create new method dialog box appears, type the name **sail to**, and click **OK**. The new method will

appear in the Editor area, and the related method tile will appear in the Details area.

3. Drag the **sail to** tile from the Details area and drop it in the default event in place of *world.my first method*.

4. Now *world.my first method* is no longer needed. Select the **world** tile in the Object tree and the **methods** tab in the Details area. Click and drag the **my first method** tile to the trash can to delete it.

Now it's time to begin writing the code for the new method. It should contain a *While* loop that matches the pseudo-code shown at the beginning of this tutorial.

NOTE □ □ □ | Even though we are learning about the sentinel loop in this tutorial, you might have noticed that the process can also be done with events and without a `sail to` method. Both techniques are acceptable.

1. Select the **sailboat** tile in the Object tree and the **methods** tab in the Details area.

2. Drag a **While** tile from the bottom of the Editor area and drop it into the `sailboat.sail to` method in the Editor area. Select **true** from the short menu that appears.

3. Next, select the **functions** tab in the Details area and find the *sailboat is within threshold of object* tile, as shown in Figure 5-19. This is a Boolean proximity function. Drag a copy of the tile and drop it in the *While* instruction in place of *true*. Select **5 meters** as the distance and **island, the entire island** as the object.

FIGURE 5-19: The Boolean proximity function *sailboat is within threshold of object*

```
sailboat is within threshold of object
```

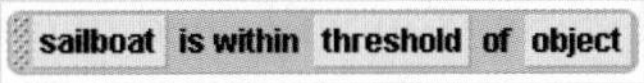

4. The *While* tile now says *While sailboat is within 5 meters of island.* However, you want just the opposite. Select the **world** tile in the Object tree and find the *not* tile on the functions tab. Drag a copy of the tile to the *While* tile, and drop it in place of the condition *sailboat is within 5 meters of island.* Now the condition should be as required, shown in Figure 5-20.

FIGURE 5-20: The modified Boolean proximity function

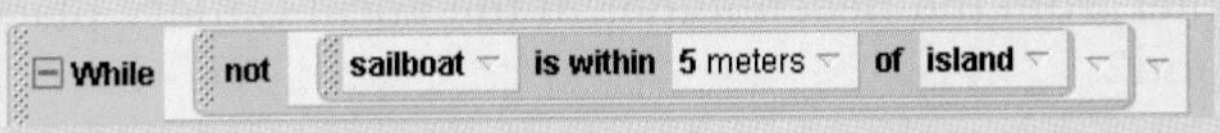

The *sailboat.sail to* method now has the correct loop structure and condition in place. Two instructions need to be placed in the event. One will turn the sailboat and one will move the sailboat. These should be executed together, so they will need to be inside a *Do together* tile.

1. Drag a **Do together** tile from the bottom of the Editor area and drop it into the *While* instruction in place of *Do Nothing*.

2. Select the **sailboat** tile in the Object tree and the **methods** tile in the Details area.

3. Drag a copy of the **sailboat turn to face** method tile and drop it in the *Do together* tile in place of *Do Nothing*. Select **island, the entire island** as the object; click **more** and change the style to **abruptly**.

4. Drag a copy of the **sailboat move** method tile and drop it in the *Do together* tile just below the *sailboat turn to face* tile. Select **forward** as the direction and **2 meters** as the amount; then click **more** and change the style to **abruptly**.

THE SAIL TO ANY OBJECT WORLD

Next, you will use the sail to island world as the basis for a new world that will allow the user to sail the boat to any object in the world. Several additional objects will be added to the world, an event will be added to allow the user to select a target object, and the `sail to` method will be modified to include a target variable instead of the island. First the world will be saved with a new name so that the sail to island world will be preserved; then several objects will be added to the world.

1. Click **File** on the menu bar, click **Save World As**, and then save a copy of the world with the new name **sail to object**.

2. Click the green **ADD OBJECTS** button to enter Scene Editor mode, and using the blue camera control arrows, pull the camera back a little farther and up a bit more so that you can see more open water. As you complete the following steps, note that it might be necessary to adjust the camera further.

3. Add several objects to the world. As you place the objects in the world, you should move them away from each other, positioning them as if they were on the edge of a large circle. Figure 5-21 shows a world with the following objects:

- An island2 from the Environments folder in the Local Gallery
- A pier from the Beach folder in the Local Gallery placed adjacent to the island2
- A lighthouse from the Beach folder in the Local Gallery
- A lifeboat from the Vehicles folder in the Local Gallery
- A shakira (a type of boat) from the Vehicles folder in the Local Gallery

FIGURE 5-21: The sail to any object world with several objects added

4. When you are happy with the collection of objects in your world, click the large green **DONE** button to return to Scene Editor mode.

Now you are ready to modify the *sailboat.sail to* method and add a new event. You will also need to delete the default event, which will actually prevent the world from playing with the changes to be made. Figure 5-22 shows the *sail to* method with the modifications you will make. The default event should be deleted first.

FIGURE 5-22: The *sail to* method with a target parameter added

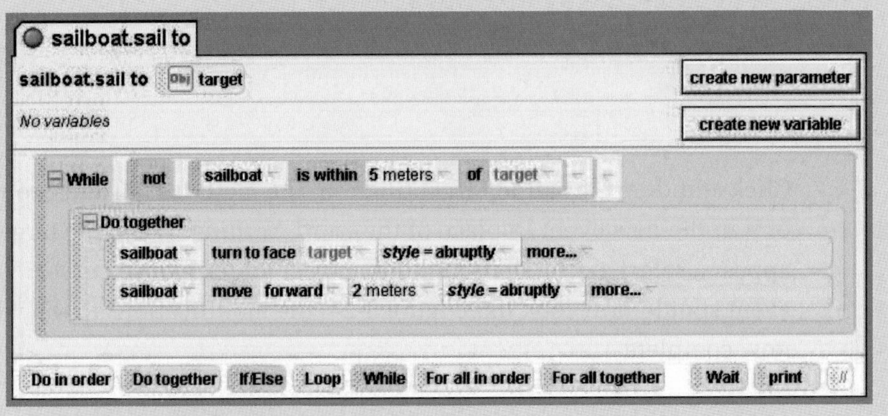

1. Right-click the default event in the Events area and select **delete** from the menu that appears. The event will be deleted.

2. Select the **sailboat** tile in the Object tree and the **methods** tab in the Details area; then click the **edit** button next to the *sail to* method tile. You should be able to see the *sail to* method in the Editor area.

3. Click the **create new parameter** button to add a target parameter to the method. When the create new parameter window appears, type the name **target,** make sure that **Object** is selected as the data type, and then click the **OK** button. A tile for the *target* object parameter will appear near the top of the method.

4. Drag the **target** object parameter tile and drop it in the *While* instruction in place of *island*.

5. Drag the **target** object parameter tile again and drop a copy of it in the *sailboat turn to face island* instruction in place of *island*. Select **target** from the short menu that appears.

6. Now you can add the new event. Click the **create new event** button in the Events area and select **When the mouse is clicked on something** from the menu of event types that appears. A new event similar to Figure 5-23 will appear.

FIGURE 5-23: A *new mouse click* event tile

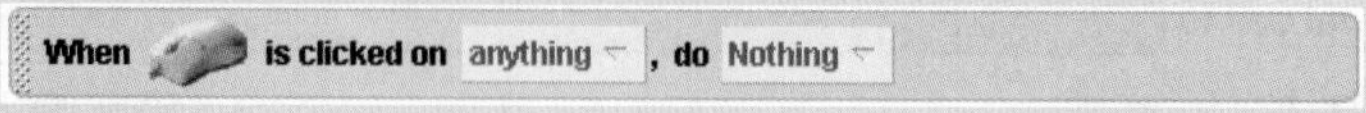

> When [mouse icon] **is clicked on** anything ⌄ , **do** Nothing ⌄

---

7. Click and drag the **sail to target** tile from the methods tab and drop a copy of it in the new event in place of the word *Nothing*. When the target menu appears, select **expressions** and then **object under mouse cursor**. Your new event should now look like Figure 5-24; the modifications to the world are now complete.

FIGURE 5-24: The new event to cause the sailboat to sail to the selected object

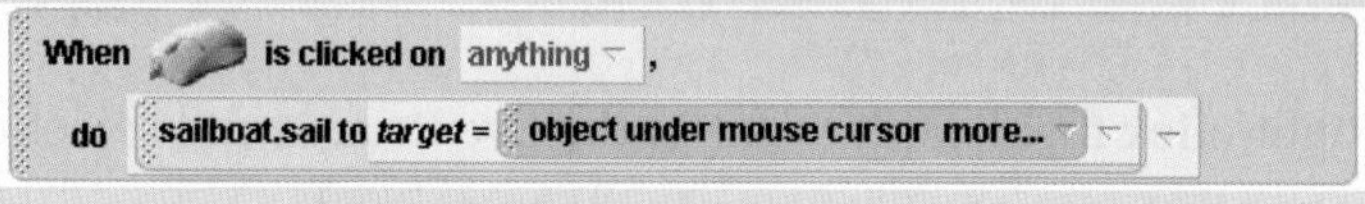

> When [mouse icon] **is clicked on** anything ⌄ ,
>
> **do** sailboat.sail to *target* = object under mouse cursor more... ⌄ ⌄ ⌄

---

8. Save the world before continuing.

You can now test your new world. The sailboat should sail to whatever object you select with the mouse. If you click the water, it will sail toward the center point of the world. If you click the sky background, then the world will stop playing, and Alice will show you an error message telling you that the target value must not be null. This means that there is no value for the target parameter because you clicked nothing.

NOTE □ □ □ | The sailboat moves rather slowly from object to object in the sail to any object world. You can use the speed **slider control** in the playing world window to speed things up a bit as you test your new world.

You might also notice that the sailboat will sail through objects to get to its target. To correct this, you would need to create methods for collision detection and avoidance in your world, which is rather time consuming; as such, it is not part of this tutorial.

CHAPTER SUMMARY

This chapter consisted of a discussion of Boolean logic, including the comparison of values and Boolean functions, followed by three tutorials. The discussion of Boolean logic included the following:

☐ Branching and looping routines both contain conditions that are either true or false. These conditions are a form of Boolean logic.

☐ Boolean logic is a form of mathematics in which the only values used are true and false.

☐ There are three basic operations in Boolean logic: AND, OR, and NOT.

☐ When two values are combined in the AND operation, the result is true only if both values are true. Otherwise, the result is false. In the OR operation, if either value is true, then the result is true.

☐ The NOT operation is a unary operation, which means that it works on only one operand. It simply reverses the true or false value of its operand: NOT true yields false, and NOT false yields true.

☐ People sometimes run into trouble converting the informality of human language into the formality needed for algorithms.

☐ Often the Boolean conditions in branching and looping routines are based on expressions that compare values.

☐ There are six logical comparison operators used in Boolean logic: equals, is not equal to, is less than, is greater than, is less than or equal to, is greater than or equal to.

☐ Numbers can be compared according to their value, but other data types, such as character strings, have their own rules for logical comparisons.

☐ Character strings are compared according to the place in a collating sequence for each character of the string. To collate means to put a set of items in order. A collating sequence is a list that shows the correct order to be used when collating a set of items.

☐ Modern computers most often use one of two codes to represent characters in the computer—either the American Standard Code for Information Interchange (ASCII), or a newer code called Unicode. These codes can also be used as collating sequences for character string values, as can the English language alphabet.

☐ A Boolean function is a function that returns a true or false value instead of a numeric value.

☐ Boolean functions can be used in any place that a true or false value can be used, such as in an If instruction or a While instruction.

☐ The AND, OR, and NOT functions in Alice can be found on the world's function tab, along with functions to compare values.

In Tutorial 5A you modified the jump user choice world from Tutorial 4A to have the computer randomly select who will jump instead of asking for user input. You created Boolean conditions that involve random numbers.

In Tutorial 5B you created a nervous penguin world with a Boolean function used in an event trigger.

In Tutorial 5C you created two worlds: one to make a sailboat sail to an Island and one to make a sailboat sail to any object. Each world contained a *sail to* method that used a sentinel loop with a Boolean condition in the loop's While instruction.

REVIEW QUESTIONS

1. **Define the following terms:**

   - American Standard Code for Information Interchange (ASCII)
   - AND
   - Boolean algebra
   - Boolean function
   - Boolean logic
   - collate
   - collating sequence
   - logical comparison operators
   - NOT
   - OR
   - Proximity function
   - Unicode

2. **Truth tables are often used to describe the result of Boolean expressions. Fill in the correct values in each of the following truth tables. For each cell in the table, apply the operation for the table to the values at the top of the row and at the beginning of the column for that cell, just as you would fill in values in a multiplication table.**

AND	true	false
true		
false		

OR	true	false
true		
false		

NOT	true	false

3. **The following three Boolean operations are composite operations, which means they can be written as combinations of AND, OR, and NOT. All three of these are important in designing the logic circuits inside computer chips. Create truth tables similar to those in Question 2 for each of these operations.**

   a. XOR –A OR B, but not both.
   b. NOR – NOT (A or B)
   c. NAND – NOT (A and B)

4. **Parentheses can be used in Boolean logic to clarify the order of operations, just as in ordinary arithmetic. Assuming that the height of a palm tree is 5 meters, the height of a lighthouse is 25 meters, and the height of a beach house is 10 meters, rewrite the following expression exactly as it is three times, but with parentheses in different places each time. Determine whether each of the new expressions is true or false.**

   Height of the beach house is less than the height of the lighthouse and not height of the lighthouse is less than the height of the tree or height of the beach house equals the height of the tree.

5. **Boolean conditions are important when using library search engines. Usually a library search engine has fields such as title, subject, author, year, and publisher. A typical search condition would be something like this: (author = "Lewis Carrol" and year < 1865). Write Boolean conditions for searches to find books about each of the following:**

    a. Martin Luther King, written between 1968 and 1978

    b. About Martin Luther King, written before 1968, but not by Martin Luther King

    c. Microsoft Excel, published by Thomson Course Technology, or accounting, published by Delmar, after 1998

    d. Careers in nursing or health care or medicine

    e. London, Ontario, not London, England, not London, Great Britain, not London, UK, written using the word NOT only once

6. **Boolean conditions are also important in Internet searches. Write Boolean conditions for searches to find Web pages about each of the following:**

    a. John D. Rockefeller and Ida Tarbell

    b. Abraham Lincoln and Jefferson Davis, but not schools or parks

    c. Cooking a turkey, but not in a microwave or deep-fat fryer

    d. George Boole and either Charles Babbage or Herman Hollerith

7. **Which of the following does not contain a valid Boolean expression, and why?**

    a. If (distance to alice < distance to caterpillar OR queen)

    b. If (count > 10 AND count < 20)

    c. While (count < 5 AND >1)

    d. While height < count OR height < 12.5

    e. If (message = "Hello, World." OR "Hello, World!")

8. **Write Boolean conditions to make While loops continue to function until the following occurs:**

    a. A car door has been opened and closed 1,000 times, or the door falls off the car.

    b. A penguin in an Alice world is within 5 meters of an igloo or an Eskimo, or is more than 100 meters away from the camera.

    c. A sailboat is moving at a speed between 5 and 10 meters per second.

9. **Write the following rule as a Boolean expression:**

    I before E except after C, or when sounding as A as in "neighbor" or "weigh."

10. **In most states in the United States, a vehicle must stop at an intersection with a traffic light when the traffic light is red, except when making a right turn, in which case the driver can pause and then make a right turn on red if the way is clear, unless otherwise posted. At a particular intersection there is a sign that says, "No right turn on red, 6 am to 6 pm, except Saturdays and Sundays." Write the set of rules and conditions for this intersection as an If/Else instruction with a single Boolean expression.**

<u>EXERCISES</u>

1. Assume that we have an Alice world similar to the nervousPenguin world, but with a strangePenguin and a motherPenguin as well as the nervousPenguin. Write code for Boolean conditions that could be used to trigger events to make the nervousPenguin react in each of the following situations:

    a. The strangePenguin is within 2 meters of the nervousPenguin and the motherPenguin is more than 2 meters away.
    b. The strangePenguin is within 2 meters of the nervousPenguin or the motherPenguin is more than 2 meters away.
    c. The strangePenguin is closer than the motherPenguin.

2. Rule 6 of the National Horseshoe Pitchers Association governing scoring for the game of horseshoes can be found on the Web at *http://www.horseshoepitching.com/rules/nhparul.shtml*. Scoring according to the American Horseshoe Pitchers Association rules can be found on the Web at *http://www.geocities.com/ahpa1949/rules/rules2.htm*. Write a single Boolean expression for each of the two organizations' rules for scoring a pitched (or thrown) horseshoe.

3. Information about leap years can be found on the U.S. Naval Observatory's Web site at *http://aa.usno.navy.mil/faq/docs/leap_years.html*. Write the rule for determining if a year is a leap year as a single Boolean expression.

4. The last paragraph in Tutorial 5A suggests that you would need to run the triple jump random world many times and keep track of how many times each character jumps to properly test the world. Modify the world to include a loop that will do this, with number variables to keep track of how many times each character jumps and print statements after the loop to show the values. Test your world to see if one character jumps more than the others, or if the jumps are uniformly distributed. How do the results compare to each other if you run the test several times?

NOTE □ □ □   For exercises 5, 6, and 7, create a new Alice world with a grass template and five objects from the people gallery: aliceLiddel, blueBallerina, handsomePrince, maleBalletDancer, and pinkBallerina. Exercises 5, 6, and 7 will refer to this world as the dancer world.

5. Using the dancer world, create a method to print the height of each character with the print instruction and the height function for that character. Using the information shown when the world is played, determine which of the following is true:

    a. aliceLiddel is taller than handsomePrince or shorter than blueBallerina.
    b. blueBallerina is taller than pinkBallerina or shorter than pink Ballerina.
    c. maleBalletDancer is shorter than handsomePrince and taller than blueBallerina.
    d. aliceLiddel is (shorter than pinkBallerina and shorter than maleBalletDancer) or (taller than Blue Ballerina).
    e. aliceLiddel is (shorter than pinkBallerina) and (shorter than maleBalletDancer or taller than Blue Ballerina).

6. Using the dancer world, create a method that will allow the user to select any two of the objects, and that will then cause the taller of the two objects to spin. If they are the same height, then both should spin. *Hint:* An object variable can be used to store the object a user has selected.

7. Using the dancer world, create a method that will allow the user to select any three of the objects, and that will then cause the tallest of the three objects to spin. If more than one is the tallest, then the first of the tallest objects selected should spin.

8. Sometimes complicated Boolean expressions can be simplified, or rewritten in a different form. One rule that explains how to do this is DeMorgan's Law. See if you can find information on the Internet about DeMorgan's Law and then use that information to rewrite each of the following using only one NOT operation:

   NOT(today is Monday) OR NOT (today is Wednesday)

   NOT(subject = History) AND NOT (subject = Biology)

9. The logic in the following code can be implemented with a single event with a compound Boolean condition, or with two events with simple Boolean conditions. What are the advantages and disadvantages of each approach? When can separate events be combined into one event, and when must separate events be kept as separate events?

   ```
   IF (mouse is clicked on island OR mouse is clicked on pier)
   THEN sail to pier
   ```

10. Create an Alice "guessing game" world according to the instructions below. The world should have two characters of your choice. *Hint:* It might be best to create a flowchart or pseudo-code to help design your world.

    a. Pick a random number X, such that $1 <= X < 100$. In the instruction to pick the random number, click "more" and select "integer only = true" so that the random number tile looks like something this: [X set value to random number (minimum = 1 maximum= 100) integerOnly = true]
    b. Ask the user to guess the number. Alice has a world level function to ask the user for a number.
    c. Have one of the characters tell the user if the guess is too low. Have the other character tell the user if the guess is too high.
    d. Set up a sentinel loop to repeat the process while the user's guess is not equal to the number the computer picked.
    e. Have both characters tell the user when the guess is correct and react, such as with a dance.

6 TEXT AND SOUND IN ALICE WORLDS

After finishing this chapter, you should be able to:

☐ Provide a brief definition of the following terms: billboard, breakpoint, dialog balloon, font, HSB, personification, RGB, tessellation, text, thought bubble, and typeface

☐ List and describe the different ways to add text to an Alice world

☐ Use the say and think methods to add text messages to an Alice world

☐ Place messages in a special zone below Alice's playing world window with the print instruction

☐ Add 3D text objects to an Alice world

☐ Create a billboard from a picture file and manipulate it in an Alice world

☐ Add sound to an Alice world

ADDING ELEMENTS OF LANGUAGE TO AN ALICE WORLD

Even in a visually rich, three-dimensional, animated, virtual world, it is still important to be able to communicate using words—both visually and verbally. Back in Chapter 1, in Tutorial 1B, the first Alice world you created was a version of the traditional Hello, World! program. As you may recall, this program contained a text message. The word **text** is used to describe the visual use of words (that is, the written language) in a computer program.

You can show text in an Alice world by:

- Using the *say* and *think* methods to show an object's speech and thoughts.
- Using the *print* instruction to show messages in a special zone below the playing world window.
- Adding 3D text as an Alice object.
- Placing a picture file with an image of text in an Alice world as a billboard.

The remainder of this chapter includes a brief discussion of each of the items in the preceding list. In addition, you will learn about sound files, which contain verbal messages that can be added to an Alice world and then played using an object's `play sound` method.

The discussions in the chapter are then followed by tutorials showing you how to use the respective techniques.

THE *say* AND *think* METHODS

Let's start with a discussion of the *say* and *think* methods. Figure 6-1 shows a scene from a playing Alice world with text produced by the *say* and *think* methods. The text created by these methods appears in what animators call balloons or bubbles, much like text appears in cartoons in a newspaper or magazine. A **dialog balloon** shows words that are supposed to have been spoken by an object, and a **thought bubble** shows words that reflect an object's thoughts. In Figure 6-1, Alice is shown saying "Simon says 'Jump'!" in a dialog balloon produced by a *say* instruction, while the Cheshire cat's thoughts are shown in a thought bubble.

FIGURE 6-1: The effects of the *say* and *think* methods

The *say* and *think* methods can be used with every object in Alice, including inanimate objects like rocks, trees, buildings, and vehicles. Figure 6-2 shows a thought balloon associated with a beach chair. Obviously beach chairs can't think. The process of giving human qualities, such as feelings, thoughts, or human-like movements, to inanimate objects is a form of **personification**.

FIGURE 6-2: A *think* method has been used to give the beach chair human-like qualities

Personification has a long tradition in literature, often being used by poets and playwrights. Shakespeare's *Romeo and Juliet* contains the line "An hour before the worshipped sun peered forth from the golden window of the East." The sun is portrayed as looking through a window, like a person would do. Shakespeare, like other writers, often used personification when describing things like a smiling moon. In cartoons seen on television, such as Warner Brothers' *Looney Tunes*, objects like trees, hammers, and anvils often walk, run, or speak. The use of the *say* and *think* methods with nonhuman objects in computer animation, such as Alice worlds, is an extension of this tradition.

The Alice *say* and *think* methods work almost identically, with a parameter to allow you to change the message itself. You can also change the font used for the text, the size of the text, the color of the text, the color of the bubble in which the text is displayed, and the amount of time that the message stays on the screen. Tutorial 6A will show you more about using the *say* and *think* methods.

THE *print* INSTRUCTION

The *print* instruction can be used to display messages or the value of variables and parameters in a special text zone at the bottom of a running Alice world. Figure 6-3 shows an Alice world with a text (or print) zone at the bottom of the window for the playing world.

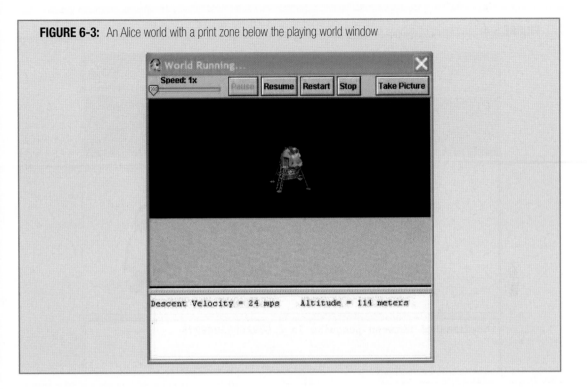

FIGURE 6-3: An Alice world with a print zone below the playing world window

The *print* instruction is often used to show someone the value of a variable while a world is playing. For example, in a world with a moving vehicle, such as a car, the object's location in three-dimensional space and its speed could be displayed.

Sometimes the value of a variable is displayed using the *print* instruction while debugging a world. The *print* instruction could then be removed once the program is debugged. For instance, this could be done in the nervous penguin world from Tutorial 5B. The world contains two penguins, a nervous penguin and a moving penguin. The nervous penguin is supposed to react whenever the moving penguin comes within 2 meters of the nervous penguin. The distance from the moving penguin to the nervous penguin could be displayed using a print command so that the programmer could see how far apart the penguins are from one another when the nervous penguin begins to react to the presence of the other penguin, as shown in Figure 6-4. Tutorial 6B will show you more about the *print* instruction.

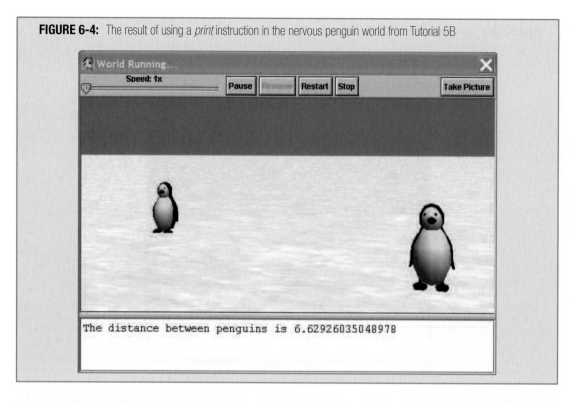

FIGURE 6-4: The result of using a *print* instruction in the nervous penguin world from Tutorial 5B

You can also use the *print* instruction when debugging a program to show that a breakpoint has been reached. A **breakpoint** is a spot in a computer program just before or just after some action occurs. For example, if a printed message shows that a point has been reached where a bunny should jump, but the bunny does not jump, then that information helps to isolate the spot in the code where the problem occurred. This is especially useful in the case where one method calls another method. The person debugging the software can tell if a problem is in the method doing the calling, or in the method being called. As with many things about learning Alice, this use of the *print* instruction is more useful in long, complex programs than in short, simple programs.

3D TEXT IN ALICE

Unlike the text used with the *say* and *think* methods or the text in a *print* instruction, 3D text is implemented in Alice as its own object. It can be used to communicate with the user or as an integral element in an Alice world. For example, the 3D text could be an object that is used as part of a story. However, most often, 3D text is used for titles, such as the opening title at the beginning of an Alice world, or for the phrase "The End" at the end of a narrative Alice world. Figure 6-5 shows an example of 3D text in an Alice world.

FIGURE 6-5: 3D text in an Alice world

The Alice Local Gallery contains a folder to create 3D text objects. Because 3D text is implemented as an Alice object, methods, such as *move*, *turn*, and *roll*, can be used to animate the text. User-created methods can also be developed to provide special effects for 3D text, just as they can with any other object. 3D text can also be resized like any other object, but it does have several special properties which other objects do not have, such as font and extrusion, which affect the way the text is displayed on the screen. The font property works like the font property of any other text, while the extrusion property controls the depth of the text, from front to back.

In Alice, unlike in many other programming languages, you cannot create an instance of an object in a world while the world is running. This means that 3D text in an Alice world must be kept off-camera or made invisible until it is needed onscreen. Each object in Alice has a Boolean *isShowing* property that can be set to false to make an object invisible. An object's *opacity* property, which determines if the object is solid or transparent, also can be changed to make an object invisible. Tutorial 6C will provide you with more details about 3D text.

PICTURE FILES AS ALICE BILLBOARDS

A picture file can be added to an Alice world as a billboard. A **billboard** is a flat two-dimensional object with length and width, but no depth. Once placed in an Alice world, the image from the picture file will be seen on both the front and back of the billboard. Like the 3D text described in the preceding section, billboards are objects that can be manipulated with primitive methods, like *move*, *turn*, and *roll*, as well as with user-created methods. Figure 6-6 shows a photograph of the Mona Lisa that has been added to an Alice world as a billboard.

FIGURE 6-6: The Mona Lisa as a billboard in Alice

The current version of Alice easily imports files in the Graphics Interchange Format (GIF) and the Joint Photographic Experts Group format (JPG), but often has difficulty with other common picture file formats, such as the bitmapped file format (BMP) and Tagged Image File Format (TIF). Anyone who adds picture files to an Alice world as billboards should keep in mind that some pictures can be very large and will add significantly to the size of the Alice world. In addition, the pictures will be rerendered (redrawn) by the Alice graphics engine and may lose some of their clarity.

Many graphics-manipulation programs, even simple programs like Microsoft Paint, allow the user to create and save text as an image file. Titles, credits, and instructions for users can be presented in an Alice world as a billboard that was created and saved as a picture file. Figure 6-7 shows a set of instructions for playing a guessing game that has been placed in an Alice world as a billboard. These instructions were first typed in Microsoft Word and then cut and pasted into an image in Microsoft Paintbrush; then the saved picture file was imported into Alice as a billboard.

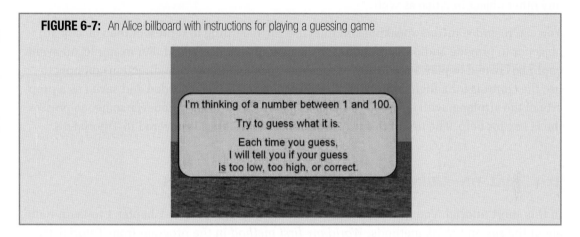

FIGURE 6-7: An Alice billboard with instructions for playing a guessing game

I'm thinking of a number between 1 and 100.

Try to guess what it is.

Each time you guess,
I will tell you if your guess
is too low, too high, or correct.

SOUNDS IN ALICE

Each object in an Alice world has a primitive *play sound* method that can be used to play a sound file. Sound files are most often used in Alice worlds to add special effects, such as the sound of a doorbell, or to play background music as a scene unfolds. A list of several sound recordings that are included with Alice is on a pop-up menu that appears when the *play sound* method is used, as shown in Figure 6-8.

FIGURE 6-8: A menu showing the prerecorded sounds for the Alice *play sound* method

sound

chicken
doorbell
drip
gong
pop
splash
thud1
thud2
whoosh1
whoosh2

import sound file...
record new sound...

Notice that the menu also includes options to import a sound file and to record a new sound. Prerecorded sound files in the WAV or MP3 formats can be imported into Alice, and new sound files can be recorded directly using the Alice interface. Sound files are stored as properties of an Alice object, but a sound file stored as part of one object can be played by any other object in Alice as well.

You can record someone speaking and then use the recording to represent the voice of an object or to provide audio instructions for the user of an Alice world. For example, an event could be created to play a recording of someone speaking to provide directions on how to use the controls for a flight simulator. The directions could be recorded and saved as a property of the airplane, with an event in place to play the recording whenever someone presses the H key for help. The use of the *play sound* method in Alice is covered in Tutorial 6E.

TUTORIAL 6A—USING THE *say* AND *think* METHODS

In this short tutorial, you will revisit the *hello world* program from Chapter 1 to learn more about the *say* and *think* methods. *World.my first method* in the program from Tutorial 1B already contains two *bunny say* tiles, as shown in Figure 6-9. In this tutorial, you will learn how to manipulate the text in these two *say* methods.

NOTE □ □ □ | The *think* method functions almost identically to the say method, except that its text is displayed in a thought bubble instead of in a dialog balloon.

FIGURE 6-9: *World.my first method* in the Alice world from Chapter 1

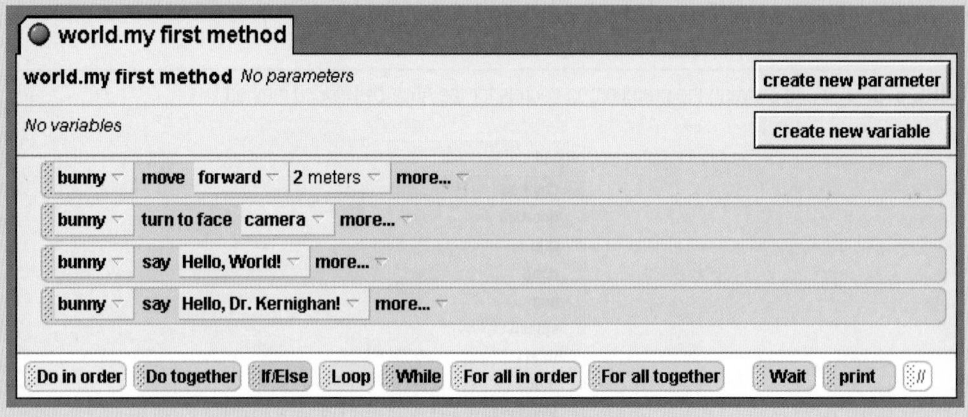

1. Open the **hello world** Alice world created in Tutorial 1C, or a copy of the world from the CD that accompanies this book.

2. If you cannot see the instructions in *world.my first method*, select the **world** tile in the Object tree and the **methods** tab in the Details area, and then click the **edit** button next to the name of the method on the methods tab. You should see the method displayed in the Editor area.

3. Click the word **more** following the phrase *Hello, Dr. Kernighan!* in the second *say* instruction. You should see a short menu, as shown in Figure 6-10, with several additional parameters for the *say* method. The *think* method has the same parameters.

FIGURE 6-10: A menu showing the parameters used with both the *say* and *think* methods

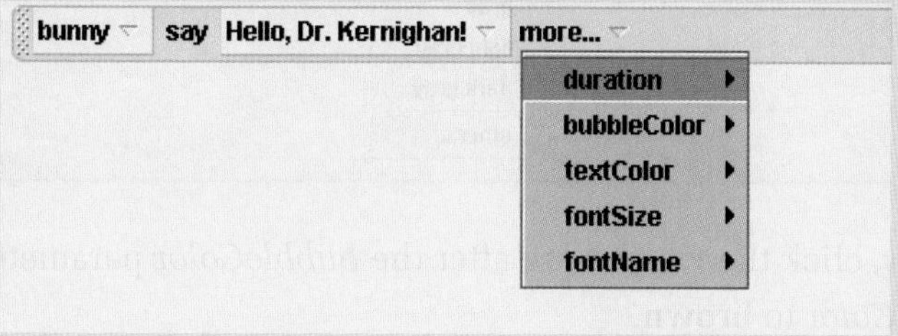

4. Select **fontSize,** and then **30**. Note that the choice of 20 is the default size for all *say* and *think* text in Alice.

5. Save the world again, and then play it to see the effect of your change.

The *duration* parameter determines how long, in seconds, the message will remain on the screen. It is used just like the duration parameter in many primitive Alice methods, such as *move* and *turn*. The *bubbleColor* parameter affects the background color, and the *textColor* parameter affects the font color for the messages displayed by the *say* and *think* methods. The default values for all durations in Alice is *1 second*; the default for say and think bubbles is black text on a white background, and the default font for all text-based items in Alice is Arial. The number for the *fontSize* parameter refers to the point size of the text, but the actual size depends on the size of the window in which the world runs, as well as the computer's screen resolution. The *fontName* parameter is the name of the chosen font.

Let's take a look at how to change these values.

1. Click the word **more** after *Hello World* in the *say Hello World* instruction, and then select **bubbleColor** from the menu that appears.

2. A color menu will appear with 16 different options, including *no color* at the top, a list of 14 colors, and *other* at the bottom, as shown in Figure 6-11. Select **yellow** as the new bubbleColor. Notice that the color of the *bubbleColor* parameter box in the *say* tile is now yellow.

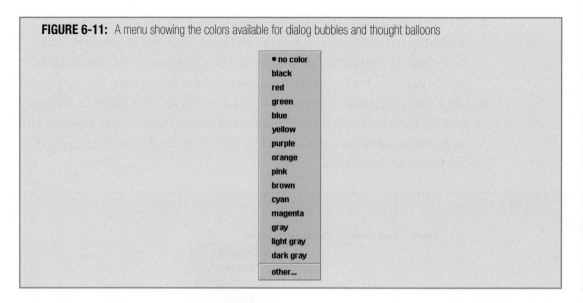

FIGURE 6-11: A menu showing the colors available for dialog bubbles and thought balloons

• no color
black
red
green
blue
yellow
purple
orange
pink
brown
cyan
magenta
gray
light gray
dark gray
other...

3. Now, click the word **more** after the *bubbleColor* parameter and change the *textColor* to **brown**.

4. Play the world to see the effect of the changes you made.

5. Leave the world open for use in the next set of steps.

The *other* option on the *bubbleColor* and *textColor* menus will take you to a custom color dialog box, which will let you set the color in one of three different ways: by picking a swatch from a predefined palette of colors, by using HSB color values, or by using RGB color values. **HSB** stands for Hue, Saturation, and Brightness. (Brightness is also called Brilliance.) **RGB** stands for Red, Green, and Blue. These are two different color models for describing the color of a pixel on a computer screen, which is determined by blending red, green, and blue light. It can also be described by setting the hue for the pixel's color, the color saturation, and its brilliance, as shown in the following steps:

1. Click the **bubbleColor** parameter in the say Hello, World! instruction tile and select **other** from the menu that appears. You should see the *Swatches* tab in the Custom Color window, as shown in Figure 6-12.

2. Pick a light green color from those available on the palette, click **OK,** and then play the world again to see the effect.

3. Next, click the **bubbleColor** parameter and select **other** again. This time, click the **RGB** tab. Figure 6-13 shows the RGB tab. You can set the color on this tab by entering values in the input boxes for red, green, and blue, or by using the slider controls. The effect of your changes can be seen in the previews at the bottom of the window. Experiment a bit with the colors before continuing.

FIGURE 6-12: The *Swatches* tab in the Custom Color window

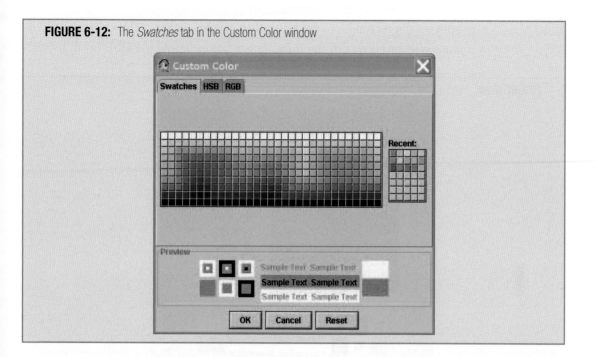

FIGURE 6-13: The *RGB* tab in the Custom Color window

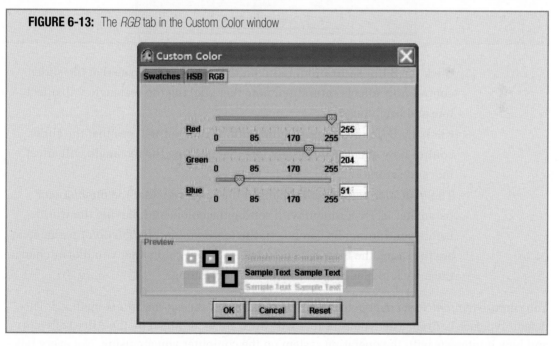

4. Select the **HSB** tab, and you will see the HSB color controls, as shown in Figure 6-14. You can enter numbers in the input boxes for hue, saturation, and brightness or slide the hue control arrow up and down, and then click

a spot on the rectangle to set saturation and brightness. The equivalent RGB values will be shown in the information boxes below the HSB input boxes.

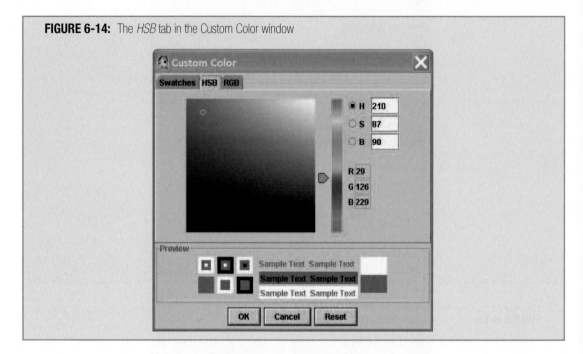

FIGURE 6-14: The *HSB* tab in the Custom Color window

5. Click the **S** (for **saturation)** radio button, and you will see that the slider control now affects saturation; note that clicking the rectangle will affect hue and brightness.

6. Click the **B** (for **brightness)** radio button, and you will see that the slider control now affects saturation; note that clicking the rectangle will affect hue and saturation.

7. The *textColor* parameter is changed the same way that the *bubbleColor* parameter is. Experiment with setting the colors and playing the world before continuing. Be careful—if the *textColor* and *bubbleColor* parameters are the same, the text will be invisible. Select colors that you like or change them back to black and white before continuing.

You can use the *fontName* parameter to set the typeface for the *say* and *think* methods. The default typeface is Arial. The typefaces that will work are determined by the Alice software and how it interacts with the operating system on the computer you are using. Not every type-face that is available on your computer system in programs like Microsoft Word or Internet Explorer will work with the Alice *say* and *think* methods. Figure 6-15 shows a few of the typefaces that have worked with the current version of Alice in different environments.

FIGURE 6-15: Some of the typefaces that work with the *fontName* parameter

Arial	**Haettenschweiler**
Book Antigua	*Monotype Corsiva*
Comic Sans MS	Palatino Linotype
Courier New	Times New Roman

The only way to be sure which typefaces will work on your system is by trial and error. Arial and Times New Roman will almost always work. The following steps will show you how to change the typeface by changing the *fontName* parameter.

1. Click the word **more** after the text in the *bunny say Hello Dr. Kernighan!* tile.
2. Select **fontName** from the menu that appears, and then select **other**.
3. You should now see a small window that will allow you to enter a string. This is one of the weakest parts of Alice. You must type the name of the typeface you want to use, rather than selecting it from a list as with other parameters. Type **Times New Roman** as the new fontName, and then click **OK**. Capitalization is not important, but spelling and spacing are.
4. Play the world, and you should see the first message in the Arial typeface and the second in the Times New Roman typeface.
5. Try experimenting with some of the typefaces shown in Figure 6-15 to see if they work on your system before continuing.

The *say* and *think* methods can be used to display information about the world, although they are more commonly used as elements of an Alice world's story or simulation. Many fonts almost have a personality of their own, and particular fonts can be used for particular characters in a story or for particular situations.

Some special typefaces for characters from languages other than English don't work, but Arabic, Hebrew, and Cyrillic characters can often be cut from Microsoft Word or from a Web browser and pasted as the text for the *say* and *think* methods. Figure 6-16 shows an example of this. The Greek phrase *Γειάσου κόσμος* (translation: *Hello World!*) has been cut from Microsoft Word and pasted into a *say* method.

FIGURE 6-16: *Hello World!* in Greek that was cut and pasted from Microsoft Word

TUTORIAL 6B—THE *print* INSTRUCTION

The *print* instruction can be used to display information in a special print zone below the playing world window, as shown in Figure 6-17. The text displayed here is very simple plain text and cannot be formatted. You can print any text string as a message in the print zone, or you may print the names of objects and the values of variables and parameters from a running world.

FIGURE 6-17: A playing world window with the print zone showing

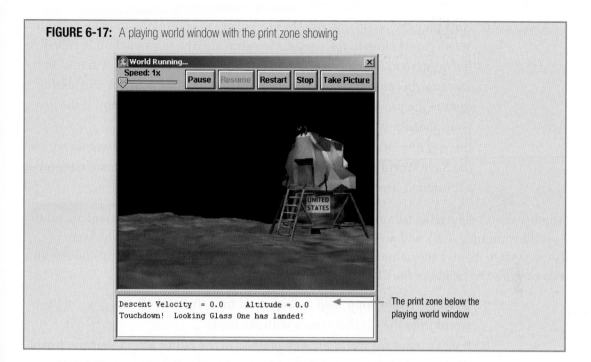

The print zone below the playing world window

In this tutorial, you will print the distance between two penguins in the nervous penguin world, and you will print a message showing when the point in the program has been reached where the nervous penguin should jump.

1. Open the **nervous penguin** world that was created as part of Tutorial 5B, or open a copy of the world from the CD that comes with this book.

2. Select the **nervousPenguin** tile in the Object tree and the **methods** tab in the Details area.

3. Click the **edit** button next to the *react* method tile on the methods tab, and the method should be displayed in the Editor area. It contains instructions to make the nervous penguin jump up and to flap its wings.

4. Drag a **print** instruction tile from the bottom of the Editor area and drop it in the method in front of the instructions that are already there.

5. A short menu will appear with two options, *text string* and *object*. Select **text string** and an Enter Text String window will appear. Type **begin reaction** and click the **OK** button.

6. Now play the world and use the arrow keys to control the moving penguin. When it gets close to the nervous penguin and the react method is called, the *begin reaction* message should be displayed in the world window. In this case, because the code should work, the nervous penguin will start to react at the same time, but you can see how this might be useful if the nervous penguin were not reacting.

7. It is not necessary to save the world before continuing, but if you do so, use the **Save World As** menu option and give the world a new name to preserve the original *nervous penguin* world.

Another useful debugging technique is to display the value of a variable or parameter while a world is running. Let's add an instruction to the triple jump while loop world from Tutorial 4D to display the value of the index variable, which is used as the loop counter and also controls the height of the Cheshire Cat's jump.

1. Open the **triple jump loop 2.a2w** world from Tutorial 4D or a copy of the world from the CD that comes with the book.

2. If you cannot see *world.my first method* in the Editor area, select the **world** tile in the Object tree and the **methods** tab in the Details area, and then click the **edit** button next to the name of the method on the *methods* tab.

3. *World.myfirst method* contains a loop to make the characters jump. The *cheshireCat jump* instruction uses index as the value of its height parameter. Drag the **print** instruction from the bottom of the Editor area and drop it in *world.my first method* just above the *cheshireCat jump* instruction.

4. When the print menu appears, select **object**, then **expressions**, then **index**. The print instruction tile should now say *print index*, as shown in Figure 6-18.

FIGURE 6-18: A message displaying the value of distance in the print zone

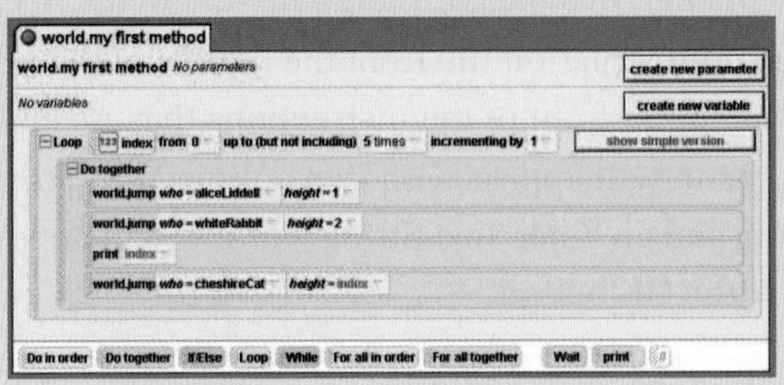

5. Try playing the world. You should see messages that display the value of the distance variable appearing in the print zone. It is not necessary to save the world, but if you want to do so, save it with a different name to pre-serve the copy of the world without the *print* instruction.

TUTORIAL 6C—THREE-DIMENSIONAL TEXT

In this tutorial, you will add opening titles to the *generic triple jump* world created in Chapter 2. Messages and titles can be added to an Alice world as three-dimensional text. Once in the world they can be animated and manipulated just like any other Alice object by using primitive methods or creating new methods of your own.

You can add 3D text to a world through the object gallery or by using the *Add 3D Text* option on the File menu. Both ways of starting the process take you to the same place and produce the same results. In the first part of this exercise, you will add an opening title using the object gallery.

1. Open the **generic triple jump** world created in Tutorial 2C, or open a copy of the world from the CD that comes with this book.
2. Click the **ADD OBJECTS** button to enter Scene Editor mode and see the object galleries. Scroll through the Local Gallery until you find the *Create 3D Text* tile. It's on the far-right side of the Local Gallery.
3. Click the **Create 3D Text** tile, and you should see the Add 3D Text window, as shown in Figure 6-19. It has a place to enter your text, a button with a pull-down menu to select a font for the text, and buttons for boldface and italicized text effects.

FIGURE 6-19: The Add 3D Text window

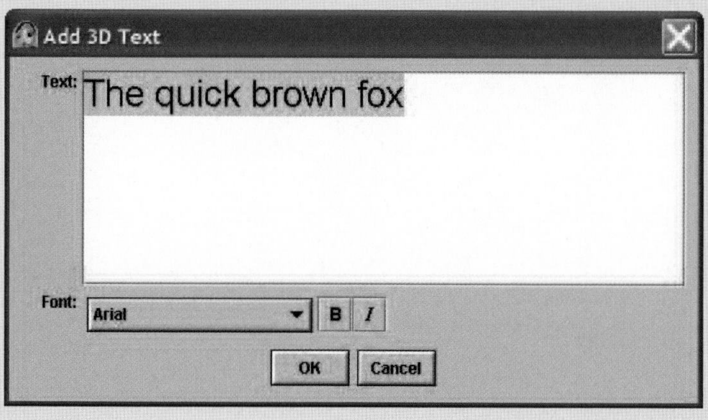

4. Type the camelCase name **openingTitle** as the text for the new object. You'll come back to the other controls in just a minute.

5. Click the **OK** button, and you will see the text appear in the Alice world. In addition, a tile for the text object will appear in the Object tree. The tile will have the name that you just typed: *openingTitle*.

6. Now that the object has been created using the text you typed as its name, you can change the text to be what the opening title should say. Click the **openingTitle** tile in the Object tree and then click the **properties** tab in the Details area.

7. Click the words **openingTitle** next to the *text* property on the properties tab and change the text from *openingTitle* to **Triple Jump**. Press the **Enter** key after you have finished changing the text. Notice that the text has changed in the Alice world window, but the object retains its original name, *openingTitle*, in the Object tree.

You can get back to a window similar to the Add 3D Text window through the *font* property on the properties tab at any time to change the typeface of the 3D text. However, there is no property for size. Because 3D text is an object in Alice, it is resized like other objects, by using the primitive *resize* method. Let's take a look at the *font* property.

1. Click the button next to the *font* tile on the *properties* tab in the Details area. The button is labeled with the name of the font, which will probably be *Arial*, but could be something different, depending on your computer system and how it has been used. This will open the Choose a Font window, as shown in Figure 6-20. Notice that it looks very much like the Add 3D Text window shown in Figure 6-19. You can see the text in the Choose a Font window, but unlike the Add 3D Text window, you cannot change the text. You can make changes to the text by using the buttons near the bottom of the window.

FIGURE 6-20: The Choose a Font window

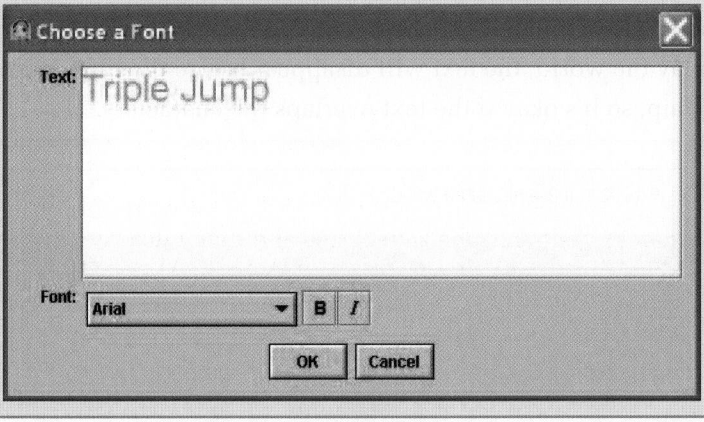

2. Click the **typeface** button, and a scrolling menu with the names of all the typefaces currently available will appear. This is much more convenient than the way in which the *fontName* parameter is changed for the text for the *say* and *think* methods, which you saw in Tutorial 6A.

3. Take a moment to try a few of the typefaces from the list. You will notice that several of the more uncommon typefaces won't work because Alice has not been programmed to render 3D text using them. More common fonts, such as Arial, Times New Roman, and Courier New, should work.

4. Before continuing, select a typeface and color for your title by changing the *font* property and the *color* property on the *properties* tab.

Next you will position the openingTitle title in the Alice world. This can be done in Scene Editor mode or by running primitive methods directly. In the next several steps, you will use the primitive methods approach.

1. Right-click the **openingTitle** tile in the Object tree, select the **openingTitle move** method, select **up**, and then select **2 meters**. If 2 meters is not an available option, select **other** and type **2** in the Custom Number dialog box, then press **Enter**.

2. Again right-click **openingTitle** in the Object tree, select **methods,** and run the **openingTitle turn to face** method to make the text face the **camera**.

3. If the entire title does not fit in the world window, right-click **openingTitle** in the Object tree, select **methods,** and run the **openingTitle move** method to move the title backward a few meters. If you go too far back, or not far enough, you can use the *move* method again to move it a little more forward or backward. Don't forget that you can also use the *Undo* button.

It may take a few minutes to line it up in a way that looks just right. Position the text so that you think it looks good in relation to the three characters. Figure 6-21 show one possibility. Keep in mind that when you play the world, the text will disappear before the three characters begin to jump, so it's okay if the text overlaps the characters.

FIGURE 6-21: A 3D text title in the Triple Jump world

A 3D text title looks nice, but normally we don't want the text to remain on the screen for the entire time a world is running. The text can be made to turn, roll, move, etc., including moving off-camera, by creating methods and events as desired. In addition, if you so choose, the text can also be left in place, but made invisible. In the next few steps, you will add instructions to make the title disappear a few seconds after the world starts playing. There are two ways to make the title invisible: by changing the *isShowing* property or by changing the *opacity* property. You will try both.

1. Select the **world** tile in the object tree and the **methods** tab in the Details area. Click the **edit** button next to *my first method*, and *world.my first method* should appear in the Editor area.

2. Drag a copy of the **Wait** instruction tile from the bottom of the Editor area and drop it into *world.my first method* as the first instruction in the method. When the menu appears, set the duration to **2 seconds**.

3. Next, click the **openingTitle** tile in the object tree, and then click the **properties** tab and drag a copy of the **isShowing** property tile into the method below the *Wait* instruction. Select **false** from the menu that appears. Dragging a property tile into a method will create an instruction to change that property's value. The method should now look something like Figure 6-22.

FIGURE 6-22: *World.my first method* with instructions to make the title disappear after 2 seconds

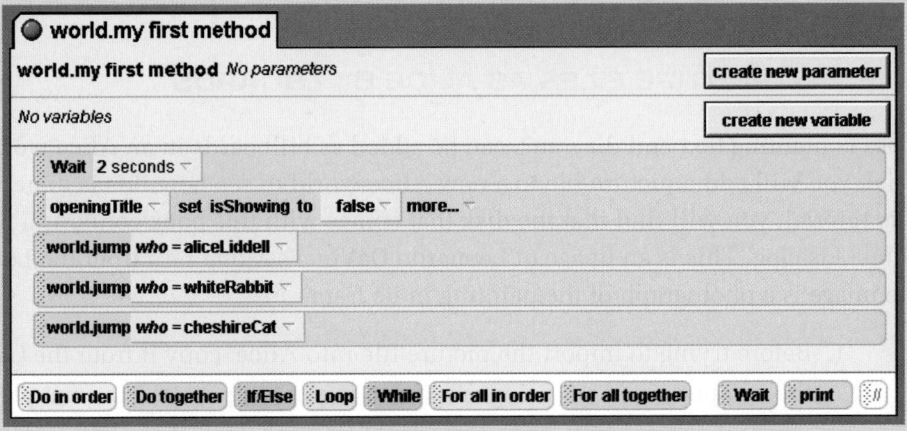

4. Now play the world and watch what happens. If you have followed the steps correctly, then the title should disappear after two seconds.

If you played the world again, you would notice that the title disappears very abruptly. In film and video production, this abrupt change is called a **cut**. A director may cut from one scene to another or cut a title from a scene. The term **fade** applies to a more subtle transition in which an object or a scene slowly disappears. In Alice, you can cause a fade to occur by using the *opacity* property.

1. First, right-click the **openingTitle set isShowing to False** instruction tile in the Editor area and select **delete** from the menu that appears. The tile should disappear from *world.my first method*.

2. Select the **openingTitle** tile in the object tree and the **properties** tab in the Details area.

3. Drag a copy of the **opacity** property tile into the method below the *Wait* instruction. Select **0%: invisible** from the menu that appears.

4. Now play the world again, and you should see the title fade away instead of disappearing abruptly.

This world will not be used further in this book, but you may want to experiment with it a little on your own. You can experiment with the font and with the bold and italics effects. You can resize the text in the Scene Editor mode, just as you would any other object. In fact, you may want to add a second title that says "created by <*your name*>", and then have the text fade or move on screen and then off from the side, from above, or even from below.

TUTORIAL 6D—PICTURE FILES AS ALICE BILLBOARDS

Picture files containing text and diagrams can be added as billboards in an Alice world. In this tutorial, you will add a picture file to a new Alice world to see how this is done. To aid you in this tutorial, you will find that the disk that comes with this book contains a file named Mona Lisa.jpg. This is an image of Leonardo DaVinci's Mona Lisa from the Louvre in Paris. The image is a photograph of the painting in its frame.

1. Before trying to import the picture file into Alice, copy it from the CD to the computer you are using. You need to put the picture file someplace where it can easily be found inside Alice, such as in the root directory on the primary hard disk drive of the computer you are using, which will probably be the C: drive. If you are doing this as part of a course, check with your instructor to see where you should place the file. The most important thing is to use a directory that you will be able to find in Step 4.
2. Start a new Alice world with a **grass** template.
3. Click **File** on the menu bar, and then click **Make Billboard**. Your screen should resemble Figure 6-23.

FIGURE 6-23: The dialog box to import a picture file for use as an Alice billboard object

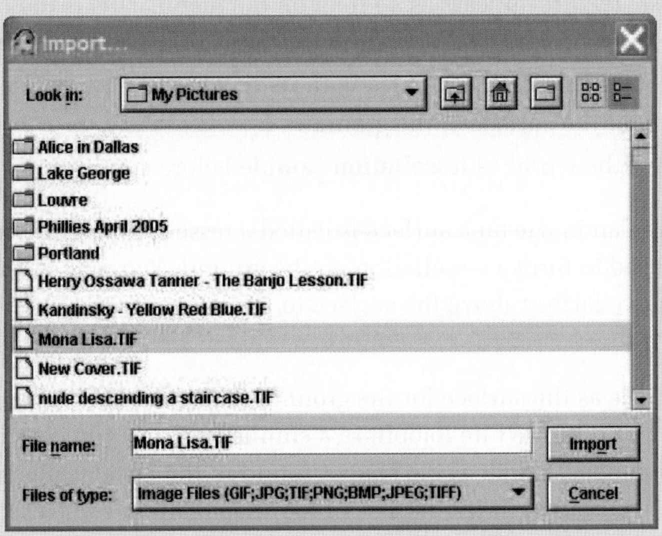

4. Find the directory where you stored the file Mona Lisa.jpg. Click the name of the file, and then click the **Import** button. The picture should appear in the world, as shown in Figure 6-6 earlier in this chapter.

The picture file may now be manipulated like any other object, using the tools in the Scene Editor mode, primitive methods, or any user-created methods that you write for the object. You may want to experiment with the Scene Editor tools and perhaps use a few methods to make the picture move around a bit. You can also use the *opacity* property to make the picture opaque or invisible, as was shown with 3D text in the previous tutorial. If you rotate the object, you will notice that it has no depth, that it is flat like a sheet of paper, and that the original image appears on both sides.

A curious side effect of adding a picture file to an Alice world as a billboard is that the image is now available as a texture map that can be used for other objects. To see how this works, you may want to try the following:

1. Click the **ground** tile in the Object tree, and then the **properties** tab in the Details area.
2. Click **ground.GrassTexture** next to the *skin texture* tile.

3. A small menu will appear, and you will notice that *Mona Lisa.Mona Lisa_texture* appears as an item on the menu. This is the image from the original *Mona Lisa.jpg* picture file. Select this as the skin texture for the ground, and the Mona Lisa with its frame will now be used as the image file for the surface of the ground.

4. Save the world as **tessellation sample** before continuing.

A repeated pattern of an image on a surface is called a **tessellation** of the surface. The Mona Lisa is now being used to form a tessellation on the ground. You may want to enter Scene Editor mode and move farther above the surface to look down to get a better view of the tessellated ground.

You can use any image as the surface for the ground. Figure 6-24 shows an Alice world tessellated with an image of the White Rabbit. In a similar manner, you could use an image file as the surface for any object, such as the shapes found in the Local Gallery's shapes folder. The image will be distorted to fit the surface of the shape, but in some cases, it may be recognizable.

FIGURE 6-24: Alice in a world tessellated with the image of the White Rabbit

NOTE □ □ □ | Using image and sound files in Alice raises the issue of copyrights. You must be careful when using copyrighted material, such as text, sound, and images in an Alice world or in other computer programs that you create. Section 107 of the U.S. copyright law (Title 17, U.S. code) describes the doctrine of fair use of copyrighted material, which covers the educational use of such material. It can be found on the Web at: *http://www.copyright.gov/title17/92chap1.html#107*. The concept of fair use is also explained on the Web at: *http://www.copyright.gov/fls/fl102.html*. The courts have generally agreed that students and teachers may use copyrighted material for instructional use provided that the material is used only for "educational purposes in systematic learning activities at nonprofit educational institutions," and that the material satisfies certain "portion limitations." An educational presentation may include the following:

- Up to 10% or 1,000 words, whichever is less, of a copyrighted text work. For example, an entire poem of less than 250 words may be used, but no more than three poems by one poet, or five poems by different poets from any anthology.
- Up to 10%, but in no event more than 30 seconds, of the music and lyrics from an individual musical work.
- Up to 10% or three minutes, whichever is less, of a copyrighted motion media work (for example, an animation, video, or film image).
- A photograph or illustration may be used in its entirety but no more than five images by an artist or photographer may be reproduced. When using photographs and illustrations from a published collective work, no more than 10% or 15 images, whichever is less.
- Up to 10% or 2,500 fields or cell entries, whichever is less, from a copyrighted database or data table may be reproduced. A field entry is defined as a specific item of information, such as a name or Social Security number, in a record of a database file. A cell entry is defined as the intersection where a row and a column meet on a spreadsheet.

One excellent comprehensive source of information about copyright and fair use is the Stanford University Libraries' Copyright and Fair Use Web site at: *http://fairuse.stanford.edu/*.

TUTORIAL 6E—SOUND IN ALICE WORLDS

In this short tutorial, you will add sound to a very simple Alice world using a sound clip that comes with Alice. In addition to using the prerecorded sounds that are supplied as part of the Alice software, you may also import sound clips from an external file or record your own sound clips.

There are three tiles for three sound clips shown in Figure 6-25: one named *Pacino*, one named *sylvester*, and one named *instructions*. Next to each there is a green triangular button that you can use to preview a sound directly before using it in your world.

FIGURE 6-25: Sound clips

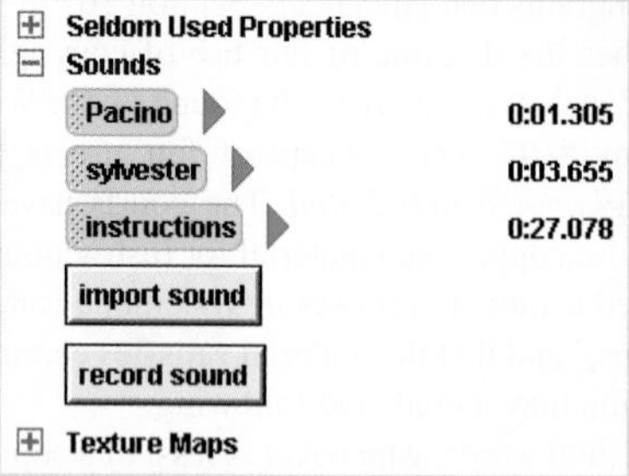

⊞ **Seldom Used Properties**
⊟ **Sounds**

Pacino ▶	0:01.305
sylvester ▶	0:03.655
instructions ▶	0:27.078

import sound

record sound

⊞ **Texture Maps**

NOTE □ □ □ | You can also rename a sound clip by right-clicking the sound clip tile and then changing the name, and you can delete a sound by dragging it to the trash can.

Of course, to play sounds in Alice you need to have a computer with an active sound card, and to record sounds, you need to have a properly working microphone connected to your computer. You will need to check with your instructor or the person who maintains the computer you are using to find out about its sound card and microphone. If your computer does not have sound, you should still read through the tutorial to get a feeling for how sound works in Alice. In these steps, you will add a chicken to a new Alice world and set up an event so that the chicken will make a chicken sound whenever the spacebar is pressed.

1. Start a new Alice world with a **grass** template.
2. Click the **ADD OBJECTS** button to enter Scene Editor mode and add a **Chicken** to the world from the Animals folder in the Local Gallery.
3. Click the **DONE** button after you have added the Chicken to the world. Notice that the *Chicken* is one of the few objects whose instance name starts with a capital letter. There is no special reason for this other than that the programmer who created the *Chicken* class of objects did so.
4. Click the **create new event** button in the Events area and select **When a key is typed** from the menu that appears.
5. Click the **any key** box in the tile for the new method and select **Space** from the menu that appears.
6. Next, make sure that **Chicken** is selected in the Object tree, and then click the **methods** tab.
7. Drag a copy of the **Chicken play sound** tile from the methods tab and drop it in the new event in place of the word *Nothing*.
8. A menu of available sounds will appear. Select **chicken** from the list that appears.

9. Play the world, and whenever you press the spacebar, the chicken sound will be played.

10. The *play sound* tile has parameters that will let you adjust the duration and volume of the sound, which can be accessed by clicking **more** on the play sound tile. You may want to experiment with the volume level, or add some instructions to your world to animate the Chicken.

CHAPTER SUMMARY

This chapter consisted of a discussion of the various uses of text in an Alice world, followed by a short discussion of sound in an Alice world and five tutorials.

The discussions included the following:

☐ There are different ways in which you can show text in an Alice world: by using the `say` and `think` primitive methods, by using the `print` instruction, by adding 3D text as an Alice object, and by placing a picture file with an image of text in an Alice world as a billboard.

☐ In addition to using visual text, sound files containing verbal messages can be added to an Alice world and then played using an object's `play sound` method.

☐ The text created by the `say` and `think` methods appears in what animators call balloons or bubbles, much like text appears in cartoons in a newspaper or magazine. A dialog balloon shows words that are supposed to have been spoken by an object, and a thought bubble shows words that reflect an object's thoughts.

☐ The `say` and `think` methods can be used with every object in Alice, including inanimate objects like rocks, trees, buildings, and vehicles. The Alice `say` and `think` methods work almost identically, with parameters to allow you to change the message itself, as well as the font used for the text, the size of the text, the color of the text, the color of the bubble in which the text is displayed, and the amount of time that the message stays on the screen.

☐ The `print` instruction can be used to display messages or the value of variables and parameters in a special text zone at the bottom of a running Alice world. It is most often used to show someone the value of a variable while a world is playing. Sometimes the value of a variable is displayed using the `print` instruction while debugging a world. You can also use the `print` instruction when debugging a program to show that a breakpoint has been reached.

☐ 3D text is implemented in Alice as its own object. It can be used to communicate with the user or as an element in an Alice world. The Alice Local Gallery contains a folder to create 3D text objects.

☐ Pictures files can be added to an Alice world as a billboard. The current version of Alice can easily import GIF and JPG files, but often has difficulty with other common picture file formats, such as BMP and TIF files.

☐ Each object in an Alice world has a primitive `play sound` method that can be used to play a sound file. Sound files are most often used in Alice worlds to add special effects, such as the sound of a doorbell, or to play background music as a scene unfolds.

☐ Several sound recordings are included with Alice. Other prerecorded sound files in the WAV or MP3 formats can be imported into Alice, and new sound files can be recorded directly using the Alice interface.

In Tutorial 6A, you explored the use of the `say` and `think` methods in Alice and how to manipulate the appearance of the methods' dialog balloons and thought bubbles.

In Tutorial 6B, you saw how the `print` instruction can be used to display the value of a variable and to show when a playing Alice world has reached a certain spot. These techniques are often used to debug a program.

In Tutorial 6C, you experimented with the creation and manipulation of 3D text as an object in an Alice world.

In Tutorial 6D, you imported a picture file into an Alice world as a billboard object that can be manipulated with methods just as other objects are.

In Tutorial 6E, you added a sound clip to an Alice world.

REVIEW QUESTIONS

1. **Define the following terms:**

   - billboard
   - breakpoint
   - dialog balloon
   - font

   - HSB
   - personification
   - RGB
   - tessellation

   - text
   - thought bubble
   - typeface

2. **List and briefly describe the different ways that text can be shown in an Alice world.**

3. **Describe how to change the typeface for each of the following: text in an Alice dialog balloon or thought bubble, Alice 3D text, and text displayed by the Alice print instruction.**

4. **Describe how to change the size of each of the following: text in an Alice dialog balloon or thought bubble, Alice 3D text, and text displayed by the Alice print instruction.**

5. **Describe how the print instruction can be useful in debugging methods in an Alice world.**

6. **Which common picture file formats work best for importing images into Alice as billboards?**

7. **How can a picture file that has been imported into Alice for use as a billboard be used to tessellate the ground in an Alice world?**

8. **Describe the notion of "fair use" of copyrighted material for educational purposes. How much of each of the following can probably be used in an Alice world or other student work based on how courts have ruled in the past on this doctrine?**
   a. Poems by Langston Hughes
   b. A recording of "Wake Me Up When September Ends" by Green Day
   c. An early recording of Gershwin's *Rhapsody in Blue*
   d. Beethoven's *Symphony No. 5* from the 1996 recording by the Vienna Philharmonic
   e. Images of artwork from the Guggenheim Museum's Web site
   f. Scanned images of pictures from a recent book about art in the Louvre

9. **List the recorded sounds that are supplied as part of Alice for use by the play sound method. How can other sounds be used in Alice?**

10. **Colors in Alice can be described using the RGB (Red, Green, Blue) color model or the HSB (Hue, Saturation, Brightness) color model. The term HSL (Hue, Stauration, Luminance) is also used for the HSB color model. Using the Internet as a research tool, see if you can find the meaning of the terms hue, saturation, and brightness (or luminance), and how these color models are related to the CMYK and Pantone color schemes.**

EXERCISES

1. Add text in dialog balloons or thought bubbles to an existing Alice world. Change the `bubbleColor`, `textColor`, `fontSize`, and `fontName` properties to give the text a look and feel that enhances the world. In addition, it should match the personality of the character with whom the text is associated or the tone of the message itself.

2. The `ask user for a string` function and the `ask user for a number` function are often used with string and number variables in a manner similar to the `ask user for yes or no` function, discussed in Chapter 4. Using these functions and the `say` method discussed in this chapter, create a simple Alice world with a dialog in which a character asks the user for his or her name, says hello to the person by name, asks how old the person is, then tells the person approximately how many days old he or she will be on his or her next birthday.

3. Create a title sequence for an existing Alice world of your choice. The titles should be added as 3D text objects, with animation sequences for the text. The world should have an entry sequence for when the text appears and an exit sequence for when the text disappears. To get some ideas for entry and exit sequences, you might want to look at Microsoft PowerPoint. The list of effects on the animations schemes or custom animations on the Slide Show menu in PowerPoint might give you some ideas for your title sequences in Alice.

4. Foreign language text can sometimes be cut and pasted from Microsoft Word, from other programs, or from a Web site into Alice `say` and `think` method tiles or as Alice 3D text. For example, the Greek language phrase "Αριστοτέλης ήταν σπονδαστής Πλάτωνα" (Aristotle was a student of Plato) can be cut and pasted from Word into Alice as the text for a 3D text object. The Altavista Babel Fish Translation Web site (*www.babelfish.altavista.com*) is one of many sites you can use to translate text from English into another language. Some of the translated text will work in Alice, and some will not, depending on the language and the typeface used to display the language. Create a simple Alice world with text in one or more languages other than English. Start by picking a few simple phrases, enter them into the Babel Fish Web site, and translate them to see how well they work. You can re-enter them into Babel Fish and cut and paste the translation from Babel Fish into Alice as needed while you develop your world.

5. Images from most digital cameras can be saved as .jpg files that can be imported into Alice as a billboard. Create an Alice world in which an image of yourself or someone you know plays a role.

6. Create an Alice world that is a short tutorial teaching the user about the sound clips built into Alice. Your world should contain keyboard events to allow the user to trigger each sound, along with either a menu of the built-in sounds, or a character who tells the user to press a particular key to hear a sound. The world should have a variety of objects to demonstrate the use of the sounds with matching animations. As always, remember to use good design techniques as you create the world.

7. You can record a dialog or narration for an Alice world using the record sound feature found on the properties tab of an Alice object. You can also import sound into Alice from an existing sound file. Select a segment of a song or other piece of music of your choice, import it into Alice as a sound file, and then create a short music video sequence in Alice with the sound you added as background. Remember to use proper design techniques as you create the world.

8. Create a 15- to 30-second animated commercial advertisement for a product or service of your choice as an Alice world. The world should use some of the features discussed in this chapter. You should begin by selecting the subject of your advertisement, and then create an outline or story-board for the advertisement. Once you have the outline or storyboard, you can write pseudo-code as refinement of the specifications for the world, and then code the world based on the pseudo-code. Remember to use good modular design as you develop your world.

9. The Television program *Sesame Street* often uses the theme of commercial endorsements to teach young children about the alphabet, such as segments on the program that are supposedly "… brought to you by the letter W…" Create an Alice world that picks up on this theme to teach children about a letter of the alphabet in a world with animation and sound.

10. Fairytales, myths, stories from history, and urban legends are all good subjects for Alice worlds with a voiceover narration. Create an outline or storyboard for such a world, then psudeo-code for the world, then the code itself. You may want to start by looking through both the Alice Local Gallery and the Alice Web Gallery to find characters for your story. There are three different approaches you can use to match the timing of the narration to the world:

   a. You could record the narration first, then make the action in the world match the narration.
   b. You could animate the story first, then record a voiceover to match the action.
   c. You could record the narration in short sound bytes that are played as required while the action is occurring.

7

RECURSIVE ALGORITHMS

After finishing this chapter, you should be able to:

- ☐ Provide brief definitions of the following terms: base case, base condition, conditional recursion, exponential recursion, infinite recursion, iteration, iterative process, linear recursion, overhead, recursion, and recursive method

- ☐ Describe what is meant by recursion in an algorithm, and how to implement recursion in Alice

- ☐ Describe how recursion differs from iteration, including the cost of recursion, and roughly how to tell when one might be more appropriate to use than the other

- ☐ Describe the difference between infinite recursion and conditional recursion

- ☐ Create a recursive method in Alice

- ☐ Convert an iterative Alice method into a linear recursive method

WHAT IS RECUSION?

This chapter is about recursion. Generally, something is said to be recursive if each of the parts that make up the thing have a structure—in other words, a design or pattern—that repeats the structure of the whole thing itself. Consider the fern in Figure 7-1. Each leaf of the fern has a pattern that is virtually identical to the overall fern itself. In fact, if you look closely at the leaf, you can see that the parts that make up the leaf have patterns that match the leaf itself. If you were to go deeper and deeper into the structure of the fern, you would see that the same pattern is repeated again and again, each time on a smaller scale, each time in more detail. The fern has a recursive structure—parts of the fern have structures that mirror the overall structure of the fern itself. There are many such examples of recursion in the natural world.

FIGURE 7-1: A fern with a recursive structure

Recursion is not a simple concept, so often it takes a while for someone who has never seen it before to really understand what it's all about. This chapter is not intended to make you an expert on recursion, but only to expose you to the topic. By the time you are done, you should have a basic understanding of what a recursive algorithm is. Before going on, let's take a look at another example. Can you see how the following very short story is recursive?

Once upon a time a young princess was sitting with her father, the king. She said to her father, "My Royal Father, can you read me a story?"

"Yes, my Royal Daughter," said the king, as he opened the *Royal Storybook*. He began to read, "Once upon a time a young princess was sitting with her father, the king. She said to her father, 'My Royal Father, can you read me a story?'"

"Yes, my Royal Daughter," said the king, as he opened the *Royal Storybook*. He began to read, "Once upon a time a young princess was sitting with her father, the king. She said to her father, 'My Royal Father, can you read me a story?' . . ."

RECURSIVE ALGORITHMS

In computer programming, an algorithm that calls itself is said to be recursive. Throughout this book you have seen how one method can call another method. Consider Figure 7-2a. The primitive method *bunny.move* is one of several methods called from within *world.my first method*. Recursion occurs when a method calls itself in the same way that *world.my first method* calls the *bunny.move* method. Figure 7-2b shows a simple example of a recursive method, *bunny.hop to carrot,* which calls itself. A part of the algorithm is identical to the overall algorithm because the method being called *is* the overall algorithm. In a sense, the method is nested within itself, just as the recursive structure of the fern is nested within itself in the example above.

FIGURE 7-2: A method that calls another method, and a method that calls itself

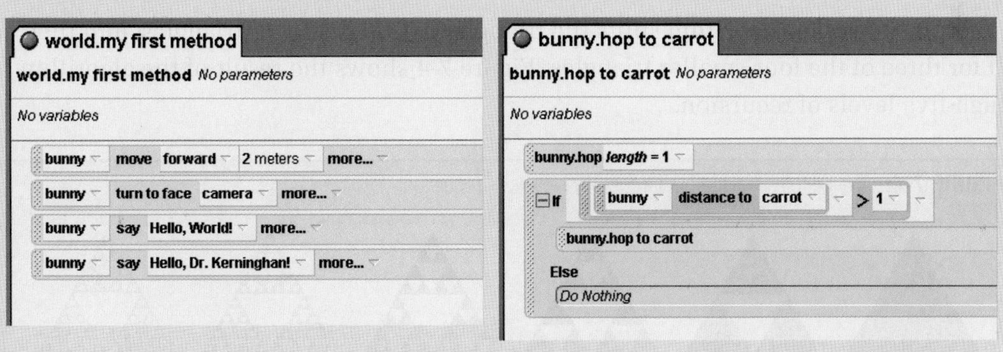

Let's take a look at another example of a recursive algorithm. Almost everyone knows about the famous ceiling of the Sistine Chapel in Rome, painted by Michelangelo, but do you know about its floor? The marble floor of the Sistine Chapel has patterns in the tiles that look like Figure 7-3. This pattern is an example of a mathematical design called a Sierpinski gasket.

FIGURE 7-3: A Sierpinski gasket

Here is the algorithm for drawing a Sierpinski gasket:

```
Begin with an equilateral triangle
Sierpinski (triangle)
    Start
    Find the midpoint of each side of the triangle
    Draw lines connecting the midpoints, which will form four
        smaller triangles that can be called triangles A, B, C,
        and D, with D in the center and the others around it.
    Color in (or cut out) the center triangle  // triangle D
    Do Sierpinski (triangle A)
    Do Sierpinski (triangle B)
    Do Sierpinski (triangle C)
    Stop
```

The Sierpinski Gasket algorithm splits the triangle into four smaller triangles, and then calls itself for three of the four smaller triangles. Figure 7-4 shows the result of the algorithm through five levels of recursion.

FIGURE 7-4: The Sierpinski algorithm through five levels of recursion

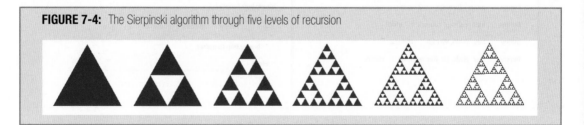

In the figure, you can see that the process of dividing the triangle into smaller triangles and then coloring in (or cutting out) one of them is repeated over and over again, each time at a smaller level, each time in more detail. The result is a complex structure created by a small, efficient algorithm.

The Sierpinski gasket algorithm demonstrates the power of recursion for drawing complex structures, but the real power of recursion in computer programming is the way in which computer scientists use recursive algorithms to analyze and solve complex problems. An algorithm is really just a set of instructions describing how to complete a process. Recursion can describe a very sophisticated process with a simple and efficient set of instructions. Many of the most important algorithms in computing, such as those used to search large databases quickly, to perform matrix algebra, and to play games such as chess, depend on the use of recursion. Unfortunately, students in introductory computer programming courses don't yet have the skills to write such programs, but you can spend some time learning about some of the basic ideas associated with recursion so that you will be able to use recursion appropriately when the time comes to do so.

It's also worth learning about recursion because of its importance in the world around us. Blood vessels in the human body have a structure that can be best described by recursion, in which they continue to divide into smaller and smaller vessels until they are tiny capillaries only a few blood cells wide. The pattern of seeds on the head of a sunflower, the geometry of a snail's shell, and even DNA gene sequencing all appear to be recursive structures. The newly emerging fields of Fractal Geometry and Chaos Theory are largely based on recursion. Seemingly random events, such as the electronic interference in a telephone circuit, can be described using recursive functions. There is also some evidence that the human brain is recursive. A basic understanding of recursion will not only help you to become a better computer programmer, but it may also help you to better understand the world around you.

RECURSION COMPARED TO ITERATION

An **iterative process** is one that uses a loop to repeat a set of instructions, so **iteration** is just another name for looping. In many cases, either iteration or recursion can be used to do the same thing. The *bunny.hop to carrot* method shown earlier in this chapter is a good example of such a case. Figure 7-5 shows the recursive *bunny.hop to carrot* method on the left, with an iterative version of the same method using a *while* loop on the right. Both methods do the same thing, but one uses recursion, and the other uses iteration.

FIGURE 7-5: Recursive and iterative *bunny.hop to carrot* methods

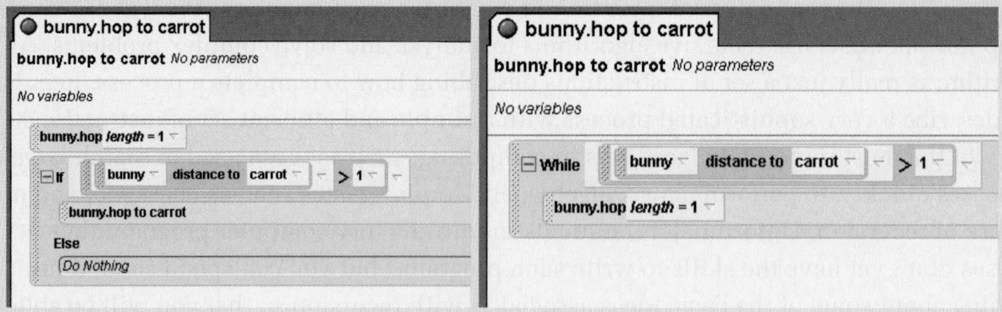

This brings us to one of the most important questions about recursion—if both iteration and recursion can be used to do the same thing, then when should iteration be used, and when should recursion be used? To be able to answer that question, you need to know a little more about some of the characteristics of recursive methods, including the cost of recursion and the difference between linear and exponential recursion.

THE COST OF RECURSION

Overhead is the extra CPU time and extra space in a computer's memory needed to manage a method as it runs. The computer must set up a section in its memory every time a new method is called—even if the new method is a copy of an existing method. We don't see this happening, yet it does take up time and space in the computer's memory. In the *bunny.hop to carrot* example, the computer must set up a new section in its memory each time the recursive *bunny.hop to carrot* method is called. If the bunny hops five times, then that means five new sections will be needed in the computer's memory to manage the five copies of the method. It if hops a thousand times, then a thousand new sections in memory will be required. The iterative *bunny.hop to carrot* method does not have such overhead, so it is more efficient when implemented on a computer.

People, such as mathematicians, who deal with theoretical algorithms, almost always think recursion is a good idea. For more practical computer programmers, the overhead associated with recursion must be considered. Often it is better to use iteration than recursion for methods that can be written using a simple loop. But before giving up on recursion completely, let's go back to the Sirepinski gasket algorithm to see the difference between linear recursion and exponential recursion.

LINEAR RECURSION AND EXPONENTIAL RECURSION

Linear recursion occurs when a method calls itself only once each time through the method. **Exponential recursion** occurs when a method calls itself more than once in each pass through the method. The graphs in Figure 7-6 shows the two compared to each other. The graph on the left shows the number of copies of the method running for each level of recursion in an algorithm that calls itself once. The graph on the right shows the same thing for an algorithm that calls itself twice. You can see that the linear recursion graph looks like a straight line. Only one additional copy of the algorithm is created at each level of recursion. Yet look how much more quickly the number of copies of the exponential algorithm grows. At each level of recursion, the number of copies of the program doubles. If it called itself three times, then the number of copies would triple at each level, and so on. A method that uses exponential recursion can very quickly generate many copies of itself to work simultaneously on smaller examples of the overall problem.

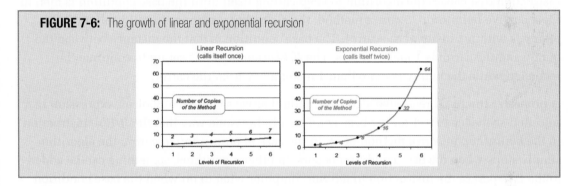

FIGURE 7-6: The growth of linear and exponential recursion

The recursive Sierpinski gasket algorithm is an example of exponential recursion because it calls itself three times. The number of triangles triples with each level of recursion. It is very unlikely that a more efficient algorithm to do the same thing could easily be written using iteration. In this case, recursion probably is the best solution. Generally, a method that uses exponential recursion—that is, a method which calls itself more than once—is often very difficult to replace with a more efficient iterative solution. Exponentially recursive algorithms are often far more efficient than iterative solutions to do the same thing because they can repeatedly break a problem into several smaller parts, then attack those smaller parts in a way that an iterative algorithm cannot. Even considering the overhead for recursion, they are usually far more efficient than iterative solutions.

So, we now have a rough answer to our question about when to use recursion. For simple tasks that can be described with linear recursion, iteration seems to be better because of the overhead of recursion, but for complex problems that can be broken down into smaller parts, exponential recursion usually works much better, even allowing for the overhead of the recursion.

INFINITE RECURSION AND CONDITIONAL RECURSION

There's one more important concept about recursion that computer programming students should understand—the difference between infinite recursion and conditional recursion. **Infinite recursion** means that an algorithm calls itself repeatedly without stopping. Infinite recursion occurs when an algorithm does not contain any instructions about when to stop the recursion. On a computer, infinite recursion continues until all available memory is used, or until it triggers some time-out mechanism in the operating system. The version of the Sierpinski gasket algorithm presented earlier is an example of infinite recursion. If you examine the algorithm carefully, you will see that the *Stop* instruction is never executed.

Recursion that is not infinite is called conditional recursion because the algorithm must contain some condition that will stop the recursion. The condition that stops the recursion is called the **base condition** or the **base case**. The algorithm usually contains an *If/Else* instruction that causes the algorithm to keep calling itself until the base condition is met. In the recursive *bunny.hop to carrot* method, the algorithm continues to call itself until the bunny is within 1 meter of the carrot. The base condition is that the distance between the bunny and the carrot is 1 meter or less. The *If/Else* command is set up to continue the recursion while the bunny is more than 1 meter away from the carrot.

A properly structured recursive algorithm should always contain a Boolean expression in a selection sequence to test for the base condition in the same way that the *If/Else* instruction in the *bunny.hop to carrot* method does. In the case of *bunny.hop to carrot,* the algorithm simply stops when the base condition occurs. In other algorithms, something can be added to the *Else* part of the instruction to tell the computer what to do when the base condition has occurred.

In conditional exponentially recursive algorithms, the recursive step breaks the problem into smaller parts, and then calls the algorithm itself for each of those parts, continuing to do so until the base case is reached. Sometimes that is enough to solve the original problem; sometimes another step is needed to combine all of the small solutions into one big solution. It is such conditional exponentially recursive algorithms that lead to sophisticated and highly efficient solutions to large programming problems. Unfortunately, they are often used with complex data structures, such as trees, graphs, and matrices, which are not easily demonstrated in introductory Alice programming, although the underlying software that runs Alice worlds does use them, especially the operating system.

In the tutorials in this chapter, you will work with simple linear recursive methods to get a feeling for recursion and to compare recursive methods to methods that do the same thing with simple loops.

TUTORIAL 7A—CREATING A RECURSIVE METHOD

In this tutorial, you will create a recursive method to make an airplane taxi from the end of a runway to a spot near an airplane hangar. Let's start with the specifications for the world. You must set up a scene with an aircraft that has just landed at an airport. The aircraft must taxi from the end of the runway to a spot near an airplane hangar. The task is to create a method that will enable an object to move from wherever it is when the method is called to a specific spot. In this case, the aircraft should taxi to within 1 meter of the part of the airport named garage02.

Immediately there are a few things that will come to mind when a good programmer is presented with this situation:

1. This seems to be the kind of programming project that is part of a larger project. You will be building a short method for a very specific task. A good programmer in this situation will think of reusable code. The method could be constructed with a target parameter instead of hard coding garage02 into the method.

2. The specifications do not call for you to build an airport, so either one already exists, or someone else will create one as a separate part of the project.

3. What's an aircraft? The vehicles folder in the local Alice object gallery has several airplanes, including a biplane, a jet, a navy jet, and a seaplane. The gallery also has a helicopter and a blimp, which might be considered aircraft. In a situation like this, the programmer would need to go back to whomever provided the specifications to get more information.

4. Finally, there are no internal specifications for the method, only functional specifications. This means that the specifications tell the programmer what the new method should do, but not how the method should do it. They don't say anything about what techniques can be used inside the method. The specifications don't say, for example, "use a loop to ...". This gives the programmer more flexibility in designing the internal workings of the method, but a good programmer will ask about this to be sure that there really is some flexibility here. Sometimes specifications don't tell you everything.

So, after reading the specifications, a good programmer will put together a set of questions for the person who provided them. Communication like this among the members of a team working on a software development project is important. In this case, the programmer would ask which airport should be used, which aircraft should be used, and whether any particular techniques should be used or avoided inside the method. The answers to these questions are that the airport in the buildings folder in the local Alice object gallery should be used; the biplane should be used as the aircraft; and there are no restrictions on the techniques to be used in the method, except that recursion should be used.

Now that things are a little clearer, you can begin. In a real situation, a programmer would probably create an iterative method or simply use the existing primitive *move to* method for this project, but your purpose in this tutorial is to experiment with recursion.

SETTING THE SCENE

First you need to build the scene for the new world.

1. Start Alice and open a new world with a **grass** background.
2. Click the **ADD OBJECTS** button to enter Scene Editor mode, and find the Airport object class in the Buildings folder within the Local Gallery.
3. Click the **Airport** tile, but pause for moment before actually adding it to the world. Notice that the Airport class information window, shown in Figure 7-7, says that the size of the object is 753 kilobytes, and that it has 44 parts. This is a large and complex object. Also notice that there are no methods listed in the window, so the object only includes the standard primitive methods. Click the **Add instance to world** button to add an airport to the world.

FIGURE 7-7: The Airport object class information window

4. Note that a tile for the airport appears in the Object tree, and the view of the airport in the World window will probably look something like Figure 7-8. The view is as if you were standing on the ground at the airport.

FIGURE 7-8: The World window after adding an airport

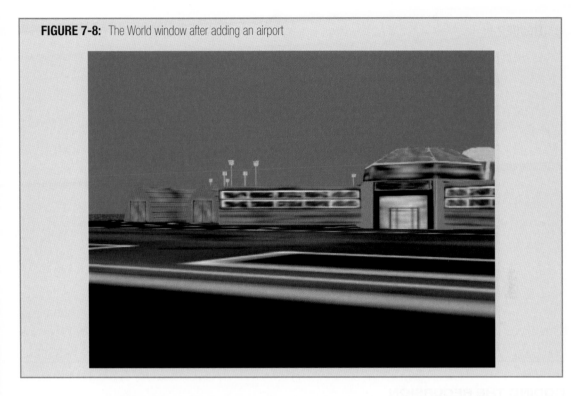

5. You need to position the camera to get a better view of the airport. Using the blue camera control arrows, move, tilt, and pan the **camera** so that the view of the airport looks more like Figure 7-9, but without the red plane. The trick is to move the camera and not the airport. This will probably take a few minutes to do unless you are very familiar with the Scene Editor. Remember the magic of the Undo button, which can be used if you are unhappy with one of your moves. Both the right end of the runway and the hangars on the left should be visible in the window when you are done.

6. Next, add a biplane to the world, and position it near the right end of the runway, similar to the way the red plane is shown in Figure 7-9. Your biplane won't be red; the one in the picture is red so that you can see it better in the printed image. The biplane should look as if it just landed and is about three-fourths of the way down the runway. You will need to move and turn the biplane.

7. Now that the scene is ready, click the **DONE** button to exit Scene Editor mode, and save the world with the name **airport setup.** This will protect you from needing to re-create the scene in case something goes wrong.

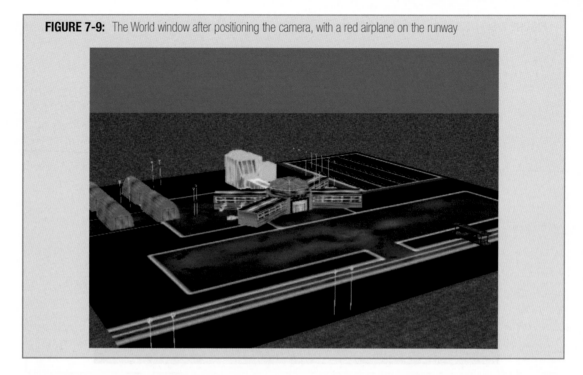

FIGURE 7-9: The World window after positioning the camera, with a red airplane on the runway

CODING THE RECURSION

Now that the scene is ready, you can create a recursive taxi method to make the biplane move as desired. Here is the pseudo-code modified for the taxi method:

```
biplane.taxi (target)
Start
If  ( [biplane.distance to target]  > 1 meter)
    {
    biplane.point at target
    biplane.move forward 1 meter
    biplane.taxi (target)
    }
Stop
```

It seems fairly straightforward, so let's create the method. You can start by creating the method and putting the *If/Else* command in place.

> 1. Select the **biplane** tile in the Object tree and the **methods** tab in the Details area.

2. Click the **create new method** button, type **taxi** as the method name, and then click the **OK** button. The method *biplane.taxi* should appear in the Editor area.

3. The method will need a parameter named *target* with the data type *object.* Click the **create new parameter** button, type the name **target,** make sure that **object** is selected as the data type, and then click the **OK** button.

4. Drag an **If/Else** tile from the bottom of the Editor area and drop it in the new taxi method in place of *Do Nothing.* Select **true** as the condition. Your method should now look like Figure 7-10.

FIGURE 7-10: The taxi method with a *target* parameter and a blank *If/Else* instruction

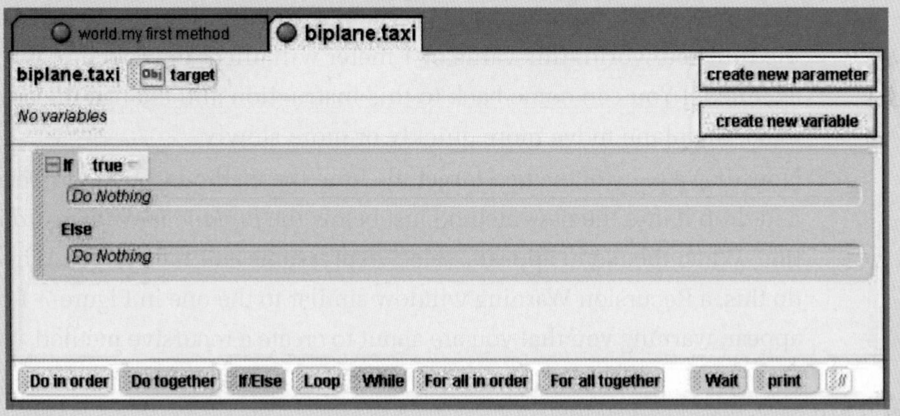

5. The Boolean condition needs to be a comparison of two values using the *greater than* operator. Select **world** in the Object tree and the **functions** tab in the Details area. One of the functions listed under math is *a > b*. Drag a copy of this tile and drop in into the *IF/Else* instruction tile in place of *true.* Select **1** as the value for *a* and **1** as the value for *b* from the short menus that appear.

6. You need to replace the first *1* with the biplane's *distance to* function. Select **biplane** in the Object tree and drag and drop a copy of the **distance to** function in place of the first number *1* in the condition in the *IF/Else* tile.

7. When the menu appears asking for an object, select **expressions**, and then **target**. The instruction should now match the pseudo-code on the previous page.

Now you need to add the instructions that belong inside the *IF/Else* structure. The pseudo-code shows that there are three of them: biplane.point at (target), biplane.move forward 1 meter, and biplane.taxi (target). You can add them in the order in which they will occur.

1. Select the **methods** tab in the Details area and drag and drop a copy of the **biplane turn to face instruction** tile into the *If/Else* tile in the Editor area in place of the words *Do Nothing* between *If* and *Else*. When the menu appears asking you for the target, select **expressions**, and then **target**. Also, click **more** and change the style to **abruptly**.

2. Next drag a copy of the **biplane move** tile from the methods tab in the Details area and drop it into the new method just below the *biplane turn to face* instruction. Select **forward** as the direction and **1 meter** as the amount; then click **more** and change the style to **abruptly**. Note that when you play the finished world, this value of 1 meter will affect the speed of the plane as it taxis. You can come back to this instruction and change the amount to make the plane move more quickly or more slowly.

3. Now drag a copy of the **taxi target** tile from the methods tab in the Details area and drop it into the new method just below the *biplane move forward* instruction. When the menu appears, select **expressions** and then **target**. When you do this, a Recursion Warning window similar to the one in Figure 7-11 will appear, warning you that you are about to create a recursive method.

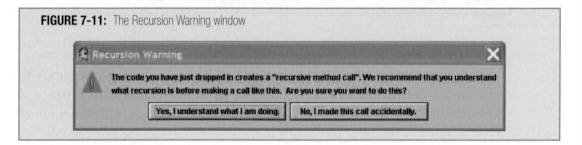

FIGURE 7-11: The Recursion Warning window

4. Click the **Yes, I understand what I am doing** button, and the instruction tile will pop into place in the method.

5. Finally, the method will work more smoothly if the *biplane turn to face* and *biplane move* and instructions happen at the same time. Drag a **Do together** tile from the bottom of the Editor area and drop it into the method between the *biplane move forward* instruction and the *biplane.taxi* instruction; then drag the **biplane turn to face** and **biplane move** instruction tiles into the *Do together* tile. The method is complete and should now be similar to Figure 7-12.

FIGURE 7-15: The completed recursive *sail to* method

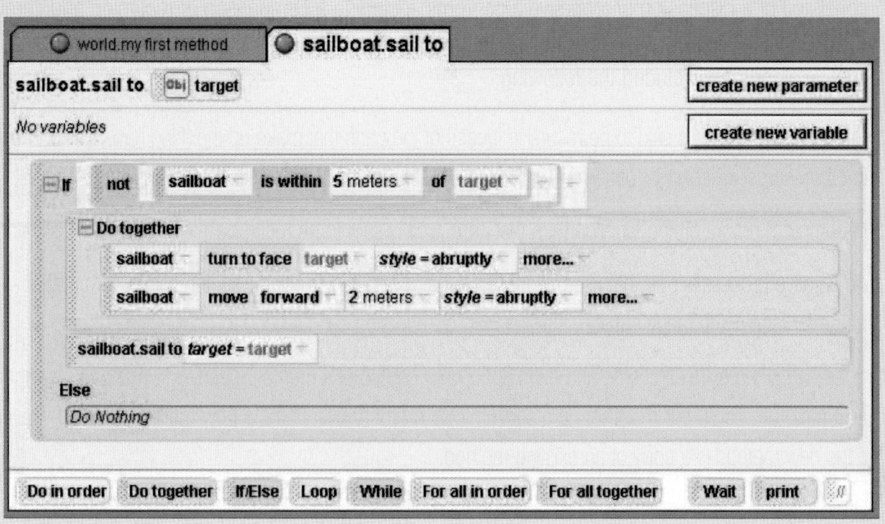

world.my first method	**sailboat.sail to**

sailboat.sail to `Obj` **target**   create new parameter

No variables   create new variable

```
If    not     sailboat    is within 5 meters    of  target

    Do together
        sailboat    turn to face  target    style = abruptly    more...
        sailboat    move  forward    2 meters    style = abruptly    more...

    sailboat.sail to target = target

Else
    Do Nothing
```

Do in order   Do together   If/Else   Loop   While   For all in order   For all together   Wait   print

Play the world and see how your new method works. If all is well, it should appear to function no differently than the old *sail to object* world did. The changes are all internal and will not really be seen by the user unless a problem occurs.

CHAPTER SUMMARY

This chapter consisted of a discussion of recursive algorithms, including a comparison of recursion and iteration, a look at linear and exponential recursion, and a look at infinite and conditional recursion, followed by two tutorials. The discussion of recursive algorithms included the following:

- ☐ Generally, something is said to be recursive if each of the parts that make up the thing have a structure—in other words, a design or pattern—that repeats the structure of the whole thing itself.

- ☐ In computer programming, an algorithm that calls itself is said to be recursive.

- ☐ An iterative process is one that uses a loop to repeat a set of instructions, so iteration is just another name for looping. In many cases, either iteration or recursion can be used to do the same thing.

- ☐ Overhead is the extra CPU time and extra space in a computer's memory needed to manage a method as it runs. The computer must set up a section in its memory every time a new method is called—even if the new method is a copy of an existing method.

- ☐ Often it is better to use iteration than recursion for methods that can be written using a simple loop because of the overhead associated with recursion.

- ☐ Linear recursion occurs when a method calls itself only once each time through the method.

- ☐ Exponential recursion occurs when a method calls itself more than once in each pass through the method. Exponentially recursive algorithms are often far more efficient than iterative solutions to do the same thing because they can repeatedly break a problem into several smaller parts, then attack those smaller parts in a way that an iterative algorithm cannot.

- ☐ For simple tasks that can be described with linear recursion, iteration seems to be better because of the overhead of recursion, but for complex problems that can be broken down into smaller parts, exponential recursion usually works much better, even allowing for the overhead of the recursion.

- ☐ Infinite recursion means that an algorithm calls itself repeatedly without stopping. Recursion that is not infinite is called conditional recursion because the algorithm must contain some condition that will stop the recursion.

- ☐ The condition that stops the recursion is called the base condition or the base case. A properly structured recursive algorithm should contain a Boolean expression in a selection sequence to test for the base condition.

In Tutorial 7A, you created a new world with a recursive method.

In Tutorial 7B, you converted an existing iterative method into a recursive method.

REVIEW QUESTIONS

1. **Define the following terms:**

   - [ ] base case
   - [ ] exponential recursion
   - [ ] linear recursion
   - [ ] base condition
   - [ ] infinite recursion
   - [ ] overhead
   - [ ] base step
   - [ ] iteration
   - [ ] recursion
   - [ ] conditional recursion
   - [ ] iterative process
   - [ ] recursive method

2. **What is the difference between recursion and iteration?**

3. **Why will a program with infinite recursion eventually crash on a computer system?**

4. **In a case where both iterative and recursive solutions to a programming problem exist, how can a programmer tell whether to use iteration or recursion?**

5. **The recursive biplane.taxi method in Tutorial 7B works only with the biplane. How can this be modified so that it will work with any object?**

6. **The following joke was all the rage in 4th grade classrooms last year. Explain how this is related to recursion.**

   "There were three men in a boat, Joe, Pete, and Repeat. Joe and Pete fell out. Who was left?"

7. **Write both iterative and recursive methods in pseudo-code that will multiply any two positive integers using only addition.**

8. **It was recently discovered that the famous graphic artist M. C. Escher used the "Droste effect" in at least one of his drawings. See if you can find out on the Internet what the Droste effect is, how it is related to recursion, and why it's called the Droste effect.**

9. **Assume that a computer student wants to impress his father, who is a computer security expert for the CIA, by writing a program like the one below. The parameter for the program is the network address of a computer system.**

```
Search for dad's account at (computer system)
     Start
     If dad has an account on this computer
            Print "Hello dad, I found your computer."
     Else
            Find two other computers connected to this one
            Search for dad's account at (first computer)
            Search for dad's account at (second computer)
     Stop
```

The preceding code is enough to cause some issues between father and son; however, assume that the student plays with it some more and then makes a mistake, leaving out the If/Else instruction so that the algorithm looks like this:

```
Search for Dad's account at (computer system )
      Start
      Print "Hello Dad, I found your computer."
      Find two other computers connected to this one
      Search for Dad's account at (first computer)
      Search for Dad's account at (second computer)
      Stop
```

a. What kind of recursion is within this program?
b. Assuming that the student knows enough systems programming to make the instructions work, what will the program actually do?
c. If it takes 10 seconds for the algorithm to run, including the time it needs to connect to other computers, how many copies of the program will be running 1 minute after the program first starts? After 2 minutes? After 1 hour? After 6 hours?
d. What would something like this do to the Internet?
e. What sentence did U.S. District Court Judge Howard G. Munson give Cornell University graduate student Robert Tappan Morris when he was convicted of doing something similar to this in November, 1988?

10. An important technique in mathematics is proof by induction. We start a proof by induction by proving that if something is true for one number, then it must be true for the next number also. In other words, if what we are trying to prove is true for n, then it must be true for n+1. This is called the inductive step in the proof. Next we show that it is true for the number 1. This is called the base step in the proof. Putting the base step and the inductive step together, we can then see that the item in question must be true for all positive integers because if it is true for 1, then it must be true for 1+1, then for 2+1, then 3+1, and so on. How is a proof by induction similar to conditional linear recursion?

EXERCISES

1. The Alice people gallery has hebuilder and shebuilder classes of objects that include a walk method. Create a simple Alice world with a few objects of your choice, including a character that you create with hebuilder or shebuilder, and create both iterative and recursive methods to make the character walk to a target object.

2. There occurs in the story *Alice's Adventures in Wonderland* a section in which Alice grows smaller, and then bigger. Create an Alice world with aliceLiddel standing between a tall flower and a short flower and with an infinitely recursive method to keep repeating the following process:

a. She touches the tall flower and then shrinks.
b. She touches the short flower and then grows.
   Hint: Use the resize primitive method.

3. Mutual recursion occurs when method *A* calls method *B*, and method *B* calls method *A.* Together, they function like a single recursive method. Rewrite the solution to Exercise 2 using mutual recursion.

4. The biplane in the taxi world created in Tutorial 7A moves right though part of the airport to get to its spot near the hangar. See if you can correct this by adding a cone to the world from the shapes gallery, positioning the cone someplace on the tarmac, then have the plane move twice, first to the cone, and then from the cone to its final spot. Once it works, you can then make the cone invisible by changing its opacity property.

5. In Tutorial 7B, you converted an existing iterative method into a recursive method. Starting with the recursive sail to world from the end of that tutorial, or the copy of it on the disk that comes with this book, convert the recursive sail to method in the world back to an iterative method.

6. A recursive algorithm can be written to draw a spiral, starting in the middle and expanding outward with each revolution. A similar algorithm can be written to draw a "spirally increasing pseudo-square" like that shown in Figure 7-16. Such an algorithm could be used for a search pattern to search for a lost object, or for a robotic lawn mower that could be left in the middle of a large field and then programmed to start mowing the field from the center outward. Create a "recursive Zamboni" Alice world with a snow background and a Zamboni with a recursive method to make the Zamboni follow the "spirally increasing pseudo-square" pattern just described. A Zamboni is the machine that is used to clean an ice-skating rink, such as at a hockey game between periods. The Alice vehicle gallery has a Zamboni.

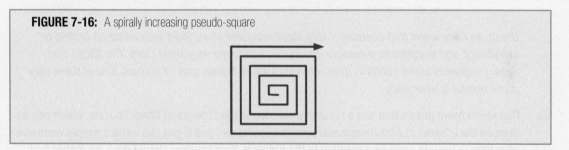

FIGURE 7-16: A spirally increasing pseudo-square

7. The Fibonacci sequence is one of the most commonly found patterns in all of nature. The sequence starts with 0 and 1, then each term in the sequence is generated by adding the previous two terms. The first few terms in the sequence are 0, 1, 1, 2, 3, 5, 8, 13, 21, and 34. Numbers that appear in the sequence are called Fibonacci numbers.

   a. Write a recursive algorithm in pseudo-code to generate the Fibonacci sequence.
   b. Write an iterative algorithm in pseudo-code to generate the Fibonacci sequence.
   c. Which algorithm would probably work better on a computer, and why?
   d. Write an algorithm in pseudo-code to test a number to see if it is a Fibonacci number.
   e. Create an Alice world with Count penguin and the Fibonacci penguin. Count penguin will simply start counting slowly when the world starts by saying each number. The Fibonacci penguin will jump up and down and flap its wings while saying "Fibonacci, Fibonacci, (n) is Fibonacci!" when Count penguin says a number that is part of the Fibonacci sequence. The Fibonacci penguin should say the actual number in place of (n).

8. **Images generated by certain recursive algorithms are sometimes called fractal images.**

    a. Draw the figure generated by the following algorithm:

    ```
    Start with a square
    Fractal (square)
        Start
        Divide the square into four smaller squares
        Fill in the upper-left square and the lower-right square
        If the squares are still big enough to draw in, then
                Fractal (upper-right square)
                Fractal (lower-left square)
        Stop
    ```

    b. Using pseudo-code, write your own recursive algorithm to generate a fractal image.

    c. Search the Internet for fractal geometry to see some very interesting fractal images.

9. **Here is an example of a very short recursive story (which was already discussed in the main part of the chapter):**

    Once upon a time a young princess was sitting with her father, the king. She said to her father, "My Royal Father, can you read me a story?"

    "Yes, my Royal Daughter" said the king, as he opened the Royal Storybook. He began to read, "Once upon a time a young princess was sitting with her father, the king. She said to her father, 'My Royal Father, can you read me a story?' . . ."

    Create an Alice world that contains a very short recursive story. Start with either an outline or storyboard, and consider how camera moves can add to the very short story. The Alice Local Gallery's Objects folder contains Book, Monitor, Picture Frame, and TV classes. One of these may prove helpful in your story.

10. **One well-known puzzle that has a recursive solution is the "Towers of Hanoi" puzzle, which can be seen on the Internet at *http://www.mazeworks.com/hanoi/*. See if you can write a simple recursive algorithm in pseudo-code as a solution to the problem. Your solution should work no matter how many discs there are. You should be warned however, that even though the algorithm is only a few instructions long, it could take a while to figure it out.**

8

LISTS AND ARRAYS IN ALICE

After finishing this chapter, you should be able to:

☐ Provide brief definitions of the following terms: array, Array Visualization Object, binary tree, data structure, index value, iterate a list, list, matrix, node, queue, root node, and vector

☐ Describe what a data structure is, and give several examples of data structures

☐ Generally describe why there are so many different data structures, and how programmers decide what data structures to use for different programs

☐ Describe the simple data structure known as a list, and how it is implemented in Alice

☐ Describe the data structure known as an array, how it differs from a list, and how it is implemented in Alice

☐ Create a list of objects in an Alice world and methods that perform operations on the list items one at a time and all at once

☐ Create methods in Alice that can manipulate the parts of objects contained in a list

☐ Describe the purpose of the Array Visualization Object in Alice

DATA STRUCTURES IN ALICE

A **data structure** is a scheme for organizing data in the memory of a computer. A set of names, addresses, and phone numbers stored as a table of data is an example of a data structure. Some of the more commonly used data structures include lists, arrays, stacks, queues, heaps, trees, and graphs. They can be simple, or they can become quite complex.

THE NEED FOR DIFFERENT DATA STRUCTURES

Computer programmers decide which data structures to use based on the nature of the data and the operations that need to be performed on that data because the way in which the data is organized affects the performance of a program for different tasks. As an example of this, let's take a look at two data structures, a queue and a binary tree, and see how the differences between the two affect how computer programmers use them.

A **queue** is a set of data items with a beginning and end, called the front and back of the queue. Data enters the queue at one end and leaves at the other. Because of this, data exits the queue in the same order in which it entered the queue, like people in a checkout line at a supermarket. A queue has many uses in the world of computers—it would, for example, be a good data structure to use in a program for keeping track of documents waiting to be printed on a network printer, as shown in Figure 8-1.

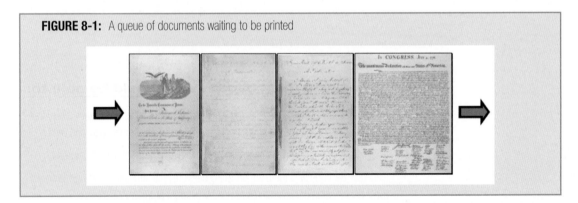

FIGURE 8-1: A queue of documents waiting to be printed

A **binary tree** is a data structure that looks like an upside-down tree. Each spot on the tree, called a **node**, holds an item of data, along with a left pointer and a right pointer, as shown in Figure 8-2. The pointers are lined up so that the structure forms the upside-down tree, with a single node at the top, called the **root node**, and branches increasing on the left and right as you go down the tree. The nodes at the bottom of each branch, with two empty pointers, are called the **leaf nodes**.

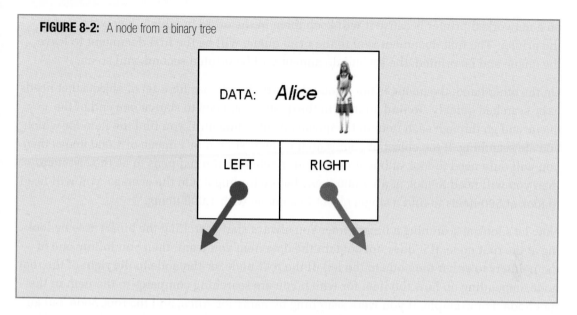

FIGURE 8-2: A node from a binary tree

A binary tree is used when it is necessary to keep a set of data items sorted in a particular order and quickly find items in the set. The middle item from the set of data is put in the root node, with anything before the middle item stored in the left branch of the tree, and anything after it stored in the right branch of the tree, as shown in Figure 8-3. It is good for storing information that needs to be searched quickly, such as a dictionary or phone directory.

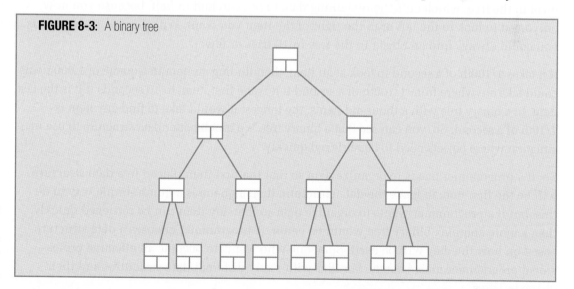

FIGURE 8-3: A binary tree

By comparing the queue with the binary tree, you can see how the structure of the data—in other words, the way in which the data is organized—affects what can be done efficiently with the data. The queue works well for keeping track of documents waiting to be printed on a networked printer because it will keep them in the order in which they were sent to the printer. The first document sent to the print queue will be the first document to leave the queue and be printed, the second document will be printed second, and so on.

On the other hand, the queue is not a good data structure to use for a set of objects that needs to be searched quickly. To find an item in the queue, you need to start at one end of the queue and go through each item in the queue one at a time until you find the item for which you are searching. If the object of your search is the first item in a queue of 1,000 items, then you will only need to look at one item to find it; whereas if it happens to be the last item, then you will need to look at all 1,000 items before finding it. On the average, you will need to look at 500 items to find a single object in a queue with 1,000 items.

Now let's look at searching a binary tree. You always start searching the binary tree by looking at the root node. If it does not contain the data item you want, then you follow one of the pointers to either the node to the left of the root node, or the node to the right of the root node, depending on how the item for which you are searching compares to the item in the root node. For example, if you were searching by name for Alice, and the root node had an object named Cheshire Cat, then you would know to go to the left branch of the tree to find Alice because it comes before the Cheshire Cat. At the next node you would do the same thing—if the node does not contain Alice, then you go to that node's left branch or right branch, and so on until you find Alice. The efficiency of the binary tree comes from the fact that each time you look at a node, you either find the item you want, or move down one level in the tree, which cuts the remaining data to be searched in half, because you now only need to look to the left or to the right of the item you want. With a set of 1,000 objects, you could always find an object in the tree in 10 tries or fewer.

If it takes 1/100th of a second to look at an item, then finding an item in a queue of 1,000 items could take anywhere from 1/100th of a second if it is the first item, to 10 seconds if it is the last item. In a binary tree with a thousand items, the longest it would take to find any item is 1/10th of a second. So, you can see that a binary tree is a much better data structure to use in a situation where objects need to be retrieved quickly.

So, if a programmer needs to organize data so that the first item placed in a data structure will be the first item to leave the data structure, then a queue is a quick simple way to do this, but if a programmer wants to organize data so that any item can be retrieved quickly, then a more complex binary tree would be better. A programmer chooses a data structure based on how the data will be used. Someone who wants to become an effective professional programmer must become familiar with many different data structures and their characteristics.

It's impossible to learn all about data structures in an introductory course in programming, although you can start to learn about the simple and commonly used data structures known as lists and arrays, which are the focus of the remainder of this chapter.

LISTS IN ALICE

One of the simplest of all data structures is a **list**, which is an ordered set of data. It is often used to store objects that are to be processed sequentially, meaning one at a time in order. In fact, lists are often used to set up queues like the print queue described earlier.

Alice has a number of instructions that can be used to manipulate lists, some of which are shown on the menu in Figure 8-4. You can see that there are commands to insert or remove items from the beginning of the list, the end of the list, or at any position in the list, which in this example is named *world.bunnies*.

FIGURE 8-4: Alice commands for manipulating lists

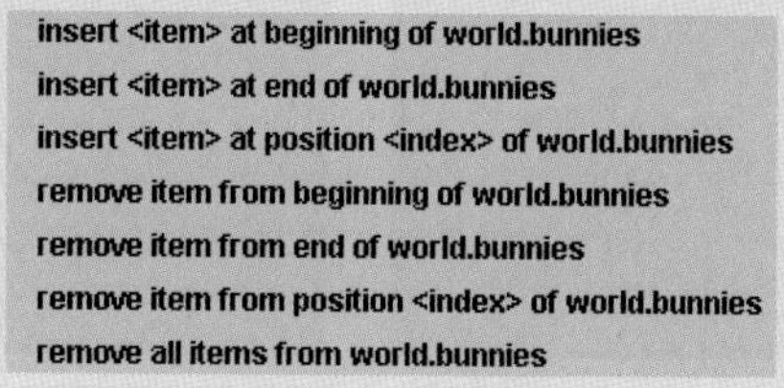

insert <item> at beginning of world.bunnies
insert <item> at end of world.bunnies
insert <item> at position <index> of world.bunnies
remove item from beginning of world.bunnies
remove item from end of world.bunnies
remove item from position <index> of world.bunnies
remove all items from world.bunnies

Alice also has two instructions among those at the bottom of the Editor area to manipulate lists—*For all in order* and *For all together*, as shown in Figure 8-5. *For all in order* will perform an operation on each item in a list one at a time, beginning with the first item in the list and going through the list in order. To **iterate a list** means to go through the list in this manner.

FIGURE 8-5: List commands at the bottom of the Editor area

● **world.my first method**

world.my first method *No parameters*   create new parameter

No variables   create new variable

Do Nothing

List instructions

Do in order   Do together   If/Else   Loop   While   For all in order   For all together   Wait   print   //

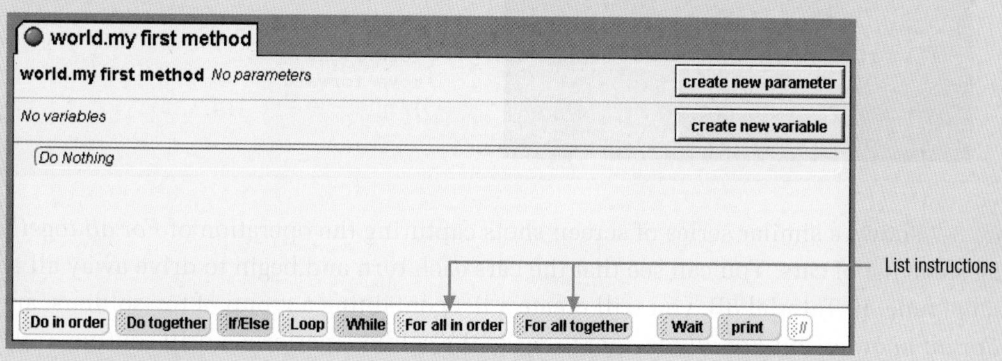

For all together will perform an operation on all of the items in a list at the same time. Notice how *For all in order* and *For all together* are different from the *Do in order* and *Do together* instructions that you saw in earlier chapters. *Do in order* and *Do together* operate on a set of instructions. *For all in order* and *For all together* operate on a set of objects. Of course, the *Do* and *For all* instructions can be combined to perform sets of instructions on sets of objects.

Figure 8-6 shows a series of screen shots from an Alice world window capturing the operation of *For all in order* on a list of cars. You can see that the cars each turn and begin to move away one at a time in order. The same instructions are being executed one at a time by each object in the list; the first car turns and moves, then the second car turns and moves, and so on.

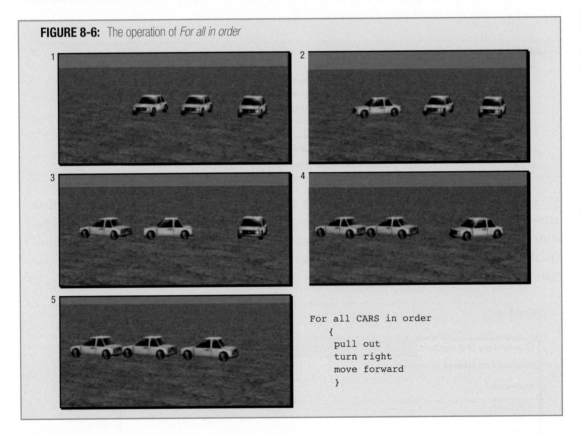

FIGURE 8-6: The operation of *For all in order*

```
For all CARS in order
{
    pull out
    turn right
    move forward
}
```

Figure 8-7 shows a similar series of screen shots capturing the operation of *For all together* on the same list of cars. You can see that the cars each turn and begin to drive away all at the same time. In Tutorial 8B, you will create a list containing a group of toy soldiers, and use *For all in order* and *For all together* to make the soldiers perform a drill routine.

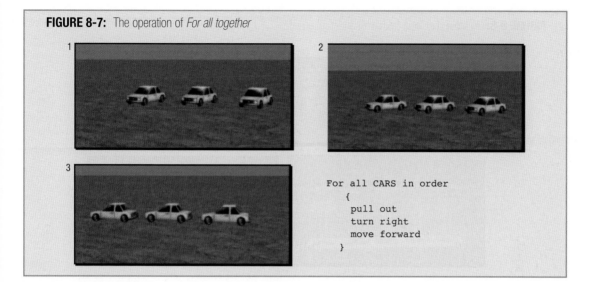

FIGURE 8-7: The operation of *For all together*

```
For all CARS in order
  {
    pull out
    turn right
    move forward
  }
```

ARRAYS IN ALICE

An **array** is a set of indexed variables, each containing objects of the same data type. For example, if we wanted to store a list of five phone numbers for use by a computer program, we might call them phone$_{[0]}$, phone$_{[1]}$, phone$_{[2]}$, phone$_{[3]}$, and phone$_{[4]}$. The value in brackets after each occurrence of phone is the **index value** for that item. There is not one phone variable, but several phone variables, each identified by its unique index value. Notice that the index values start with 0 rather than 1. This is true in almost all programming languages.

> **NOTE** ▫ ▫ ▫ | In mathematics, especially matrix algebra, index values for elements in an array are usually subscripted—which means they are placed half a line below the other characters in the name of the variable, much like the *2* in H_2O, the chemical formula for water. In many programming languages, however, they are simply placed in brackets. An array of the names of four cities might be referred to as city$_0$, city$_1$, city$_2$, and city$_3$, or as city[0], city[1], city[2], and city[3]. Sometimes both brackets and subscripting are used. In any case, such variables are often referred to as subscripted variables, even when brackets are used without true subscripting.

At first glance, it might seem that there is little difference between an array and a list, but actually, a list is a set of objects, while an array is a set of variables that hold objects. It is as if a list were a collection of things, and an array were a collection of boxes that hold things. If we remove an item from the middle of a list, then the list simply gets smaller by one object; whereas, if we remove an item from a "box" in an array, then that "box" is simply empty. Figure 8-8 shows this. If we remove the second item in a list, then the old third item becomes the new second item, and so on for all of the rest of the items in the list. If we remove the second object from an array, then the second "box" in the array is simply empty. The third item will remain in the third "box," and so on throughout the array.

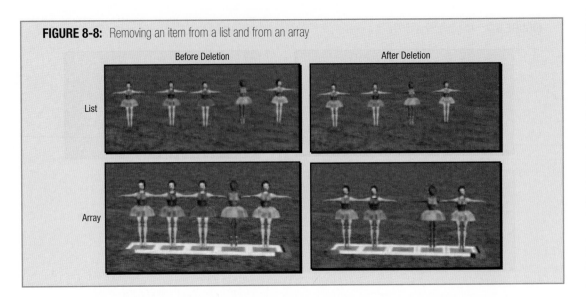

FIGURE 8-8: Removing an item from a list and from an array

There is one other crucial difference between an array and a list: a list is linear, while an array may be multi-dimensional. To say that a list is linear means that we can think of it as a straight line. It has one item, then a second, then a third, and so on, as if in one continuous straight line. To say that an array has more than one dimension means that each object in an array could have more then one subscript, referring to its location in the array in different dimensions. You might recall from Chapter Two that a dimension is simply a way of measuring something, such as the length, width, and height of three-dimensional objects. A two-dimensional array, for example, could be thought of as having rows and columns, with one subscript for the row and one for the column. Such a two dimensional array is sometimes called a **table** or a two-dimensional **matrix**. A simple one-dimensional array is sometimes called a **vector**.

You won't be working with any two-dimensional arrays in Alice, but in Tutorial 8D, you will look at a world that sorts the objects in a simple linear array. The world uses a special object in Alice called an **Array Visualization Object**, which is used to show us an array in an Alice world, rather than just creating it in the memory of the computer.

TUTORIAL 8A—EIGHT BALLERINAS

In this tutorial you will create a list with eight ballerinas in the list, and then write a method to make the ballerinas perform movements individually and all at once. The purpose of the exercise is to learn how to create lists in Alice and how to use the *For all in order* and *For all together* instructions tiles.

EXPLORING THE BALLERINA MOVEMENT METHODS

You will begin by opening a world that already has eight ballerinas in it, with methods to enable the ballerinas to perform some individual movements. You will explore the methods this world contains before creating and working with a list of the ballerinas.

1. Start the Alice software and open the **eight ballerinas** world from the CD that comes with this book.

2. Notice that the world contains eight ballerinas, whose names can be seen in the object tree: *Bronwyn, Ava, Addie, Mardi, Evelyn, Daphne, Kristen,* and *Meagan.* The opening scene from the world is shown in Figure 8-9. Click the **world** tile in the Object tree and the **methods** tab in the Details area, and you will see that in addition to *my first method,* there are generic instructions to make any ballerina jump, put its arms up or down, spin, jump and move at the same time, and bow. Before creating a list of the ballerinas, you will try each of these methods with different ballerinas.

FIGURE 8-9: The eight ballerinas world

3. Click the **edit** button next to the *my first method* tile, and you will see *world.my first method* appear in the Editor area.

4. First, drag a copy of the **jump who** tile from the methods tab into *world.my first method* in the Editor area. When the menus appear, select **Bronwyn, the entire Bronwyn.**

5. Next, drag a copy of the **armsUp who** tile into *world.my first method* and drop it below the *world.jump who = Bronwyn* instruction tile. When the menus appear, select **Ava, the entire Ava**.

6. Now, drag a copy of the **armsDown who** tile and drop it below the *world.armsUp who = Ava* instruction tile in *world.my first method*. When the menus appear again, select **Ava, the entire Ava**.

7. Drag a copy of the **spin who** tile into *world.my first method* and drop it below the *world.armsDown who = Ava* instruction tile. When the menus appear, select **Addie, the entire Addie**.

8. Drag a copy of the **jumpMove who direction** tile into *world.my first method* and drop it below the *world.spin who = Addie* instruction tile. When the menus appear, select **Daphne, the entire Daphne**, and **left** as the direction.

9. Drag another copy of the **jumpMove who direction** tile into *world.my first method* and drop it below the first *world.jumpMove* instruction tile. When the menus appear again, select **Daphne, the entire Daphne**, but this time choose **right** as the direction.

10. Finally, drag a copy of the **bow who** tile *into world.my first method* and drop it below all of the other instruction tiles. When the menus appear, select **Mardi, the entire Mardi**.

11. Now *world.my first method* contains an example of each of the instructions for the individual movements for a ballerina. Save the world with the name **ballerina movements**, and then play it to see what each of the movements looks like. You may want to try it a few times or to experiment with the various instructions for the ballerinas before continuing.

CREATING A LIST OF THE BALLERINAS

Your next task is to create a list containing the eight ballerinas so that you can try the *For all in order* and *For all together* instructions. You won't need the sample instructions you just tried, so they can be discarded. It's actually easier to restart the eight ballerinas world than to delete each of the instructions in `world.my first method`. You will begin by reopening the eight ballerinas world and creating a list of the ballerinas.

1. Close and reopen the Alice software. This will ensure that memory is clear before creating the new world. If the system warns you that the world has been modified and asks you if you want to save it, select **no**.

2. Reopen the original **eight ballerinas** world from the CD provided with this book.

3. Save the world with the name **ballerina company** so that your changes will not affect the original eight ballerinas world.

4. Select the **world** tile in the Object tree and the **properties** tab in the Details area.

5. Click the **create new variable** button on the properties tab and the create new variable dialog window should appear. Type **company** as the name, select **Object** as the type, and make sure that the **make a** option is checked and **list** is selected in the values section of the window. Do not click the OK button at this time.

6. Next, you will add the ballerinas to the new list. Click the **new item** button in the create new variable dialog window, and a line for *item 0* should appear just above the button, as shown in Figure 8-10.

FIGURE 8-10: The create new variable dialog window

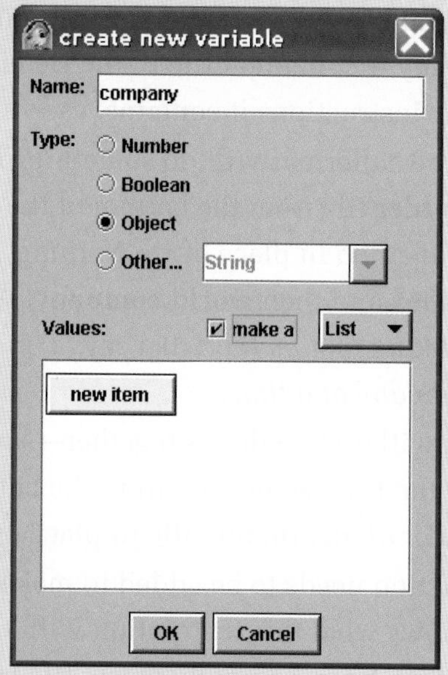

7. Click the word **None** next to *item 0*, and select **Bronwyn**, then **the entire Bronwyn** from the menus that appear.

8. Click the **new item** button again, and a line for *item 1* will appear. This time, click the word **None** next to item1, and select **Ava**, then **the entire Ava** from the menus that appear.

9. In a similar manner, add **Addie** as **item 2**, **Mardi** as **item 3**, **Evelyn** as **item 4**, **Daphne** as **item 5**, **Kristen** as **item 6**, and **Meagan** as **item 7**.

10. When you are finished, click the **OK** button in the create new variable dialog window, and a new tile for the company list should appear in the properties tab. You now have a list containing the eight ballerinas.

11. Save the world before continuing.

CREATING A DANCE ROUTINE FOR THE BALLERINAS

Now that you have a list with the eight ballerinas in the list, you can place some instructions in world.my first method to create a routine for the ballerina company. The routine will be a fairly simple one, just enough for you to learn how to use the *For all in order* and *For all together* instructions.

One at a time, each of the ballerinas will spin while saying her name, then the ballerinas will perform a few movements together. When they are finished, each will bow, and then the entire company will bow together.

1. Click the **methods** tab in the Details area, and the blank *world.my first method* should appear in the Editor area. If it does not appear, click the **edit** button next to my first method tile in the Details area. If it is not blank, then delete any instructions it contains.

2. First, each of the ballerinas will do something one at time, so drag a copy of the **For all in order** tile from the bottom of the Editor area and drop it into *world.my first method* in place of *Do Nothing*. When the menus appear select **expressions** and then **world.company**. An instruction tile will appear in *world.my first method* that says *For all world.company, one item_from_company at a time.*

3. Each ballerina will do two things together—say her name and spin—so drag a copy of the **Do together** tile from the bottom of the Editor area and drop it in the *For all* instruction tile in place of *Do Nothing*.

4. Now an instruction needs to be added to make the ballerina say her name. Figure 8-11 shows what this instruction will look like when it is complete. Drag the **one item_from_company** object tile from the *For all world. company, [obj] one item_from_company at a time* tile, and drop it into the *Do together* tile in place of *Do Nothing*.

FIGURE 8-11: Instructing a ballerina to say her name

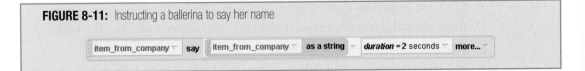

5. A menu will appear allowing you to select which of the primitive methods you want to have the *item_from_company* perform. Select **item_from_company say**, and then **hello**.

6. However*, item_from_company* should say its own name, not *hello.* You must use a function to do this. Select the **functions** tab in the Details area, find **what as a string**, then drag and drop a copy of it in the *item_from_company say hello* instruction in place of the word *hello.*

7. When the menu appears, select **expressions**, then **item_from_company**. Now the instruction looks as it should.

8. Save the world again and test it before continuing. Each ballerina should say her own name in turn.

If everything works okay so far, then you can continue. If not, then you need to find and fix the error before continuing. Once everything is okay you can proceed with creating the dance routine. To do this, you need to add the spin instruction to the *Do together* tile; then you can start adding the dance routine.

1. Click the **methods** tab in the Details area so that you can again see the list of generic methods in the world.

2. Drag a copy of the **spin who** tile from the methods tab and drop it below the *item_from_company say* instruction in the *Do together* tile in *world.my first method*. When the menu appears, select **expressions**, then **item_from_company**.

3. A spin takes two seconds to complete, so, to synchronize the spin and say instructions, click the word **more** in the *item_from_company say* instruction tile and set the **duration** to 2 seconds.

4. Test the world again, and this time each ballerina should say her name while spinning. If it looks correct, then save the world again.

Next you will add instructions to *world.my first method* to create the dance routine. All of the ballerinas will perform the routine together, so the instructions will be contained in a *For all together* tile. The ballerinas will jump, spin, jump left, jump right, and then spin again. After they are finished, they will each bow while saying their names, and then the company will bow together.

1. Drag a copy of the **For all together** tile from the bottom of the Editor area and drop it into *world.my first method* below the *For all world.company, one item_from_company at a time* tile. When the menus appear, select **expressions,** and then **world.company**. An instruction tile will appear in

> *world.my first method* that says *For all world.company, every item_from_company together.*

2. Drag a copy of the **jump who** tile from the methods tab and drop it in the *For all world.company, every item_from_company together* tile in place of *Do nothing*. When the menu appears, select **expressions**, then **item_from_company**.

3. Drag a copy of the **spin who** tile from the methods tab and drop it in the *For all world.company, every item_from_company together* tile below the *world.jump who = item_from_company* instruction. Again select **expressions**, then **item_from_company** when the menu appears.

4. In a similar manner, add instructions to **jump move left, jump move right**, and then **spin** again.

5. Save the world before continuing.

Now you can add the instructions to make the ballerinas each say their names and bow at the end of the routine. They will drop their arms after bowing, and then all bow together.

1. Drag a **For all in order** tile from the bottom of the Editor area and drop it into the bottom of *world.my first method* after all of the other instruction tiles in the method. When the menu appears, select **expressions** and **world.company**.

2. Drag the second object tile that says *one item_from_company* from the top of the new *For all world.company, one item_from_company at a time* tile, and drop it into the tile in place of *Do Nothing*.

3. Select **item_from_company say**, and then **hello** from the menus that appear.

4. Select the **functions** tab in the Details area, and then scroll through the functions until you find the **what as a string** function. Drag a copy of it from the functions tab and drop it in the *item_from_company say hello* instruction in place of the word *hello*. When the menu appears, select **expressions**, then **item_from_company**. The *say* instruction is now complete.

5. Select the **methods** tab in the Details area and drag a copy of the **bow who** instruction from the methods tab and drop it just below the *item_from_company say* instruction tile. When the menu appears, select **expressions**, then **item_from_company**.

6. Drag a copy of the **armsDown who** instruction from the methods tab and drop it below the *world.bow who item_from_company* instruction tile. When the menu appears, select **expressions**, then **item_from_company**.

Finally, the last movement that needs to be added to the routine is the company bowing together.

1. Drag a copy of the **For all together** tile from the bottom of the Editor area and drop it into *world.my first method* below all of the other instructions. When the menus appear, select **expressions**, and then **world.company**.

2. Drag a copy of the **bow who** instruction from the methods tab and drop it in the new *For all world.company* tile in place of *Do Nothing*. When the menu appears, select **expressions**, then **item_from_company**.

3. That's it! Save the method, and then play the world to see what happens. If everything is correct, the ballerinas should each say their name while spinning, complete several moves together, bow individually while saying their names, and then bow together. If they do not, then find and fix the error before continuing.

This concludes the exercise. You should now know how to create a list and how to use the *For all in order* and *For all together* instructions to perform operations on lists.

TUTORIAL 8B—MARCHING TOY SOLDIERS

In this tutorial, you will work with a list of toy soldiers to make them complete a marching drill routine. You will use the *For all in order* and *For all together* instructions to make the soldiers complete marching maneuvers sequentially and concurrently in the routine.

THE TOY SOLDIERS WORLD

On the CD that comes with this book, there is a toy soldier world containing a list of four toy soldiers with methods to make each of them march. You probably could create such a world on your own, but it is a tedious process, so you will start with a world in which this has already been done. You will start by exploring the existing world to become familiar with its features.

1. Start the Alice software and open the **toy soldiers** world from the CD that accompanies this book. When the world loads, you should see a squad of four toy soldiers on the screen, as in Figure 8-12. The first toy soldier has black pants, and the rest have blue pants. Perhaps the first toy soldier is an officer. You should also notice that there are tiles for four toy soldiers in the Object tree, named *toySoldier1* through *toySoldier4*.

FIGURE 8-12: The toy soldiers world

2. Before doing anything else, save the world with the name **toy soldiers marching** so that your changes do not affect the original toy soldiers world.

3. Click the **properties** tab in the Details area, and you will see that there are two variables: a list of objects named *squad*, and a Boolean variable named *marching*, which is initialized to *true*, as in Figure 8-13.

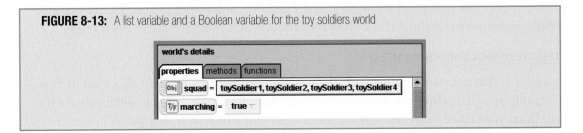

FIGURE 8-13: A list variable and a Boolean variable for the toy soldiers world

4. Click the button after the equals sign following the *squad* tile on the properties tab, and you will see the Collection Editor window open, as shown in Figure 8-14. The Collection Editor window shows that the list contains the four toy soldiers, with *toy soldier1* as the first element, and so on up to *toy soldier4* as the last element in the list. Click the **OK** button to close the Collection Editor window.

FIGURE 8-14: The Collection Editor window

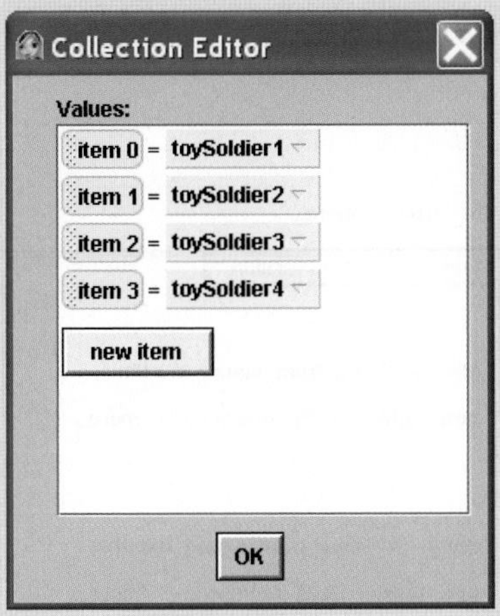

5. Look in the Events area and you will see that there is an event to run the method *world.squadMarch* while the world is running.

6. Click the **methods** tab in the Editor area and then the **edit** button next to *squadMarch* to see what this method does. If you look at the method in the Editor area, you will see that if the Boolean variable *world.marching* is true, then each of the four toy soldiers will march, and if it is not true, then nothing happens—in other words, they will not march. *world.marching* is a state control variable, which controls the status of the toy soldiers. When it is true, they will be marching; when it is false, they will not be marching.

7. Because the Boolean variable *marching* is initialized to *true*, the squad should march if the world is played. Play the world and you should see the soldiers march off the screen. Once they have marched away, you can stop the world.

8. From now on, the soldiers should not march away when the world starts, so click the **true** button next to the *marching* tile on the world's properties tab in the Details area, and change it to **false**.

CREATING A MARCHING ROUTINE

You are now ready to create a method to make all of the soldiers complete a marching drill routine. They will start marching, then after two seconds they will turn right one at a time, then after another two seconds, they will turn right all at once. This process will be repeated four times, which should create an interesting marching routine using only a few simple instructions. Figure 8-15 shows what this method will look like when it is finished.

FIGURE 8-15: A marching routine for the toy soldiers

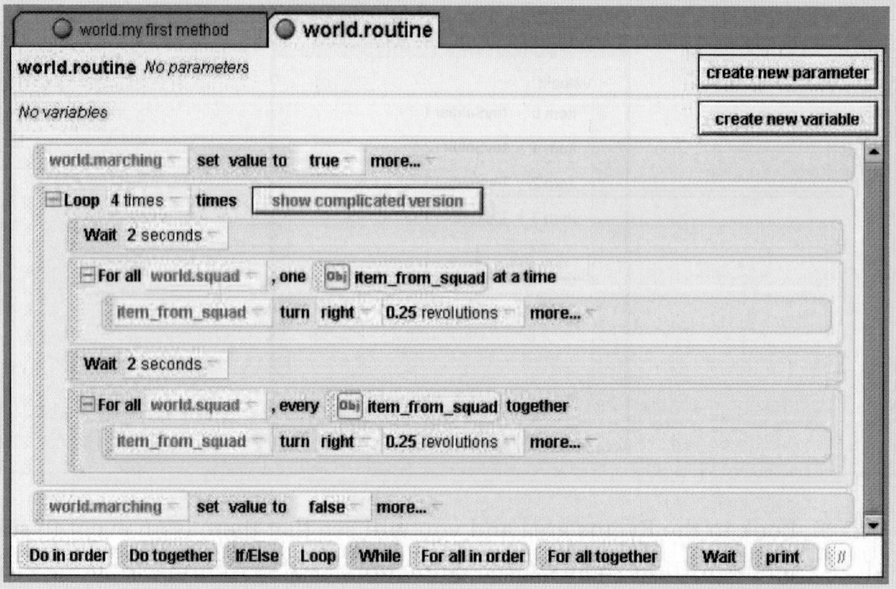

1. Click the **world** tile in the Object tree, and then the **methods** tab in the Details area.

2. Click the **create new method** button on the methods tab, type the name **routine** in the new method dialog window that appears, and then click the **OK** button.

3. Click the **properties** tab and drag a copy of the **marching** Boolean variable tile from the properties tab and drop it into the *world.routine* method in place of *Do Nothing*. Select **true** from the menu that appears. Setting the *marching* variable to *true* will have the affect of a "Forward, march!" command and will start the soldiers marching when the routine is run.

4. The routine will contain a process to be repeated four times, so drag a copy of the **loop** instruction from the bottom of the Editor area and drop it in the *world.routine* method below the *world.marching set value to true* instruction. Select **other** from the menu that appears, enter the value **4** using the calculator style keypad that appears, and then click the **Okay** button.

5. Drag a copy of the **Wait** instruction from the bottom of the Editor area and drop it into the *loop* instruction in place of *Do Nothing*. Set the duration for the *wait* to **2 seconds**.

6. Drag a copy of the **For all in order** tile from the bottom of the Editor area and drop it into the *loop* instruction below the *wait* instruction. When the menus appear, select **expressions**, and then **world.squad**.

7. The new instruction now says *For all world.squad one [obj] item_from_squad at a time*. Drag a copy of the **item_from_squad** parameter in this instruction and drop it in the same instruction in place of *Do Nothing*.

8. When the menus appear, select **item_from_squad turn,** then **right**, then ¼ **revolution**.

9. Next, right-click the **wait** tile in the *world.routine* method and select **make copy**. Move the copy of the **wait** instruction to the end of the *loop* instruction, inside the *Loop* tile but below the *For all* tile.

10. Drag a copy of the **For all together** tile from the bottom of the Editor area and drop it into the *loop* instruction below the second *wait* instruction. When the menus appear, select **expressions**, and then **world.squad**.

11. The new instruction now says *For all world.squad every [obj] item_from_squad together*. Drag a copy of the **item_from_squad** parameter in this instruction and drop it in the same instruction in place of *Do Nothing*.

12. When the menus appear, select **item_from_squad turn,** then **right**, then ¼ **revolution**.

13. Finally, drag a copy of the **marching** Boolean variable tile from the properties tab and drop it into the *world.routine* method at the very bottom, below the *loop* instruction tile. Select **false** from the menu that appears. This will have the affect of a "Halt" command and will stop the soldiers from marching.

14. Your new method is now complete. Save the world again before continuing.

Finally, to make the soldiers carry out the routine when the world starts, you need to put a *routine* instruction in `world.my first method`.

1. Click the **world.my first method** tab in the Editor area and the method should become visible. It should be blank except for *Do Nothing.*

2. Drag a copy of the **routine** tile from the methods tab in the Details area and drop it into *world.my first method* in place of *Do Nothing*.

3. Save the world again before continuing.

4. Play the world and watch what happens. The soldiers should complete two circuits of their routine before stopping. Each iteration through the loop in the *routine* method is only one-half of the routine's circuit, which is why they will complete two circuits when the loop is set to repeat four times. If the method does not perform as expected, then find and fix any errors before continuing.

TUTORIAL 8C—SALUTING TOY SOLDIERS

In this tutorial, you will create a method to make the toy soldiers from the previous tutorial salute, which will provide you with practice in manipulating the parts of objects that are contained in a list. Manipulating the parts of an object can be the most tedious part of programming objects in three-dimensional virtual worlds like Alice, but the result is that the objects function more like similar items in the real world.

You will actually create two methods. First, you will create a generic salute method to make any soldier salute; then you will the use the *For all together* instruction to create a method to make the entire squad salute. It is necessary to use several *move* and *turn* instructions to manipulate the right arms of the toy soldiers to make them salute.

CREATING A GENERIC SALUTE METHOD

To salute, a soldier needs to raise its arm into a saluting position, then drop the arm back to its original position. You will first create a generic method with a *who* parameter to enable any soldier to salute.

1. If necessary, start the Alice software and open the **toy soldiers marching** world that you saved in the previous tutorial, or open the world from the CD that accompanies this book. When the world loads, you should see a squad of four toy soldiers on the screen, as shown in Figure 8-12.
2. Save the world with the name **toy soldiers salute** before continuing so that you do not change the existing toy soldiers marching world.
3. Click the **create new method** button on the methods tab in the world's Details area, type the name **salute** in the New Method dialog window that opens, and then click the **OK** button. A new method named *world.salute* will appear in the Editor area.
4. Click the **create new parameter** button at the top of the new method in the Editor area, and the Create New Parameter window will open. Type the name **who**, make sure that **Object** is selected as the parameter type, and then click the **OK** button.

Figure 8-16 shows what the first part of the *salute* method will look like. This is the part that will cause the soldier to raise his arm into a saluting position.

FIGURE 8-16: The first part of the *salute* method

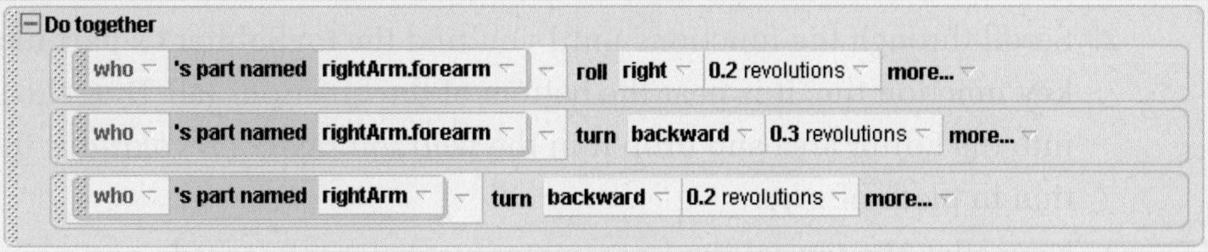

You can see that three things need to happen to make the soldier salute:

- The right forearm needs to roll right .2 revolutions.
- The right forearm needs to turn backward .3 revolutions.
- The entire right arm needs to turn backward .2 revolutions.

The numeric values for the amounts of these movements were determined through calculation combined with trial and error. All three of these instructions need to be carried out at the same time, so they will be placed inside a *Do together* tile. Because the method will be a generic method to make any soldier salute, you will also need to use an object parameter in the method to indicate which soldier should salute.

There is one complication that you will encounter in creating the salute method. To manipulate parts of an object in a generic method, such as a soldier's arm or forearm, it is often necessary to use a function that points to the object's part by name. The two parts you need to manipulate are the *rightArm*, and the *rightArm.forearm*. When the time comes below to use these, you will need to type in their names, so be careful: The capitalization and spelling are important.

1. Drag a **Do together** tile from the bottom of the Editor area and drop it into the *world.salute* method in place of *Do nothing*.
2. Drag a copy of the **who** parameter tile from the top line of the *world.salute* method and drop it in the *Do together* tile in place of *Do Nothing*.
3. When the menus appear, select **world.salute who roll**, then **right**, then **other**. Use the calculator style keypad to enter **.2**, and then click the **Okay** button.
4. The last instruction in the method now reads *who roll right .2 revolutions*. This needs to be modified, because you do not actually want *who* to roll, but *who's forearm* to roll. You will now need to use the function that points to an object's part. To get to this function, you will need to look at the functions tab for one of the toy soldiers.

1. Click the **toySoldier1** tile in the Object tree and then the **functions tab** in the Editor area.

2. Scroll through the functions until you find the **toySoldier1's part named key** function tile. It is near the bottom of the functions tab. Drag the tile into the Editor area and drop it in the *who roll right .2 revolutions* instruction in place of *who*.

3. Now click the **toy soldier1** parameter just before the words *part named*, and select **expressions**, then **who** from the menu that appears.

4. Finally, click the **empty white box** just after *part named* in the same instruction, select **other** from the menu that appears, and the Enter a string dialog window will appear. Carefully type **rightArm.forearm** in the box, and then click the **OK** button. The instruction should now look like the roll instruction in Figure 8-17.

FIGURE 8-17: The instruction to move a soldier's right forearm

Now you will add the instruction to make the forearm turn backward .3 revolutions.

1. Drag a copy of the **who parameter** tile from the top of the *world.salute* method and drop it in the *Do Together* tile just below the *roll* instruction.

2. When the menus appear, select **world.salute who turn,** then **backward**, then **other**. Use the calculator style keypad to enter **.3**, and then click the **Okay** button.

3. You need to again use the part name function, but this time you can copy it from the previous instruction. Drag a copy of the purple box that says *who's part named rightArm.forearm* from the *roll* instruction and drop it on the clipboard; then drag it from the clipboard and drop it into the *who turn* instruction at the bottom of the *Do together* tile in place of *who*. Your turn instruction should now look like the turn instruction in Figure 8-18.

FIGURE 8-18: The instruction to turn a toy soldier's forearm

who ⬇ 's part named **rightArm.forearm** ⬇   ⬇   **turn backward** ⬇ 0.3 revolutions ⬇   **more...** ⬇

Next, you will add the instruction to make the entire arm turn backward 0.2 revolutions. You will do this by copying and modifying the instruction that you just completed.

1. Drag a copy of the **who's part named rightArm.forearm turn backward .3 revolutions** instruction to the clipboard; then drag it from the clipboard and drop it into the bottom of the *Do together* tile as the last instruction in the tile.

2. Click the **rightArm.forearm** box in the last instruction and select **other** from the menu that appears. Carefully type **rightArm** in the Enter a string dialog window that appears, and then click **OK**.

3. Click the **.3 revolutions** box in the last instruction and select **.2 revolutions** from the menu that appears. Your method should now look like Figure 8-19.

FIGURE 8-19: The first part of the *salute* method

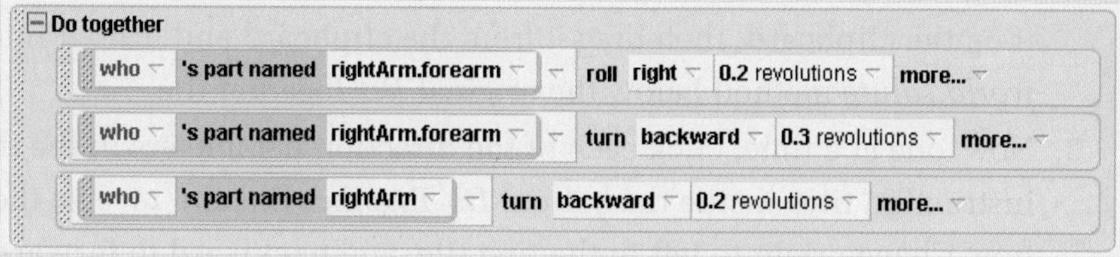

The `salute` method is not finished yet, but you can unit test it to see what it does so far. It should cause a soldier to raise its arm into a saluting position. To test the method, you will need to modify `world.my first method`, and then play the world. `World.my first method` currently contains the `routine` instruction, which the soldiers carry out in their marching routine. You will temporarily disable the `routine` instruction to unit test the `salute` method.

1. Click the **world** tile in the object tree and then the **methods** tab in the details area.

2. Click the **world.my first method** tab in the Editor area, and the method should become visible.

3. Right-click the **world.routine** instruction tile and select **disable** from the menu that appears.

4. Drag a copy of the **salute who** method tile from the methods tab and drop it into *world.my first method* in the Editor area above the *routine* instruction so that it becomes the first instruction in the method.

5. Select **toySoldier1, the entire toySoldier1**, from the menus that appear.

6. Now play the world. The first soldier should raise his arm into a saluting position. If it does not, then check your work and fix the problem in the *salute* method. If the method runs but the salute looks funny, then you should check the direction and amount of the parameters in the *turn* and *roll* instructions in the *salute* method. If you get a "*subject must not be null*" error message, then the name of one of the parts you typed as the *part named* parameters in the *turn* and *roll* instructions may be wrong.

7. Save the world again before continuing.

The method makes the toy soldier raise its arm into a saluting position, but it also needs to make it drop its arm. To add this to the method, you will simply make a copy of the *Do Together* tile in the salute method, and then reverse the direction of each of the arm movements.

1. Click the **world.salute** tab in the Editor area.

2. Drag a copy of the **Do Together tile** from the *world.salute* method and drop it on the clipboard, then drag it from the clipboard and drop it into the *world.salute* method below the original *Do Together* tile.

3. Now, one at a time, click each of the direction parameters in the three instruction tiles inside the bottom *Do Together* tile and reverse the direction. Change **right** to **left** in the first tile, and **backward** to **forward** in each of the other two tiles. When you are finished, the second *Do together* instruction should look like Figure 8-20.

FIGURE 8-20: The second part of the *salute* method

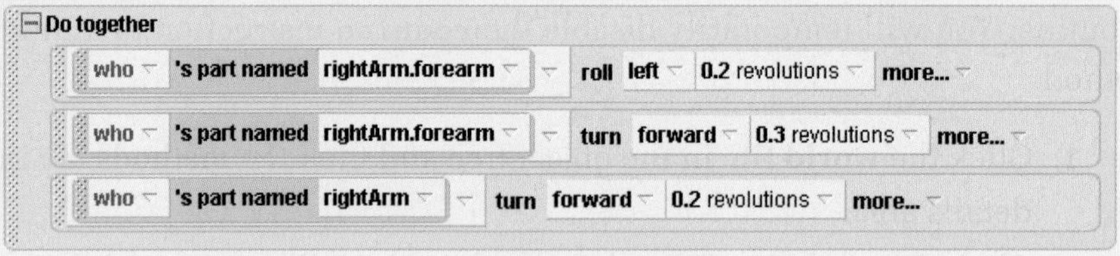

4. Now the soldier should raise its salute, and then drop its salute. Play the world again to see if it works, fix any errors you encounter, and then save the world again before proceeding.

MAKING ALL OF THE SOLDIERS SALUTE

Now that you have a generic method to make any soldier salute, you need to create a method to make the entire squad of soldiers salute together. To do this, you will create a *squadSalute* method that contains the generic *salute* method inside a *For all together* instruction for the squad of soldiers. Your finished method should look like Figure 8-21.

FIGURE 8-21: A method to make all of the toy soldiers salute

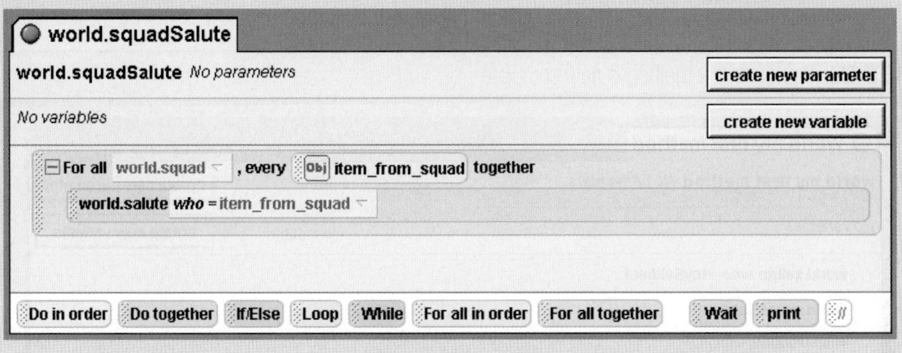

1. Click the **create new method** button on the **methods** tab in the world's Details area.
2. Type the name **squadSalute** in the New Method dialog window that opens, then click the **OK** button. A new method named *world.squadSalute* will open in the Editor area.
3. You will use a *For all together* instruction to have the soldiers all salute at the same time. Drag a copy of the **For all together** tile from the bottom of the Editor area and drop it in the *squadSalute* method in place of *Do Nothing.*
4. When the menus appear, select **expressions,** and then **world.squad**.
5. Drag a copy of the **salute who** tile from the methods tab and drop it into the *For all* tile in place of *Do Nothing*.
6. When the menus appear, select **expressions**, then **item_from_squad**.
7. The *squadSalute* method is finished and should resemble Figure 8-21. Save your world before continuing.

You are now ready to test the `world.squadSalute` method.

1. Click the **world.my first method** tab in the Editor area to see the method. The method still contains the instruction *world.salute who = toySoldier1* and the disabled *routine* instruction.
2. Drag a copy of the **squadSalute** method from the Editor area and drop it into *world.my first method* between the two instructions.
3. Now play the world to see if it works as expected. If it does, then the first soldier should salute, followed by all of the soldiers saluting together.

Finally, you need to enable the disabled `routine` instruction in `world.my first method`.

1. Right-click the disabled **world.routine** instruction and select **enable** from the menu that appears. *world.my first method* is now complete and should resemble Figure 8-22.

FIGURE 8-22: world.my first method is now complete

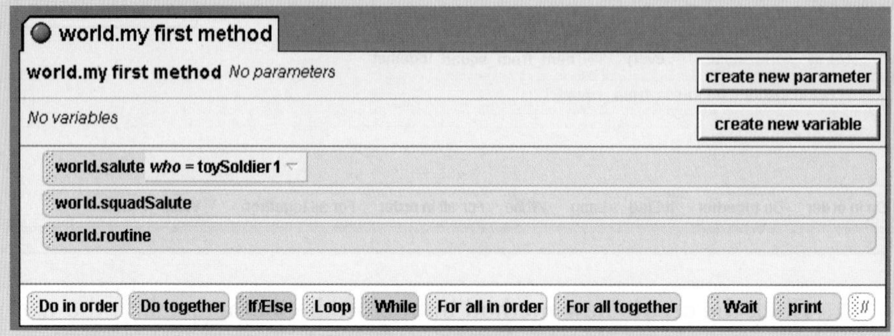

2. Save the world again, and then play the world to see if it performs as expected. The first soldier salutes, all soldiers salute, and then they complete their routine. If the world does not perform as expected, then find and fix any errors before continuing.

If you would like, you could copy and paste from the existing instructions in `world.my first method` to make the soldiers turn and salute again when they are finished their marching routine.

TUTORIAL 8D—SORTING AN ARRAY OF SIXTEEN BALLERINAS

This tutorial is a little different from the others because you will not create any new worlds but simply examine a world from the CD provided with this book. The world, named sixteen ballerinas, has an array that contains sixteen ballerinas. The array exists as an Array Visualization Object in Alice, which will let you see the array as a set of adjacent boxes in the Alice world much like the way an array would be stored as a set of consecutive locations in a computer's memory.

The array has room for sixteen elements, with one ballerina stored in each spot in the array. The ballerinas are different sizes, and the world contains a method to sort the ballerinas in the array according to their height. The sorting method uses the bubble sort technique, which is not the most efficient sort, but it is fairly easy to understand.

1. Start the Alice software and open the world named **sixteen ballerinas** that is on the CD supplied with this book.
2. You will see that the world has a set of sixteen ballerinas, all lined up in separate "boxes" in an array. The ballerinas are all different heights, as seen in Figure 8-23.

FIGURE 8-23: The sixteen ballerinas world

3. Play the world, and you will see that the ballerinas are sorted into order according to their heights.

4. Click the **array** tile in the Object tree and the **methods** tab in the Details area. You will see that there are two different user-created methods for the array—*swap* and *bubbleSort*.

5. Click the **edit** button next to the *swap* method; the method becomes visible in the Editor area. There are two spots in the method where the *duration* is set to .1 seconds. Changing these to a larger number will slow down the sort.

6. Click the **edit** button next to the *bubbleSort* method; the method becomes visible in the Editor area.

Notice that there are two loops in the *bubbleSort* method, a *while* loop and a *count-controlled* loop. The count controlled loop goes through the array once, comparing each element in the array to the next element. This is done by using the index variable from the loop to refer to the element in the array. *array[index]* and *array[index +1]* are adjacent elements in the array. If *index* is 2, for example, then *index +1* will be 3, and the two elements being compared will be *array[2]* and *array[3]*. If the two elements are out of order, then they are swapped. Each time through the loop, comparing each item to its adjacent item, is called a pass though the loop.

The method continues to make passes through the loop until no more swaps occur. The Boolean variable called *changed* is used to keep track of when a swap occurs. It is set to *false* at the beginning of the While loop, and is only reset to *true* if a swap occurs when going through the inner count-controlled loop. This will cause the program to keep repeating passes through the list until no swap occurs; then the program stops.

In other words, here is how the bubble sort works: The computer goes through the array, comparing each value to the one that follows it. If they are out of order, then they are swapped; otherwise, they are left in place. The computer continues to make passes through the array until it makes one pass where no swaps occur. Once it can do this, the list is all in the correct order, and the sorting stops. As stated earlier, this is not the most efficient way to sort an array, but it is a reasonably easy-to-understand technique that correctly sorts an array.

If you look through the various parts of this world, you will see that it contains both an array and a list. The world is really just included for demonstration purposes so that you can see a program that operates on an array.

Close the Alice software when you are finished examining the **sixteen ballerinas** world.

CHAPTER SUMMARY

This chapter consisted of a discussion of data structures, followed by four tutorials. The discussion of data structures included the following:

☐ A data structure is a scheme for organizing data in the memory of a computer. Some of the more commonly used data structures include lists, arrays, stacks, queues, heaps, trees, and graphs.

☐ Alice has instructions that will allow you to manipulate two of the most basic data structures—lists and arrays.

☐ Computer programmers decide which data structures to use based on the nature of the data and the processes that need to be performed on that data because the way in which the data is organized affects the performance of a program for different tasks.

☐ A queue is a set of data items with a beginning and end, called the front and back of the queue. Data enters the queue at one end and leaves at the other. Because of this, data exits the queue in the same order in which it entered the queue, like people in a checkout line at a supermarket.

☐ A binary tree is a data structure that looks like an upside-down tree. Each spot on the tree, called a node, holds an item of data along with a left pointer and a right pointer. The pointers are lined up so that the structure forms the upside-down tree, with a single node at the top, called the root node, and branches increasing on the left and right as you go down the tree.

☐ By comparing the queue with the binary tree, you can see how the structure of the data affects what can be done efficiently with the data.

☐ One of the simplest of all data structures is a list, which is an ordered set of data. It is often used to store objects that are to be processed sequentially.

☐ Alice has a number of instructions that can be used to manipulate lists, including *For all in order* and *For all together*.

☐ *For all in order* will perform an instruction on each item in a list one at a time, beginning with the first item in the list and going through the list in order. This is known as iterating the list.

☐ *For all together* will perform an operation on all of the items in a list at the same time.

☐ An array is a set of indexed variables, each containing objects of the same data type.

☐ Each variable in the array is identified by its unique index value.

☐ A list is a set of objects, while an array is a set of variables that hold objects. It is as if a list were a collection of things, and an array were a collection of boxes that hold things.

☐ A list is linear, while an array may be multi-dimensional. A two-dimensional array, for example, could be thought of as having rows and columns, with one subscript for the row and one for the column. A two-dimensional array is sometimes called a table, or a two-dimensional matrix. A simple one-dimensional array is sometimes called a vector.

☐ Alice has a special object called an Array Visualization Object, which is used to show us an array in an Alice world, rather than just creating it in the memory of the computer.

In Tutorial 8A, you created a list of ballerinas and used the `For all in order` and `For all together` instructions to perform operations on the list.

In Tutorial 8B, you again used the `For all in order` and `For all together` instructions to perform operations on a list of toy soldiers so they would complete a marching routine.

In Tutorial 8C, you created a generic method that performs operations on the parts of objects contained in a list to make the toy soldiers salute.

Tutorial 8D demonstrated the use of an Array Visualization Object in a method that uses the bubble sort technique to sort a set of objects stored as an array.

REVIEW QUESTIONS

1. **Define the following terms:**

☐ array	☐ index value	☐ node
☐ Array Visualization Object	☐ iterate a list	☐ queue
☐ binary tree	☐ list	☐ root node
☐ data structure	☐ matrix	☐ vector

2. **How do programmers decide what data structures to use for different programs?**

3. **Why is a queue a good data structure to use for keeping track of documents to be printed on a network printer?**

4. **Why would a binary tree be a good data structure to use for storing a dictionary on a computer?**

5. **What is the difference between a list and an array?**

6. **What is the role of index values in an array?**

7. **What does it mean to say that an array can be multi-dimensional?**

8. **What is the difference between using the *Do together* and the *For all together* instructions in an Alice world?**

9. **The swap method in Tutorial 8D contains an object variable called temp. Why is it needed in this method?**

10. An encapsulated data structure is one that has functions available to programmers who use it, such as adding an element to the data structure, but the details of those methods are hidden from the user. In other words, they can use the methods, but they cannot see inside them. List several encapsulated methods that would be useful for all of the following data structures: a queue, a binary tree, a list, and an array. List several methods that would each be useful for one of the data structures but not necessarily the others.

EXERCISES

1. Create an Alice world with four helicopters and a list containing the helicopters. Program the world to make the helicopters each lift off from the ground one at a time, then all turn and fly away together.

2. The Animals folder in the Alice Local Gallery contains several different kinds of fish, including a goldfish and a shark. The Ocean folder contains an ocean floor background. Using these items, create an Alice world with a school of goldfish that swim around together, then scatter when a shark appears. You may be tempted to use the Lilfish in the Ocean folder instead of the goldfish, but be careful—each instance of the Lilfish requires more than 2 megabytes of memory, while each Goldfish requires only 30 kilobytes.

3. Create a drill routine of your own for the toy soldiers world from Tutorial 8B that demonstrates the use of the *For all in order* and *For all together* instructions, along with good modular programming techniques.

4. Create an Alice world with several objects from the People gallery. Place some of the objects in one list and some of the objects in another list. Create a method to make each object in the first list say hello to each object in the second list, and vice-versa.

5. Create several new generic movement methods for the eight ballerinas world, then demonstrate their use in methods that use the *For all in order* and *For all together* instructions.

6. Create a series of keyboard and mouse events for either the eight ballerinas world that will allow the user to control a ballet routine, or for the toy soldiers world that will allow the user to control a marching drill routine while the world is running.

7. Open the generic triple jump world from the CD that accompanies this book and add a set of five different heights to the world as a list of numbers. Create a method to iterate through the list and have the three characters jump each of the heights contained in the list.

8. Create a search method for the sixteen ballerinas world that will do all of the following:
   a. Allow the user to input a ballerina's name.
   b. Go through the list to find the ballerina in the list that has the name from Step 8a.
   c. Have the ballerina respond by performing a dance maneuver.

   If the list does not contain a ballerina with the name that the user entered, then one of the ballerinas should tell the user that this is the case.

9. **The Bugs folder inside the Animals folder in the Alice Local Gallery contains a Butterfly class of objects. Complete the following:**

   a. Create an Alice world with six butterflies in the world.
   b. Create a generic method to make any butterfly flap its wings.
   c. Create a generic random movement method that will use random numbers to pick a direction and an amount, and then cause a butterfly to move accordingly.
   d. Place the six butterflies in a list, and create methods and events to make all of the butterflies fly around gently in an Alice world, flapping their wings and moving about randomly.

10. **The National Institute for Standards and Technology has a Dictionary of Algorithms and Data Structures on the Web at _http://www.nist.gov/dads/_. Look up the definitions for the data structures stack and queue, and then describe the differences between a stack and a queue.**

In this appendix, you will learn the basics of acquiring and installing Alice.

ACQUIRING THE ALICE SOFTWARE

Alice Version: 2.0 04/05/2005 is included on the CD supplied with this textbook. It is also freely available from Carnegie Mellon University. The software may be downloaded directly from the link found on the Web at *www.alice.org*.

At the time this book was published, versions of Alice were available for IBM PC compatible computers running the Windows operating system and Apple MacIntosh computers running OSX.

System requirements for the PC version of Alice are as follows:

- Windows ME, Windows 2000, or Windows XP
- A CPU running at 500 MHz or better (A 1.0 GHz or better CPU is recommended.)
- A VGA graphics card capable of 16-bit color and video resolution of 1024 × 768 pixels (A video card with at least 16MB of memory is recommended; some newer laptops still have 8MB video cards.)
- At least 128 MB of RAM (256 MB or more is recommended.)
- A sound card to use Alice's sound features

The Apple version of Alice was new at the time this book was published and was still undergoing testing. It is intended to work on an iMac, Mac mini, Power Mac, iBook, or PowerBook with the following:

- OSX 10.3 or higher
- a G4 or G5 processor
- At least 256 MB of RAM
- At least 16MB of video RAM

INSTALLING THE ALICE SOFTWARE

To install the Alice software, simply unzip the software into the folder of your choice on your computer. A new folder named Alice will be created, containing two program icons named *Alice* and *SlowAndSteadyAlice* and a subfolder named *required*. You should not move or delete these three items, but you may copy the entire Alice folder from one place to another, such as onto a CD and then from the CD to another computer, and it will still work properly.

When the *Alice* program icon is clicked, the standard version of Alice will load and run on your computer. This is a hardware accelerated version of Alice that will use the circuitry in your computer's video card to render Alice on your computer screen.

The *SlowAndSteadyAlice* icon is for a special software rendering version of Alice that will run code through your machine's CPU to render Alice on the screen rather than trying to take advantage of the machine's video card. As the name implies, it is slower than the hardware accelerated version of Alice, but it is more reliable, especially on machines with older video cards. The developers of Alice recommend that you try the standard version of Alice first, and if it does not run well, then try the slow and steady version. The standard version of Alice should run well on almost any personal computer that is less than two years old.

The Alice software has been carefully designed so that it will not interfere with your system's registry, DLL files, or any other parts of your system software. However, to accomplish this, the Windows feature that allows you to run a program simply by clicking the icon for a saved file will not work for Alice worlds. You must run Alice first and then load saved worlds from inside Alice. You must also connect any storage devices that you want Alice to see, such as flash ROM drives, to your system before running Alice.

One final tip: To make Alice easier to use, you can create a shortcut to either version of the Alice software and place the shortcut on your desktop. To do this, copy and paste the icon in the same Alice folder where the original resides, then drag the new shortcut icon to your desktop. This is an easy way to keep the original Alice program in its folder so that it will run properly, while still being able to access it from your desktop. The shortcut can also be placed on the taskbar at the bottom of your computer screen.

APPENDIX B

Almost all modern high-speed digital electronic computers are based on the binary numbering system. At the heart of the computer, inside the central processing unit (CPU), there are one or more arithmetic logic units (ALUs) that process information by performing binary arithmetic. Everything associated with modern computers—all of the audio, video, word processing, Internet access, and so on—is processed with binary arithmetic inside the CPU by these relatively simple electronic circuits. All data to be handled by the computer and all of its instructions must be processed in the CPU as streams of binary numbers.

The set of binary digits, or bits, that the CPU understands as an instruction set is called the computer's machine code. Eventually, everything that a computer does must be translated into its machine code. Each CPU, or each family of CPUs, such as the Intel Pentium family, has its own machine code. There are as many machine codes as there are families of processing units.

When a new processor is first invented and manufactured, it only understands its machine code. Systems programmers work with these binary codes to create a new language called assembly language. They do this by using machine code to build an assembler, which is a program that translates assembly language into machine code. Assembly languages are made up of very primitive instructions, just like machine code, but they can be written using the following: numbers other than base two; mnemonics, or short words that sound like the instructions they represent, such as ADD for addition or SUB for subtraction; and symbolic names instead of numbers to refer to memory locations.

Writing sophisticated software, such as word processors and video games, is still rather difficult and very time-consuming in assembly language, so computer scientists and software engineers build translators that can handle high-level languages, which are closer to human languages. They are easier for people to understand, but harder to translate into a computer's machine code. Java, JavaScript, VB.net, C, C++, and Python are all examples of modern high-level computer programming languages. COBOL, FORTAN, BASIC, and Pascal are all examples of once-popular high-level languages that are seldom used.

The translators that convert high-level languages into machine code fall into two categories: compilers and interpreters. Using a compiler, a programmer ends up with two stored copies of the program. The first, in the original high-level programming language, is called the source code. The second stored copy of the program, which is the same program after translation into a particular machine code, is called the object code. Even after translation into machine code, a program may still need to be processed so that it will run on a particular computer with a particular operating system. A program that has been translated into machine code and prepared to run on a particular system is called executable code or an executable file.

An interpreter is much simpler than a compiler. Rather than translating an entire source code program into object code all at once, the compiler translates each instruction one at a time and then immediately feeds it to the CPU to be processed before translating the next instruction. The only stored copy of the program is the original source code program. Often scripting languages, such as JavaScript or Visual BASIC for Applications (VBA), work this way. Scripting languages are simplified high-level programming languages that allow someone to program in a particular environment. JavaScript can be added to the HTML code for Web pages to provide them with some primitive data-processing capability. VBA allows someone to program features in Microsoft Office products, such as Microsoft Word or PowerPoint.

Interpreters are often used for teaching languages. Serious computer programming languages, such as Java and C++ that are used by professional programmers, are sometimes referred to as production languages. Teaching languages are languages that are not generally used in production environments but are instead used to teach someone the logic of computer programming or the processes used in creating computer software before attempting to teach them to use production languages. Alice is an example of a teaching language. Its primary purpose is to be used as a tool to introduce people to computer programming.

One of the first high-level languages in existence was the FORTRAN language, created in the 1950s by the U.S. Government in cooperation with IBM, which, at the time, was by far the world's largest computer company. FORTRAN was intended to be used by scientists and engineers working on large, primitive mainframe computers of the day—about 20 years before the first personal computers appeared—to program mathematical formulas and processes. In fact, the name FORTRAN comes from the two words "formula translator."

Before FORTRAN, all software had to be created using assembly language and machine code. Once FORTRAN appeared, people began to use it for much more than science and engineering. The increasing use of FORTRAN in the business world led to the development of the COBOL language in 1960. Like the name FORTRAN, COBOL is an acronym that comes from the words "common business-oriented language." It was based on work by Grace Hopper, who rose to become an admiral in the United States Navy before she retired more than 30 years later. It is estimated that as of the year 2000 there were more lines of code written in COBOL than in any other computer programming language. However, during the last five years, the use of COBOL has declined rapidly as other programming languages and applications software, such as electronic spreadsheets, have become more common.

Over the years, many high-level programming languages have evolved, each with different features that have changed the way people create and use computer software. Algol, BASIC (Beginner's All-purpose Instruction Code), Pascal, Smalltalk, ML, LISP, Prolog, and C are some of the most well known of these. Today Java, C++, and VB.NET are probably the most important languages for professional programmers to know. New languages continue to emerge, such as the Python and Haskel languages that first appeared in the 1990s. As of January 2006, The Association for Computing Machinery's Hello World! Page, on the Web at *http://www2.latech.edu/~acm/HelloWorld.shtml*, had sample Hello World! programs in almost 200 different programming languages.

APPENDIX C

Although Alice does not contain a menu-driven set of commands like Microsoft Word, it is useful to be familiar with the features on the four Alice menus: File, Edit, Tools, and Help. This appendix contains a short summary of the options on the menus for Alice Version 2.0 04/05/2005. The Alice 2.0 CourseCard (ISBN 1-234-56789-0), available from Course Technology, provides a more extensive reference for Alice. It is available from your Course Technology representative or on the Web at *www.course.com/*.

THE FILE MENU

The File menu has the following submenus:

- **New World**: Starts a new Alice world. It will take you to the Templates tab of the Welcome to Alice! window, as described in Chapter 1.

- **Open World...**: Opens an existing Alice world. It will take you to the Open a world tab of the Welcome to Alice! window, allowing you to navigate the system's directories, as described in Chapter 1.

- **Save World**: Saves the current Alice world. If used with a world that has not yet been saved, it will function like Save As; otherwise, it resaves the current world without further user interaction, as described in Chapter 1.

- **Save World As...**: Saves the current Alice world with a new name or location. The Save World As window will appear, allowing you to select the location and enter the name of the file in which the world will be saved, as described in Chapter 1.

- **Export As a Web Page**: Exports the current Alice world as a folder with an HTML file, an a2w file, and an applet.jar file. A Save World for the Web window will open with options for the title of the Web page, the author's name, the size of the viewing window on the Web page, the location of the saved files, and whether or not to include code from the world on the page.

- **Export Movie**: This option is disabled in Alice 2.0 and is not expected to be reactivated. Video capture software, such as Camtasia, can be used to capture a playing Alice world.

- **Export Code for Printing**: Exports code from Alice methods and events to an HTML Web page for viewing or printing. A dialog box will appear allowing you to select which items to export and where to save the resulting HTML file, as described in Chapter 1.

- **Import...**: Used to import external files into an Alice world. Most commonly, it is used to import objects saved from other worlds as a2c files. Right-clicking an object's tile in the Object tree will let you save an object, which can be imported into another world by using this option. Other files, including sound files and graphic image files, can also be imported, and they will show up as options on the appropriate menus.

- **Add 3D Text**: Creates 3D text objects in Alice, as described in Chapter 6.
- **Make Billboard**: Creates billboard objects from image files, as described in Chapter 6.

THE EDIT MENU

The only item on the Edit menu is Preferences, which will open a Preferences window with four tabs: General, Rendering, Screen Grab, and Seldom Used. A description of these tabs follows:

- **General**: Has options allowing you: to change the number of worlds displayed on the Recent Worlds tab of the Open a World Window; choose whether to display Alice code in the Editor area as Alice style code, black-and-white Java style code (looks most like true Java programming), or color Java style code; to set the default directory for opening and saving files; and to choose the size of the font used to display code in the Editor area.

- **Rendering**: Has options for forcing software rendering that will cause Alice to run in the slow and steady mode, show the number of frames per second being rendered as an Alice world plays, numerically change the World window position and size, lock the window's aspect ratio, make sure the window is always visible, and select the rendering order for Alice so that it will try to render a world using either DirectX or Java3D rendering first.

- **Screen Grab**: Has options that affect the function of the Take Picture button on the playing world window, including which directory to use when saving an image, the base filename for the image file, how many digits to append to the base filename, whether to use the JPG or PNG image file format, and whether or not to show a dialog box when the *Take Picture* button is pressed while an Alice world is playing.

- **Seldom Used**: Has nine check boxes that affect different aspects of Alice and options to change the number of clipboards available on the Alice interface, the number of minutes to wait before reminding a user that the current world has not been saved, and the number of backup copies of each world to maintain. The nine radio boxes allow you to turn features of Alice on or off, including showing the startup dialog when Alice launches, showing warnings when browsing the Web Gallery, opening tabs that were previously open when a world loads, picking up tiles while dropping and dragging, using alpha blending in picked-up tiles, saving thumbnails with saved world files, showing world statistics on the bottom of the Alice interface, clearing text output each time a world is played, and enabling a special high-contrast video mode for use with projectors.

THE TOOLS MENU

On the Tools menu, you will find the following submenus:

- **World Statistics**: Shows a variety of statistics about the current Alice world, such as the number of objects in a world, how much memory the texture maps in the world use, how many times a world has been run, how many times it's been saved, and the total amount of time the world has been open.

- **Text Output**: Shows a copy of the text log file for this world, including information about the version of Alice and the operating system in use, a record indicating each time the world was started or stopped, any messages that appeared in the print zone, and any error messages that were generated. The text in the window can be copied to the system's clipboard and then pasted in Microsoft Word or other programs with an option to paste text from the clipboard.

- **Error Console**: Functions the same as the Text Output option.

THE HELP MENU

On the Help menu, you will find the following submenus:

- **Example Worlds**: Opens the Examples tab on the Welcome to Alice window.

- **Tutorial**: Opens the Tutorial tab on the Welcome to Alice window.

- **About Alice**: Opens a window showing the version number of the Alice software being used, along with a reference to the Alice Web site.

GLOSSARY

absolute direction—A direction in relation to a scale of measurement, as opposed to a direction from the point of view of a particular object.

algorithm—A step-by-step process. Every computer program is an algorithm.

American Standard Code for Information Interchange (ASCII)—A set of characters used in computer programming based on the English language. It includes letters, numeric digits, and some "hidden" characters, such as the Enter key and the Escape key. Each character is given a numeric value, and the binary equivalents of those numeric values are used to store characters in the computer.

AND—A Boolean logical operation of form <A> AND < B>. When two values are combined in the AND operation, the result is true only if both values are true. Otherwise, the result is false.

array—A set of indexed variables, each containing objects of the same data type. An array can be thought of as a set of numbered boxes each containing a value.

Array Visualization Object—A special object in Alice used to show an array in an Alice world, rather than just creating it in the memory of the computer. The name of the object in Alice is *ArrayVisualization.*

ASCII—*See* American Standard Code for Information Interchange.

axis—In Euclidean geometry, and hence in Alice worlds, a fixed scale of measurement at a right angle to another fixed scale of measurement. The values of coordinates in Euclidean 3-space and in Alice virtual worlds are measured from one axis along or parallel to another axis.

base case—*See* base condition.

base condition—The condition that stops a recursive algorithm from continuing.

BDE event format—A format for defining an event that includes specifications for three event handlers to be executed when the event trigger Begins, in the time During which the event trigger continues, and when the event trigger Ends.

billboard—A pictures file that has been added to an Alice world as an object. It is a flat two-dimensional object with length and width, but no depth. Once placed in an Alice world, the image from the picture file will be seen on both the front and back of the billboard. Billboards are objects that can be manipulated just as as other objects can be.

binary branching—In an algorithm, a branching routine with two possible exit paths. In Alice, a binary branching routine is most often associated with an If/Else instruction.

binary bypass—A binary branching routine in which an instruction (or set of instructions) is either executed or bypassed completely. This is implemented in Alice by using an If/Else instruction with a blank Else clause.

binary choice—A binary branching routine in which one instruction (or set of instructions) or another is always executed, but not both. This is implemented in Alice by using an If/Else instruction with an active Else clause.

binary tree—A data structure that looks like an upside down tree, in which each node on the tree holds an item of data along with a left pointer and a right pointer. The pointers are lined up so that the structure forms an upside down tree, with a single node at the top, called the root node, and branches increasing on the left and right as you go down the tree.

Boolean algebra—A symbolic language for representing Boolean logic.

Boolean function—A function that returns a value of either True or False.

Boolean logic—A formal system of logic dealing with true and false values, first described by George Boole in his 1854 work, *"An investigation into the Laws of Thought, on which are founded the Mathematical Theories of Logic and Probabilities."*

branch—A particular path of logic through an algorithm. The term is often used to mean one of several paths followed as a result of a branching or looping instruction.

branching routine—A set of instructions in an algorithm in which the path or flow of sequential logic splits into two or more paths. A branching routine is also known as a selection sequence.

breakpoint—An identifiable a spot in a computer program just before or just after some action occurs.

CamelCase—The practice of writing compound names without using blank spaces, but capitalizing the first letter of each name that forms the compound name, like the name CamelCase itself.

camera—The object in Alice that provides the view seen in the Alice world window.

Cartesian coordinates—A system of quantification for two dimensions developed by French mathematician René Descartes and extended to include more than two dimensions. With two-dimensional Cartesian coordinates, the location of each point is referred to by an ordered pair of the form (x, y), in which x represents the point's location along an X-axis and y represents its location along a Y-axis perpendicular to the X-axis.

Cartesian triplet—A three-valued set of coordinates of the form (X,Y,Z) representing the X-axis, Y-axis and Z-axis values for a point in a three-dimensional Cartesian coordinate system.

class—A group of objects with the same properties and the same methods. Objects in the same class are virtually identical to each other, except that the values stored in some of their properties may be different. In true object-oriented programming, unlike Alice, class level methods can be created that are available to all objects in a class.

coding—The process of implementing a new method by entering instructions (and data) on the computer in a particular programming language. It is the phase in a program development cycle in which an algorithm is expressed in a particular programming language.

collate—To put a set of items in order according to particular criteria.

collating sequence—A list that shows the correct order to be used when sorting a set of items.

command-driven interface—A user interface in which people control a computer by entering text-based commands, as opposed to a Graphical User Interface.

computer program—A step-by-step set of instructions telling a computer how to perform a specific task. Every computer program is an algorithm and most are sequential in nature.

computer programming language—A particular instruction set for programming a computer, along with the syntax and grammar for using those instructions.

concurrency—The process of running multiple threads of a parallel algorithm at the same time.

concurrent execution—*See* concurrency.

control variable—A variable whose value controls whether or not a repetition sequence or selection sequence will be executed in a particular pass through an algorithm.

count-controlled loop—A repetition sequence in which a process is to be repeated a specific number of times.

counter—The control variable for a count-controlled loop. It needs to have an initial value, a final value, and an increment.

cut—To abruptly change scenes, or make an object abruptly appear in or disappear from a scene. The term also means to delete an item from an Alice world or from a program.

data structure—A scheme for organizing data in the memory of a computer.

data type—The classification of an object according to its properties and the methods that may be performed on the object.

Details area—The section of the standard Alice interface with tabs to show properties, methods and functions for the currently selected Alice object. The Details area is located below the Object tree.

dialog balloon—A box with rounded corners appearing in an Alice world showing words that are supposed to have been spoken by an object.

dimension—A way of measuring something. The word dimension is a derivative of the ancient Latin word *demetiri*, meaning to measure out. We create a dimension whenever we assign a value on a continuous scale to some property.

Editor area—The section of the standard Alice interface where methods are assembled and edited by clicking and dragging tiles from other parts of the interface.

encapsulated method—A method whose details are hidden from the user.

encapsulation—*See* encapsulated method.

Euclidean 3-space—A three-dimensional space, such as the physical world around us, in which each point can be located by its X, Y, and Z coordinates along mutually perpendicular X, Y and Z axes.

event—A condition, called an event trigger, and the name of a method, called an event handler. Whenever the event trigger occurs, the event handler is called into action.

event handler—A program that is executed in response to the occurrence of an event trigger.

event listener—Hardware or software that detects when an event trigger occurs. Users of Alice software define event triggers, but the actual event listeners are built into the system.

event trigger—A condition that causes an event to occur.

Events area—The part of the Alice interface that shows existing events and is used to create new events. It is located above the Editor area.

exponential recursion—Recursion in which a method calls itself more than once in each pass through the method. As a result, the number of copies of the world that are running grows exponentially.

fade—To slowly change scenes, or make an object appear in a scene or disappear from a scene gradually.

flowchart—A diagram used to show the structure of an algorithm. A flowchart can be used to show the path or flow of logic in an algorithm as different branches of the algorithm are selected in branching and looping routines.

font—A design for a set of characters that includes typeface, size, style, and weight of characters. Although the terms "typeface" and "font" are not synonymous, they are often used interchangeably. For example, Times New Roman is a typeface, whereas Times New Roman, 10 point, italics, bold is a complete specification for a font.

frame an object—To position the camera so that an object fills the World window. Several objects could also be framed as a group.

function—A method that returns a value. A function may be used in place of an actual value. For example, there is an Alice function to return the height of an object. It can be used any place a number can be used, such as in an instruction like this: rabbit jump [height of tree] meters.

Graphical User Interface (GUI)—A user interface with icons on the computer screen and a mouse to control a pointer that can be used to operate the computer. Most modern software, such as word processing, electronic spreadsheets, Internet browsers, and computer games, depends on the use of a GUI.

ground—An object that corresponds to the XY plane in an Alice virtual world. Every new Alice world has a ground with one of six skin textures: dirt, grass, sand, snow, space, or water.

HSB—A color model for computer graphics in which the color of a pixel is expressed in terms of hue, saturation, and brilliance.

If/Else—The branching instruction in Alice that provides the basic unit of Boolean logic. It has the form If <Boolean condition> then <A> else <B>. If the condition is true, then <A> is executed; otherwise, <B> is executed.

increment—The amount by which something is increased, such as the amount by which a counter in a loop is increased each time through the loop.

index value—The value of a variable used to identify either an element in an array or an iteration of a loop.

infinite recursion—Recursion that continues without ending on its own.

instance—A copy of an object from a particular class.

instantiation—The process of adding an instance of a class of objects to an Alice world.

integration test—A software test that checks to see if a method works when it is placed into a larger program in combination with other methods.

iterate—To go through a set of items, such as the elements of an array or the instructions in a loop, one at a time.

iteration—Each pass through of the body of instructions in a loop. The term is also used to refer generally to looping as opposed to recursion.

leaf node—A node at the end of a branch in a tree or tree-like data structure. A leaf node has null pointers, which means that it has no child nodes.

linear recursion—Recursion in which a method calls itself only once each time through the method. Consequently, the number of copies of the method running grows linearly.

linear sequence—The simplest element of logical structure in an algorithm, in which one instruction follows another as if in a straight line.

list—An ordered set of data. In Alice, a list may be implemented as an object or as a variable.

Local Gallery—A collection of folders with Alice objects that is supplied with the Alice software.

logical comparison operators—Operators used to create a Boolean condition by comparing two values, such as the less than operator in the condition (hours < 40).

loop—An algorithmic structure in which a set of instructions is repeated.

matrix—An array, most commonly a two-dimensional array, of numeric values.

method—A program that manipulates an object by changing one or more of its properties. In object-oriented programming, software is written as a collection of methods.

method header—Information at the top of a method, including the method name and any parameters needed to run the method. In Alice methods, the parameters are in the form of tiles showing a parameter's name and data type.

method parameter—*See* parameter.

module—A unit of software organization that is logically independent, performs a well-defined single task, and is compatible with other modules.

modular development—Development of a large project as a collection of smaller projects organized as related modules.

modular programming—The application of principles of modular development to computer programming, resulting in the development of a collection of small, specialized, related modules instead of a single larger program.

multiple branching—In an algorithm, a selection sequence with more than two possible exit paths. All multiple branching routines can be rewritten as a collection of binary branching routines. Alice has no instruction for multiple branching.

node—An organizational unit in a data structure, such as a graph or a tree, with a data element and one or more pointers to other nodes.

NOT—A Boolean logical operation of the form NOT <A>, in which the true or false value of the operand <A> is reversed; NOT <true> yields false; NOT <false> yields true.

object—A collection of related properties and the methods available to manipulate those properties.

object-oriented programming—A modern approach to computer programming that emphasizes objects and the development of software as a collection of methods that are each associated with a particular object. True, or complete, object-oriented programming languages must allow for encapsulation, inheritance, and polymorphism. While Alice is a good tool to use for an introduction to object-oriented concepts, it is not a complete object-oriented system.

object-relative direction—A direction from the point of view of a particular object, as opposed to a direction in relation to a scale of measurement. The six major object-relative directions are forward, backward, left, right, up, and down.

off-camera—Not visible in the image captured by a particular camera. In Alice, objects in the world that cannot be seen in the World window are said to be off-camera.

OOP—*See* object-oriented programming.

opacity—A property of an Alice object that determines how solid or transparent an object will appear to be. It is measured as a percentage, with 100% representing completely solid (opaque) and 0% completely transparent (invisible).

OR—A Boolean logical operation of the form <A> AND < B>. When two values are combined in the OR operation, the result is true if either one of the values is true, and false only if both values are false.

ordered pair—A two-dimensional set of Cartesian coordinates of the form (x, y), in which x represents the point's location along an X-axis and y represents its location along a Y-axis. Ordered pairs can be used to map any two sets of coordinated values.

organizational chart—A diagram used to show the overall structure of separate units that have been organized to form a single complex entity. In computer programming, an organizational chart can be used to show how individual software modules are part of a larger, more complex module.

orientation—The direction in which an object is facing.

overhead—The extra CPU time and space in a computer's memory needed to manage a method as it runs.

pan—To turn a camera left or right without changing its position, although it is possible that you could pan and move at the same time.

parallel algorithms—An algorithm in which multiple paths of sequential logic, called threads, are each being executed at the same time.

parameter—A parameter is a variable whose value is passed from one method to another.

personification—The process of giving human qualities such as feelings, thoughts, or human-like movements to inanimate objects.

point of view—A property combining an object's location and orientation.

post-test loop—A loop in which the test to determine whether or not to repeat the loop comes after the instructions that are to be repeated.

pre-test loop—A loop in which the test to determine whether or not to repeat the loop comes before the instructions that are to be repeated.

primitive method—One of a set of standard encapsulated Alice methods that provide basic behaviors for objects added to an Alice world.

program development cycle—The four-phase software engineering process of designing, coding, testing, and debugging computer programs. A cycle is formed when debugging leads back to the design phase.

property—A value that describes an object in some way, such as the height of a tree or the balance in a bank account.

proximity function—A function that returns information about the distance between two objects. Some proximity functions return Boolean values and some return numeric values.

pseudo-code—Formal language that is similar to a computer programming language. Psuedo-code is a tool used to describe algorithms more precisely than ordinary language.

quantification—The process of forming a dimension by assigning a value on a continuous scale to some property of an object.

queue—A simple linear data structure with a beginning and end, called the front and back of the queue, in which data items enter the back of the queue and leave from the front of the queue in the same order in which they entered the queue. The front and back of the queue are also referred to as the queue's head and tail.

recursion—*See* recursive method.

recursive method—A method that calls itself.

repetition sequence—An element of logical structure in an algorithm, in which the flow of instructions to be executed branches backward to a previous instruction, repeating part of the algorithm. A repetition sequence forms a loop in an algorithm.

RGB—A color model for computer graphics in which the color of a pixel is expressed in terms of quantification of its red, green, and blue light components.

root node—A node at the top of a tree, to which no pointers in the tree are directed. Setting a pointer in a leaf node to point at the root node of a tree turns the tree into a graph.

Scene Editor mode—A mode for the Alice Interface used to add and position objects in an Alice world.

selection sequence—A set of instructions in an algorithm in which the path or flow of sequential logic splits into two or more paths. A selection sequence is also known as a branching routine or selection structure.

sentinel—A condition or value that causes a repetition sequence to stop repeating.

sentinel loop—A repetition sequence that repeats until a condition or marker, called a sentinel, is encountered.

side effects—Unintended results produced by two or more overlapping events or methods.

skin texture—A graphic image file that is layered over the surface of an object to affect its appearance.

state of an object—The values stored in the properties of an object at any one time.

structured language—Formal language with elements of logical structure similar to a computer programming language. Structured language is used to describe an algorithm.

tessellation—A repeated pattern of an image on the surface of an object.

test for correctness—A test to determine whether or not a software method functions according to its original specifications.

testing shell—A short software method that simulates the environment in which a newly developed method will be used. This is especially important if the new method will be receiving values from other methods, or passing values to other methods as parameters. A testing shell is also called a testing hull.

thought bubble—A cloud-like box appearing in an Alice world showing words that are supposed to represent the thoughts of an object.

thread—One of several paths of logic being executed concurrently in a parallel algorithm.

tilt—To turn a camera up or down without changing its position, although it is possible that you could turn and move at the same time.

top-down design—A process of decomposition in which a problem is broken into parts, those parts are solved individually, and then the smaller solutions are assembled into a big solution. This is also known as stepwise refinement, or as a divide and conquer approach to problem solving.

top-down development—The application of top-down design principles to the development of computer software.

typeface—A design for a complete set of characters in a particular alphabet or character set. Although the term "font" is a more specific term than "typeface," they are often used interchangeably. For example, Times New Roman is a typeface, whereas Times New Roman, 10 point, italics, bold is a complete specification for a font.

Unicode—A 16-bit computer code for alphabetic characters, numeric digits, and some "hidden" characters, such as the Enter key and the Escape key. Each character is assigned a numeric value, and the 16-bit binary equivalents of those numeric values are used to store characters in the computer. Unicode is a newer and larger code than the ASCII code, and includes characters for alphabets other than English, such as Greek, Hebrew, Arabic, and the Cyrillic alphabet used for Russian and Eastern European languages. The ASCII code is now actually a subset of the longer Unicode.

unit test—A test of a software method that checks to see if the method works as expected all by itself.

user-defined method—A method that can edited by someone creating an Alice world. Some of the objects in the Alice gallery, such as the penguin, include user-defined methods. They are also known as user-created methods.

variable—A name for a memory location that temporarily holds a value while a method is running.

vector—A one-dimensional array.

virtual world—In Alice, a Euclidean three-dimensional space, complete with objects, that exists only in the memory of the computer. It is possible to create and manipulate virtual worlds with other than three dimensions or in non-Euclidean space using other software.

World window—That part of the Alice interface through which the user sees the current Alice virtual world.

zoom—To move the viewer closer in to an object or farther out away from an object. Real cameras often allow the operator to do this by manipulating the lens of a camera, whereas zoom effects in Alice must be created by actually moving the camera.

■ ■ ■ ■ INDEX

Please note that bolded numbers indicate where a key term is defined in the text.